TURBO C: MEMORY-RESIDENT UTILITIES, SCREEN I/O AND PROGRAMMING TECHNIQUES

Al Stevens

MANAGEMENT INFORMATION SOURCE, INC.

COPYRIGHT

Copyright © 1987 by Management Information Source, Inc.
1107 N.W. 14th Avenue
Portland, Oregon 97209
(503) 222-2399

Third Printing

ISBN 0-943518-35-0

Library of Congress Catalog Card Number: 87-12343

All rights reserved. Reproduction or use, without express permission of editorial or pictorial content, in any manner is prohibited. No patent liability is assumed with respect to the use of the information contained herein. While every precaution has been taken in the preparation of this book, the publisher assumes no responsibility for errors or omissions. Neither is any liability assumed for damages resulting from the use of the information contained herein.

Apple-DOS is a trademark of Apple Computer, Inc.
BDS C is a trademark of BD Software
BIX is a trademark of McGraw-Hill Inc.
CP/M is a trademark of Digital Research
Homebase is a trademark of Brown Bag Software
IBM PC/XT/AT is a trademark of IBM Corporation
Intel MDS is a trademark of Intel, Inc.
MS-DOS is a trademark of Microsoft Corporation
ProKey is a trademark of RoseSoft
Sidekick is a trademark of Borland International, Inc.
Sidekick Plus is a trademark of Borland International, Inc.
SuperKey is a trademark of Borland International, Inc.
Tiny-C is a trademark of Scott B. Guthery and Thomas A. Gibson
TRSDOS is a trademark of Tandy Corporation
Turbo Basic is a trademark of Borland International, Inc.
Turbo C is a trademark of Borland International, Inc.
Turbo Pascal is a trademark of Borland International, Inc.
UNIX is a trademark of AT&T Bell Laboratories
Wizard C is a trademark of Wizard Systems Software, Inc.
WordStar is a trademark of MicroPro International Corporation

ACKNOWLEGMENTS

I wish to acknowledge the contributions of Nan Borreson, Paul Chui, and Brad Silverberg of Borland International. They answered my questions and provided the Beta copy of Turbo C that allowed me to start this project.

DEDICATION

This book is dedicated to those who find and share the secrets:

barryn, comeau, demo6, dmick, dondumitru, drifkind, dthielen, geary, mjk, mws, pittore, rduncan, rschnapp, sazer, sjg, skluger, tanj, tdinger, and wardw.

These names are the only ones I know for most of the people I wish to thank. They live as messages on my screen, coming to me down skinny wires from the insides of a bigger machine. Most of what I know about the last two chapters of this book comes from the efforts of these people. They delve into the mysteries of DOS; curse its anomalies; discover its quirks, habits, and secrets; and post their findings in shreds of code and comment. By now, there are more nicknames on the list, more secrets to tell, more problems to solve. They say "<grin>," "aarrggh," ":-)," and "foobar." Their gift is priceless.

TABLE OF CONTENTS

Foreword vii
    Chapter Overviews ix

Chapter 1: Interactive, Display-directed Software 1

Chapter 2: The C Language 9
    A Brief History of C 10
    C Language Characteristics 12
    C Language Strengths 13
    The Acceptance of C 14
    References to C 15

Chapter 3: Turbo C 17
    Two Turbo Cs 19
    Customizing the Environment 20
    The Turbo C Editor 21
    The Turbo C Link Utility 22
    The Turbo C Project Make Utility 22
    The Compiler/Linker Error Traps 23
    Low-level Software Support 23
    Installation 24
    Memory Models 25
    Library Source Code 25
    Summary 25

Chapter 4: General-purpose Functions 27
    General-purpose Source Listings 31
        Listing 4.1: ibmpc.c 32
        Listing 4.2: keys.h 37
    Summary 38

Chapter 5: Screen Windows 39
    The Video Window 40
    Video Memory Architecture 44
        Listing 5.1: vidpoke.c 47
    Snow and Video Retrace 48
    Summary 51

Chapter 6: The Windows Function Library 53
   Stacked Windows 54
   Layered Windows 56
   Window Functions 59
   Window Listings 66
      Source Listing: twindow.h 66
         Listing 6.1: twindow.h 67
      Program Description: twindow.h 72
      Source Listing: twindow.c 72
         Listing 6.2: twindow.c 73
      Program Description: twindow.c 90
   Window Examples 95
      Moving a Window 95
         Listing 6.3: move.c 47
         Listing 6.4: testmove.c 98
         Listing 6.5: move.prj 99
      Promoting and Demoting Windows 99
         Listing 6.6: prom.c 101
         Listing 6.7: promote.c 102
         Listing 6.8: prom.pjr 103
      Assigning Titles and Changing Window Colors 103
         Listing 6.9: color.c 104
         Listing 6.10: ccolor.c 105
         Listing 6.11: color.prj 106
      Comparing Stacked and Layered Windows 106
         Listing 6.12: fast.c 107
         Listing 6.13: fasttest.c 108
         Listing 6.14: fast.prj 108
      Moving, Promoting, Hiding, Intensity, and Menus 109
         Listing 6.15: poetry.c 111
         Listing 6.16: poems.c 112
         Listing 6.17: poetry.prj 117
   Summary 117

Chapter 7: Context-sensitive Help Windows 119
   Programming for Help Windows 121
   The Help Window Text File 123
      Listing 7.1: tcprogs.hlp 126
   Help Functions 127
   Changing the Help Function Key 128
   Changing the Help Function 128
   Disabling Help 129

Source Listing: thelp.c 129
    Listing 7.2: thelp.c 130
Program Description: thelp.c 133
An Example of Context-sensitive Help 134
    Listing 7.3: sayings.c 136
    Listing 7.4: maxims.c 137
    Listing 7.5: sayings.prj 138
Summary 138

Chapter 8: Data Entry Windows 139
Data Entry Template 140
    Data Entry Field 140
        Position 141
        Attribute 141
        Buffer 141
        Validation 141
        Help 142
        Data Entry Mask 142
    Field Prompts 142
Data Entry 143
Data Collection Functions 143
Source Listing: entry.c 149
    Listing 8.1: entry.c 150
Program Description: entry.c 161
An Example: Order Entry 164
    Listing 8.2: order.c 167
    Listing 8.3: ordent.c 168
    Listing 8.4: order.prj 170
Summary 171

Chapter 9: The Window Text Editor 173
Text Editor Commands 175
    Cursor Movement 176
    Page Movement 176
    Text Block Commands 177
    Editing Commands 178
The Text Editor Function 178
Source Listing: editor.c 179
    Listing 9.1: editor.c 180
Program Description: editor.c 199

  An Example: The Notepad 203
    Listing 9.2: note.c 204
    Listing 9.3: notepad.c 205
    Listing 9.4: note.prj 206
  Summary 207

Chapter 10: Window Menus 209
  Menus 210
  The Window Menu Executive Process 212
  The Menu Function 213
  Source Listing: tmenu.c 214
    Listing 10.1: tmenu.c 215
  Program Description: tmenu.c 219
  Window Menu Example 220
    Listing 10.2: menu.c 220
    Listing 10.3: menu.prj 221
    Listing 10.4: exec.c 222
  Summary 225

Chapter 11: Memory-resident Programs 227
  Interrupts 231
    Interrupt Vectors 231
    Hardware Interrupts 232
    Software Interrupts 232
  DOS, the Single-task Operating System 233
  Terminate-and-Stay-Resident Programs 236
    Interrupt Service Routines 238
    Memory-resident Utilities 238
    What Should be Resident? 238
  Building TSR Utilities 241
    Getting Resident 242
    Is the TSR Program Already Resident? 242
    Capturing an Interrupt 244
    Chaining Interrupts 244
    How Big is the TSR Program? 245
    Context Switching 248
    The Stack 249
    The Program Segment Prefix (PSP) 250
      INT Call to Process Terminator (PSP:0) 250
      Top of Memory Segment Address (PSP:2) 250
      Terminate Handler Address (PSP:0xa) 250
      Ctrl-Break Handler Address (PSP:0xe) 252
      Critical Error Handler Address (PSP:0x12) 252

- Segment of Parent's PSP (PSP:0x16) 252
- File Handle Table (PSP:0x18) 253
- Environment Block Segment Address (PSP:0x2c) 253
- Stack Address during DOS Function Calls (PSP:0x2e) 253
- Size of File Handle Table (PSP:0x32) 253
- Address of File Handle Table (PSP:0x34) 253
- File Control Block #1 (PSP:0x5c) 254
- File Control Block #2 (PSP:0x6c) 254
- Command Tail/Disk Transfer Area (PSP:80) 254
- Context-Switching the PSP 255
- The Disk Transfer Area (DTA) 257
- The Keyboard Interrupt (9) 258
- The Timer Interrupt 259
- The DOS Reentrancy Problem 260
- The Two DOS Stacks 260
- The DOS Busy Flag (0x34) 261
- The DOSOK Interrupt (0x28) 261
- The Disk ROM-BIOS Interrupt (0x13) 262
- The DOS Critical Error Interrupt (0x24) 263
- The DOS Ctrl-Break Interrupt (0x23) 264
- Running the TSR Utilility Program 264
- Terminating a TSR Utility Program 265
- Suspending and Resuming a TSR Utility Program 267
- Summary 267

Chapter 12: Building Turbo C Memory-resident Programs 269
- A TSR Example: The On-line Clock 270
  - Making the Program Resident 271
  - The Divide-by-Zero Interrupt Vector 271
  - Executing the Timer ISR 273
  - Chaining to the Old Timer 273
  - Saving and Switching the Stack Context 274
  - Computing the Time 274
    - Listing 12.1: clock.c 276
    - Listing 12.2: clock.prj 278
- The TSR Driver Programs 278
  - Operation of the Three Program Modules 279
  - Size of the TSR 279
  - Hot Key Assignment 280
  - The TSR Signature 281
  - The Communications Interrupt Vector 283
  - Preparing for Residency 284
  - The Disk ISR 284

    The Critical Error ISR 286
    The Keyboard ISR 286
    The Timer ISR 286
    The DOSOK ISR 287
    Executing the TSR Utility 287
    Terminating the TSR 287
    Memory Blocks and Memory Control Blocks 288
Source Listings: popup.c, resident.c 289
        Listing 12.3: popup.c 290
        Listing 12.4: resident.c 293
The TSR Application Program 301
        Listing 12.5: popup.prj 302
Testing a TSR Program 303
Summary 304

Epilogue 305

Index 307

FOREWORD

As a reader of this book, you are probably a C programmer who has acquired or plans to acquire the Turbo C compiler for the IBM PC. This book assumes you know the C language fairly well, and you understand DOS and its functions. A knowledge of 8086 assembly language and the PC's address and register architecture is helpful but not mandatory. Much of this book contains C language source code functions that will help you write video windows into your code and make your programs into memory-resident utility programs.

Programs that use video windows and memory-resident utility programs are the mainstream of today's IBM PC programs. The PC's nature is one of interactive systems. It resides on the desk and offers the user access to a host of interactive tools. The PC hardware and operating system environments encourage the development of programs that use windows and menus that pop up when a key is pressed. Most PC packages that users buy today incorporate one or both of these features. This book explains the basics of these features and provides functions in C source code that allow you to build such programs. With the lessons and software contained in this book, the Turbo C compiler, and a basic foundation in C language programming, you will be prepared to design and write memory-resident utility programs that use video windows for the user interface.

This book is about a computer language, a software development environment, and some practical applications of the language within the environment for use in developing screen-oriented, interactive computer programs. It is not another book about the IBM PC, but the PC figures significantly in the subjects presented here. A few years ago, the PC acronym designated a specific machine, but today, it signifies an architecture that has been spawned by a giant and embraced by an industry. The PC that is the object but not the subject of this book is anything that sits on your desk, runs MS-DOS, and calls itself a PC, an XT, an AT, or a clone.

C is the language—the wonderful language—used in this book. Most programmers love it. Some don't and can be vocal about it, but most love it. You can write programs in C that do what you want programs to do. By not getting in the way, the language encourages you to code. It seems that other PC languages have congenital productivity obstacles, and C has none. C has evolved into a language that greases the way to a working program: it is fast, efficient, and predictable. Once you are comfortable with C, you can do anything the computer can do, which is perhaps because C was designed by one programmer to be used by other programmers. Other languages have other birthrights. COBOL was designed so that managers could read code; BASIC was designed for people who are not programmers; FORTRAN is for scientists; ADA comes from a committee—a government committee, no less; PILOT is for teachers; Pascal is for students; LOGO is for children; APL is for martians; FORTH, LISP, and PROLOG are specialty languages; C, however, is for programmers.

If C is the language, Turbo C is the software development environment used in this book. This package is the first of a new generation of C compilers. Turbo C combines a user-configured editor, a project-oriented make process, a fast linker, and the PC's fastest C compiler into an integrated, window-oriented, program development environment. Turbo C also provides functions and language extensions that support the development of interrupt service routines and other memory-resident programs. This support is appropriate because Borland International, the creator of Turbo C, is the premier producer of memory-resident utility programs.

This book contains functions you can use in programs that will be run in the interactive user environment. These functions will advance the user interface of your software. They include video windows, menus, data entry templates, a window text editor, and a complete memory-resident package that allows you to develop desktop utility programs that pop up at the press of a key.

Besides providing these functions, this book explains the hardware and software principles that underlie the development of video drivers and memory-resident programs. There are detailed discussions of interrupt structures, video display memory, and the internals of DOS, including a number of DOS functions that are indispensable in a memory-resident program yet are not documented or otherwise acknowledged by the authors and vendors of DOS.

Chapter Overviews

Chapter 1 introduces you to the concept of interactive, display-directed software systems in which the user language is as important as the applications algorithms.

Chapter 2 contains the obligatory discussion of the C language.

Chapter 3 describes Turbo C and its programmer's environment.

Chapter 4 introduces the first layer of functions, those that deal with the PC's hardware architecture.

Chapter 5 explains video windows, including a discussion of video architecture in general and the problems of writing windows into the PC's video memory.

Chapter 6 presents the window library of functions. These window functions are useful for displaying many kinds of information in many user environments and, as such, are the foundation of the menu, editor, and data entry template functions that follow in later chapters. Chapter 6 includes several example programs that illustrate the use of the window library's features.

Chapter 7 provides a description of context-sensitive help windows and includes software functions that allow you to incorporate such help windows into your programs.

Chapter 8 introduces the use of windows for data entry templates, which are driven by the definition of a set of data entry fields within an assigned window. Functions are provided that support this capability in your applications software. An on-line order entry program is given as an example.

Chapter 9 contains a window text editor. This function is a general-purpose text editor for entering and modifying free-form text. It includes many of the commands of larger word processors, such as automatic paragraph formation, word wrap, block operations, and so on. An on-line notepad program is included as an example of using the text editor.

Chapter 10 covers menus and includes functions that let you build the kind of menus you see in professional programs—the sliding bar menu at the top, with the pop up menu under each selection of the sliding bar. To illustrate its use, all the other example programs are integrated into one program with a menu to let you select from the examples.

Chapter 11 explains memory-resident programs and their implementation. The subject is given comprehensive treatment, with explanations of the undocumented DOS functions—which ones you should use, which ones you should avoid, and why. The problem of DOS reentrancy is explained and its solution described. The problems of concurrent memory-resident utilities are also addressed. Finally, there is a discussion of the single-task properties of DOS and why memory-resident programs are never totally safe.

Chapter 12 uses examples that show how you can use Turbo C to build a memory-resident utility program. The first example is a memory-resident clock utility that maintains a constant time-of-day display in the upper right corner of the screen. Then, a general-purpose Terminate-and-Stay-Resident (TSR) driver program is provided that will allow you to develop utility programs, test them as transient Turbo C environment programs, and link them into working memory-resident executable modules. To illustrate this technique, Chapter 12 integrates the menu-driven window examples from Chapter 10 into a memory-resident utility program that executes at the touch of a hot key.

In summary, this book contains the explanations and the source code that support two of the most popular features in PC software—video windows and memory residence. With these tools and the rich development environment of Turbo C, you will improve your programming productivity and significantly enhance the human factors and usefulness of your programs.

Al Stevens
September, 1987
Merritt Island, Florida

CHAPTER 1

INTERACTIVE, DISPLAY-DIRECTED SOFTWARE

1 Interactive, Display-directed Software

Most of the PC software written and purchased today is developed for an interactive environment where the user language is expressed in keystrokes and screen displays. A program uses the facilities of the PC's video terminal to speak to the user. The user responds with typed words and numbers. This medium of expression has become second nature to a new generation of computer users. The use of this medium in a computer program involves the development of a style of display and response, which has come to be called the "look and feel" of a computer program, and it is usually designed and developed by programmers. The computer's medium of expression is a language as much as French, COBOL, and Morse Code are languages, and often, each new program is a new language or a radical dialect of an earlier one. Language is for communication, and the more effective and efficient the language, the clearer the understanding between the meaning of the user and the action of the machine.

These languages are not designed; they evolve as the programmer builds the program. A programmer is concerned with several different matters: the programming environment, the data structures, the functional algorithms, and the user language. As a program develops, the programmer adds a prompt here, an error message there. The amount of consistency in the user interface is a function of the programmer's understanding of a need for consistency and the software tools that are available to help build the language.

Programmers can use many different techniques to manage the language between the PC and the user. These techniques vary, and each of them is more appropriate for some applications than for others. But they have common purposes: they tell the user what information he or she needs to know, and they provide a medium of expression for the user's input.

Interactive, Display-directed Software 1

At first thought, you might decide that entering alphanumeric data is a simple problem to solve. The PC displays a prompt, and you type an answer. You can use **printf** and **scanf**, and little else is necessary. When computers had typewriter-like console terminals, such an approach was about all a software system could offer as a user interface. That technique was acceptable because computers were run by computer operators, while users were others who entered data values on code sheets and read printed reports. Today, however, PCs are on users' desks, and user languages must be more complex than those that existed before. Because the user must effectively communicate with the PC, and because today's user is someone with interests other than talking to the computer, languages must be provided that advance the human-machine communication rather than restrict it.

In an interactive system, the program arrives at a place where it needs some information known to the user, and the program asks for the information by displaying a prompting message. The program must wait until the user can provide the requested information. If the program can determine the validity of the information, the program can accept the data entry and proceed, or it can display an error message and wait for the user to enter a new data value. If the user does not understand what is expected next, the user can ask the program for help. A smart program will include a set of helpful messages that explain what the program is requesting and will display an appropriate help message when the user asks for help.

Data entry takes many forms because there are many kinds of data to be entered. These kinds of data can be broadly classified into two categories: commands and data values.

A **command** can be as simple as the single function key that forms a paragraph in a word processor. On the other hand, a command can be as complex as the cryptic string of letters, numbers, and symbols that characterize many of the MS-DOS commands. Some commands are requested by the program, such as the "y" and "n" responses you enter when the PC asks if you really mean to have the PC do what you just asked it to do. Other commands are user-initiated, such as when you tell the word processor to save the document to the disk file. The program in the PC isn't waiting for this command but watches for it and executes it when requested. Sometimes the program will provide a list of optional commands that you can peruse and select from. This list is called a **menu**.

1 Interactive, Display-directed Software

Data values are different from commands and can be further classified as data elements or text. **Data elements** are specific data items with precise formats and purposes. They are dates, account numbers, names, addresses, tire sizes, and shades of paint. The data values that are entered for data elements can be validated as to their format, content, and length. Conversely, **text** is narrative without a predefined form, content, or length. Data base systems usually deal with data elements, and word processors deal with text.

An interactive system should have a user language that makes good use of the keyboard and screen when the programs process different types of data entry. The IBM PC has a video and keyboard architecture that contribute to the design of a wide range of user languages, and, as you might expect, these capabilities have been fully exploited by the many successful PC software packages.

No one way exists to display menus, help messages, error messages, and data entry prompts. No one way exists to read the text and data values that the user enters into the program. The programmer can select from a variety of techniques in the design of a user language. The tools in the programmer's library will influence the design of the software. If the tools support an effective set of display and data entry primitives, the programmer can use them to build an effective software system.

Of the many techniques that support a user language, the approach called **video windows** is one of the most popular. A video window is part (or all) of the computer's video screen that is used for a particular kind of display. The window is displayed in a manner that sets it apart from whatever else is on the screen. A window is usually a rectangular area of the screen that has a visible border. Windows are used for all kinds of information displays—to display menus, to serve as areas for entry of data elements and text, to display messages, and to provide help information as requested by the user.

Another technique that enhances the quality of an interactive system is the ability of the user to rapidly jump from task to task without disturbing work in progress or making tedious retreats to the operating system. In an integrated software system, these side trips are often a part of the operating environment of the program being run. But when a number of unrelated tasks are involved, the business of rapidly switching from one to another in asynchronous abandon is beyond the ability of the single-task DOS of the PC. To provide the appearance of a task-switching capability, a class of programs known as **memory-resident programs** has evolved. These programs do not constitute true multitasking, but they allow the installation of certain routine utility functions into an otherwise bland (to the user) DOS command environment.

The software in this book provides a library of software tools that use video windows to support text entry, data entry, user help, and menus. The functions can be installed into a memory-resident utility program. The functions in the library are written in Turbo C to be used by programs that are written in Turbo C. To understand and use the software in this book, you should understand the concepts of DOS and the functions it provides to the programmer. This book will describe some of the internals of DOS and some of the undocumented functions that support memory-resident programs. An excellent reference book on the documented features of DOS and the ROM-BIOS is *Advanced MS-DOS* by Ray Duncan (Microsoft Press, 1986). This book is without equal in its subject matter and is an indispensable item in a programmer's library. With tongue-in-cheek, Duncan describes his book as just that, but the endorsement you are reading here is a serious one.

The software in this book is presented in six layers as shown in Figure 1.1. The presentation is from the top down, but your exposure to the layers will be from the bottom up, which is how the layers will be described here.

1 Interactive, Display-directed Software

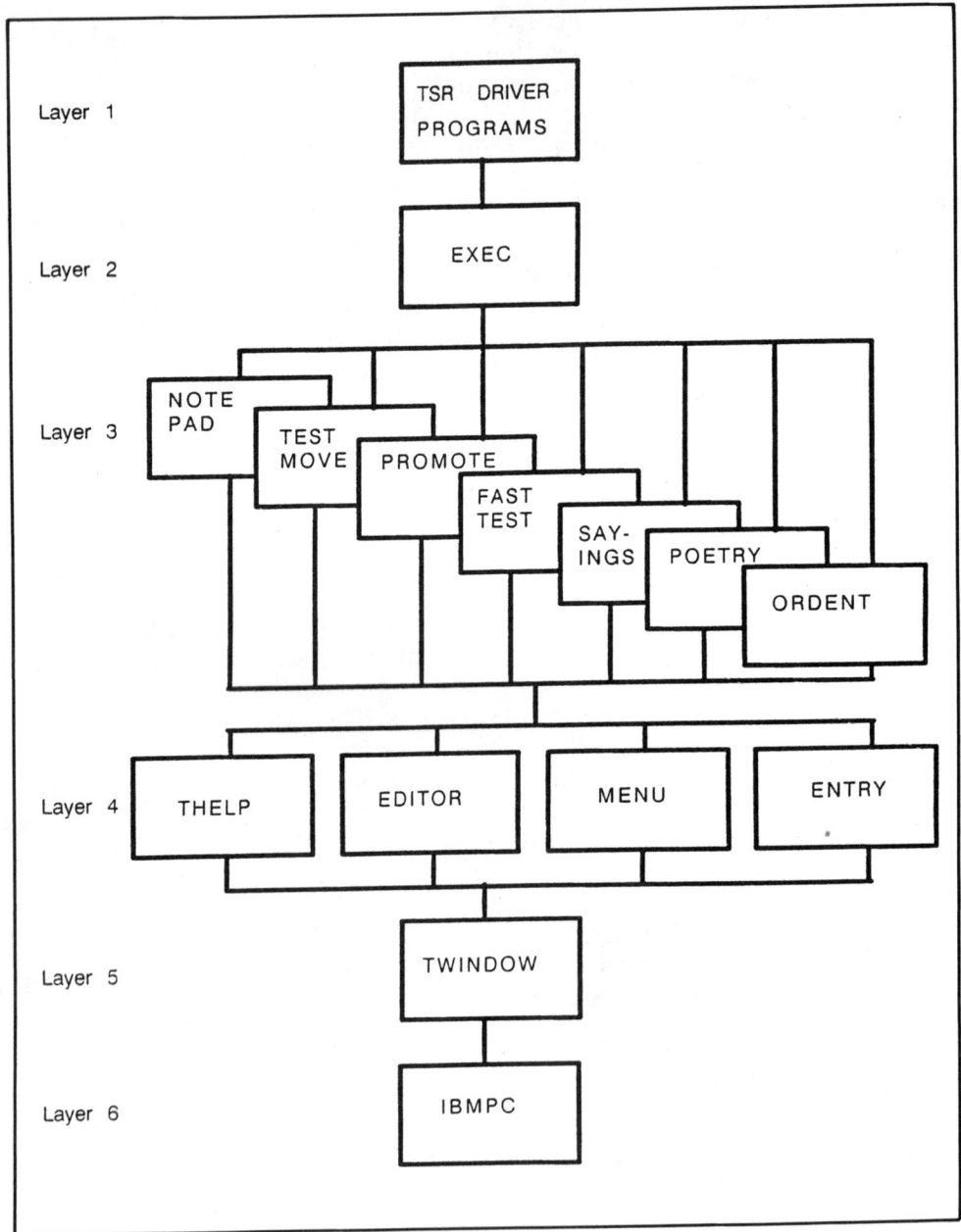

Figure 1.1 The Layers of Software

Interactive, Display-directed Software 1

Layer 6 is the library of low-level functions that manage the IBM PC-specific operations.

Layer 5 is the library of video window functions that control the display, placement, and integrity of screen windows.

Layer 4 contains functions that use windows to support applications. These functions manage the context-sensitive help windows, the text editor windows, the menus, and the data entry template windows.

Layer 3 represents your applications programs and is depicted here by the example programs that illustrate each of the features of the lower libraries. These examples can be run independently or as an integrated program with one of the higher layers.

Layer 2 is the executive example that ties the applications examples together in a single, menu-driven program. This example can run as a stand-alone program or be integrated into a memory-resident utility in the highest layer.

Layer 1 is the TSR driver program that builds a Terminate-and-Stay-Resident program from a transient program. It is used in the example to integrate the other example programs into a single memory-resident utility program.

Before jumping into the depths of window and memory-resident programming, you might want to read something about the C language and why it is chosen for the work presented in this book. Chapter 2 is a brief history of the C language and an attempt to explain why programmers love it so. Chapter 3 continues with a look at Turbo C, the compiler chosen for this book.

CHAPTER 2

THE C LANGUAGE

2 The C Language

Every book about C praises and chronicles the C language. This chapter continues that tradition; it outlines reported C chronology, describes fundamental C characteristics, talks about C's strengths as a programming tool, and attempts to explain why C has become almost universally accepted by programmers and managers. At the end of the chapter is a list of reference materials for the study of C and its application.

A BRIEF HISTORY OF C

The C language was developed in the early 1970's by Dennis Ritchie at Bell Telephone Laboratories. The ancestry of C can be traced through a design lineage that started with Algol and includes Pascal and PL/I.

C was developed to be a programmer's language for use on the new UNIX operating system. UNIX had been written in assembly language on the PDP-7 and ported to the PDP-11. C was influenced by its predecessor, B, which was written by Ken Thompson and descended from BCPL. BCPL, written in 1969 by Martin Richards, was an outgrowth of the Combined Programming Language project from London and Cambridge Universities.

UNIX was soon rewritten in C, and in 1974-75, UNIX was first distributed outside of the Bell Laboratories environment, giving credibility to the notion that an operating system can be successfully written in a language other than assembly language if the other language has sufficient power and flexibility.

In 1978, Brian Kernighan and Dennis Ritchie wrote *The C Programming Language* (Prentice-Hall). This work, called "the white book" by insiders and "K&R" by the rest of the world, became the standard definition of the C language. When "K&R" was written, C compilers were available on the PDP-11, the Interdata 8/32, the Honeywell 6000, and the IBM 370. Before long, the list would grow.

The C Language 2

In the late 1970's, C language products began to appear for the CP/M-based 8080 and Z80 microcomputers. Scott Guthery and Jim Gibson developed and marketed **Tiny-C**, an interpreted language based loosely on a subset of the C language but with an interactive programming environment resembling that of the enormously successful Microsoft BASIC. In 1980, Ron Cain published his **Small-C** compiler for CP/M and the 8080. Small-C compiled a subset of the C language, and the compiler was written in Small-C itself, a chicken-and-egg feat made possible when Cain wrote the first version of the compiler with the Tiny-C interpreter. After that, Small-C "bootstrapped" itself into existence as Cain and others added to the compiler, using earlier versions of the compiler to compile the improvements. Small-C compiles the C language source code into 8080 assembly language, and Cain has placed the compiler and its source code into the public domain.

At about the same time, Leor Zolman introduced the CP/M-based **BDS C** compiler, also a subset of the C language. The compiler's strengths were its speed and its compilation of relocatable object modules linked together into an executable module.

Shortly after BDS C was introduced, full-language compilers became available for CP/M. The impact of C on microcomputer programming had begun, and in 1981, the world of microcomputing took a mighty leap forward as IBM introduced the PC.

As soon as it was apparent that the PC was going to take hold, C compilers began to appear. Several C compilers were upgrades from 8080 ancestors, and many others were developed specifically for the PC marketplace. Today, at least seventeen C compilers are actively marketed for the PC.

In 1983, the American National Standards Institute (ANSI) formed the X3J11 Technical Committee, which has as its charter the development of a C Language standard. The standard will address not only the language but the compiler environment and the standard function library as well. The committee participants include representatives from major vendors of C compilers—including those for the PC—as well as many luminaries from the world of C. The efforts of the X3J11 committee have received a great deal of media attention, and the proposed standard has been published for review and comment by all interested parties. (It is doubtful that a brilliant programmer could fix a language designed by a committee, but it seems that a committee is doing an acceptable job of improving a language designed by a brilliant programmer.)

2 The C Language

Because of their participation in the X3J11 committee's work, most PC compiler vendors are releasing new versions incorporating changes in the proposed standard. (Turbo C, one of the newest PC compilers, includes most language and library enhancements of the proposed standard.)

C LANGUAGE CHARACTERISTICS

This book's purpose is not to teach you to program in C, but it is helpful to understand the characteristics of C that make it the language of choice for so many programmers.

C is a language of functions, data types, assignments, and flow control. To program in C, you must call a function, and most functions return values. The value returned from a function, the value of a data variable, or the value of a constant can be used in an assignment statement to change the value of another variable. With the addition of flow control—**if**, **while**, **for**, **do**, **switch**—the C language takes on the structure of a high-level language, enabling and promoting good programming style.

C has a small set of data types: integers, floating point numbers, characters, bit fields, and enumerated types. In C, you can declare a **pointer** variable that points to any data type. The address arithmetic of C is sensitive to the properties of the pointer being adjusted. Pointers to functions are also supported. You can extend the data types by building structures that are hierarchies of members, each member being one of the data types or an earlier-declared structure. **Unions** resemble structures but define a different kind of hierarchy in which all data types occupy common memory.

Arrays of data types can be declared. An **array** can consist of any data type, including a structure or union. Arrays can have multiple dimensions.

C functions are recursive by default; you can code a function that does not work in a recursive operation, but the language tends to naturally support recursion and requires little recursion programming effort.

The code in a C function is grouped into **blocks**; each block can have its own local variables. Blocks can be executed as the result of a single flow control operator. Blocks can be nested within blocks.

Variables and functions can be global to the program, global to the source module, or local to the block in which they are declared. Local variables can be declared so they retain their value through all invocations of their block (static), or they can be considered as new entities for each invocation (automatic).

C allows you to develop a program in multiple source files that are independently compiled. The relocatable object modules of individual source files are linked into a single executable program. This feature allows a compiler to support object libraries of reusable functions as well as large programs made up of many small source code components.

The C language has no input/output operations. The compiler compiles a language of functions, and all input and output is done with functions. Because of this feature, a standard library of functions has evolved, and this standard is what gives C its most endearing quality—C language code can be portable.

C LANGUAGE STRENGTHS

Portability is the most publicized advantage of C. If you write code that is obedient to the rules of C and avoids compiler-specific library extensions or machine-specific operations, your code stands a reasonable chance (more than with any other language) of being successfully ported to other compiler/operating system/computer environments.

The software presented in this book does not strive for portability. The screen window library is specific to the PC's video memory architecture, and the memory-resident utility functions use the interrupt structure of the PC, specific characteristics of DOS, and the Turbo C library extensions that support the development of interrupt service routines. A few functions contain a small amount of in-line assembly language.

2 The C Language

Extensibility in a computer language is the potential for the language to be extended by the programmer. C is extensible primarily because of the small number of C operators. Remember, the language itself does little more than change the value of variables and control the flow of execution. Everything of significance in a C computer program is performed by functions, and the language itself has no intrinsic functions other than the main function. The first extensions to C are found in the standard library; others are in nonstandard extensions that individual compilers include, and still others are in the third-party function libraries (such as the ones in this book) that add functional properties to C. The final layer of extensions is provided by the programmer who writes programs and uses reusable C language functions.

Besides its functional extensibility, C allows you to extend its repertoire of data types by declaring structures, unions, and **typedef** statements.

Programmers are particularly fond of the concise expression of algorithms permitted by C. C is an expressive language. Most statements that do not control process flow return a value, whether the statement is an assignment, a condition, a function call, or an expression. This property allows embedded expressions that result in a concise and efficient use of the language.

C is noted for efficient code generation. Its roots lie in languages that were close to the memory and register architectures of the hardware for which they were designed. C is often described as a high-level, portable assembly language. The nature of the language allows a compiler to produce efficient, optimized code.

THE ACCEPTANCE OF C

There can be no question of the overwhelming acceptance of C as the language of choice among software developers. Programmers like C for the reasons previously mentioned. The management of software development companies like C for the apparent independence it gives them from specific hardware and operating system environments. Today's managers, many of whom are yesterday's programmers, are sensitive to both advantages. C is the development language for most of the world's best-selling PC software packages.

C REFERENCES

Following is a list of C reference works that can help you learn more about the language and the ways in which it can be used:

The C Programming Language, Brian W. Kernighan and Dennis M. Ritchie, Prentice-Hall, 1978.

C Programming Standards and Guidelines, Thomas Plum, Plum Hall, 1982.

Learning to Program in C, Thomas Plum, Plum Hall, 1983.

Programming in C, Stephen G. Kochan, Hayden Book Company, 1983.

C Programming Guide, Jack Purdum, Que Corporation, 1983.

C: A Reference Manual, Samuel P. Harbison and Guy L. Steele, Jr., Tartan Laboratories, 1984.

The C Programmer's Handbook, Thom Hogan, Brady, 1984.

The C Toolbox, William James Hunt, Addison-Wesley, 1985.

Reliable Data Structures in C, Thomas Plum, Plum Hall, 1985.

MIX C Compiler, Mix Software, Inc., 1985. (This product is marketed as a compiler and priced like a book. Whether you use the compiler or not, the tutorial and C reference manual are well worth the price.)

Learning C with Tiny C, Scott B. Guthery, Tab Books, 1985.

Data Handling Utilities in C, Robert A. Radcliffe and Thomas J. Raab, Sybex, 1986.

C Development Tools for the IBM PC, Al Stevens, Brady, 1986.

Dr. Dobbs Toolbook of C, Editors, *Dr Dobb's Journal*, Brady, 1986.

C Data Base Development, Al Stevens, MIS:Press, 1987.

Advanced Graphics in C: Programming and Techniques, Nelson Johnson, Osborne McGraw-Hill, 1987.

C Tutor, Diskettes #577 and #578 of the PC-SIG Library. (This package is an on-line tutorial that consists of text lessons and example programs that you compile with your own compiler.)

CHAPTER 3

TURBO C

3 Turbo C

In December, 1986, a small company by the name of Wizard Software Systems, Inc. announced their relocation from Arlington, Massachusetts to Monte Sereno, California. They had created and marketed a $450 C compiler named **Wizard C**.

Wizard C was a respected C compiler—always faring well in reviews—and was even called the "best" C compiler by at least one reviewer. Its strengths were its quick compile times, efficient code optimization, compliance with the proposed ANSI standard, and a number of extensions to C to support the development of interrupt service routines. These extensions included a special interrupt function type, in-line assembly code, and pseudo-variables that allowed direct access from C language to the microprocessor's machine registers.

In February, 1987, Borland International of Scotts Valley, California, announced the introduction of **Turbo C**, the long-awaited companion product to the highly successful Turbo Pascal compiler. The announcement included claims for performance that few experts believed. It had to be hype, they reasoned—even the fastest C compilers were incapable of anything near the 7000-lines-a-minute compile time that Borland claimed for Turbo C. The performance windows for C compilers had been pushed to the limit by established, mature compilers, and no one was going to improve those numbers, the experts thought.

That same month, Wizard ran its last magazine advertisement.

In May, 1987, Version 1.0 of Turbo C was shipped (complete with T-shirts). The lid was off, and the competition had to take notice; Turbo C turned out to be everything its developers claimed and more.

Actually, Borland International had acquired Wizard Software Systems to implement Turbo C. The industry had been speculating about when Borland would enter the C compiler market with a low-end, fast compiler to go with the company's maiden product, Turbo Pascal, and the more recent, highly popular Turbo Basic. Rather than undertake such a major development effort from scratch, Borland made a wise choice; they bought the best C compiler available and committed the resources to make it even better.

At the time of Borland's announcement, 17 C compilers were marketed for the IBM PC; few people thought the world needed another one. There is something about Philippe Kahn's Borland International, however, that captures the imagination and demands attention. When claims about Turbo C were published, many doubted and few knew, but all wanted to see for themselves. The C world was ready for one more compiler — if it was coming from Borland. It was well worth the wait. Borland was not in business to introduce another ho-hum C compiler; Borland intended to redefine what the C language development environment looked like.

TWO TURBO Cs

Turbo C is two compiler products: the usual UNIX-style command line make/compiler/linker combination and the Turbo C **Integrated Development Environment**.

The command line package includes a make utility, the **tcc** compiler, and a custom linker. Future versions will undoubtedly include an object librarian. The command line compiler is similar to that of most other C compilers for the PC, but it is much faster. Programmers who prefer this environment will find everything they need in Turbo C combined with a favorite editor. Having bought this book, you probably have bought or will buy Turbo C. Everything you will need to know about the command line environment is documented in the User's and Reference Guides.

The Integrated Development Environment is a program named **tc**, and it integrates a programmer's editor, an on-line, project-oriented make utility, and a program execution utility in one package. Future plans probably include an integrated, source-level debugger — a necessary addition to Turbo C. The Environment, as it is called, is what separates Turbo C from the competition (other than its impressive performance, of course).

3 Turbo C

The Environment is the showcase of Turbo C. Its strongest asset is the level of integration achieved between the editor, the compiler, and the linker. In the Environment, a programmer can edit a program, compile it, link it with other source modules and libraries, and run it. This capability represents the first of the new generation of C compilers. It is similar to what Borland achieved with Turbo Pascal over three years ago, but until now, no C compiler has attempted to emulate it. Expect most major contenders to introduce similar capabilities in the future.

CUSTOMIZING THE ENVIRONMENT

You can customize the Environment. Everything from colors on the screen to the level of error-checking can be modified. Some modifications are made by running the **TCINST** program; others are available in pop-up menus at the top of the Environment's interactive entry screen. Following are some items that can be customized in the Environment:

- memory model — tiny, small, medium, compact, large, or huge
- function calling convention — C or Pascal
- microprocessor — 8088/8086 or 80186/80286
- floating point — none, coprocessor, or emulated
- levels of optimization
- level of error-handling

You can customize more Turbo C options. Turbo C is capable of rigorous error- and warning-checking such that older programs will, when compiled, deliver numerous warnings. You can use the Options menu to stifle much of this warning-reporting. You can insist on rigid ANSI compliance, or settle for K&R lenience. You can require warnings if the most common functions lack declarations and prototypes, or you can let implicit function declarations and haphazard parameter specifications prevail as they did in the earlier, so-called K&R compilers.

You will probably want to modify the colors. The three preprogrammed color packages you can select include a default color set (gaudy), a turquoise color set (ugly), and a magenta color set (simply awful). Don't despair; the **TCINST** program allows you to select color and intensity for each individually defined component of the Environment. Remember, these observations are based on how the color sets appear to a picky programmer on a CGA system. You might love them.

THE TURBO C EDITOR

At one level, the Turbo C editor resembles WordStar's nondocument mode text editor. This editor architecture has prevailed in many of Borland's products, including the Sidekick Notepad and Turbo Pascal editor. If you can use WordStar, you can also use the Turbo C editor. Many users, however, will take advantage of the **TCINST** program to customize the editor. You can change the default window sizes and editor command keys. Programmers who regularly use a different editor will appreciate the opportunity to make Turbo C behave more like the other editor, sparing them the mental confusion over remembering two editor command sets. The extent to which you can modify the editor is limited; certain function keys and Alt/key combinations are reserved as Environment Hot Keys and cannot be used as editor commands.

The editor is not as powerful as some specialty programmer's editors, but it is adequate for small editing tasks. The editor has a nonconfigurable tab spacing of eight characters per tab, which was annoying while working with the code in this book because its tabs are set every four spaces to accommodate limitations of the printed page. Borland has posted a **PATCH.COM** program and several bug-repair patches on Compuserve and BIX, and among these is a patch allowing you to change the tab stops to every four positions. The editor thus became immediately useful for this project. Perhaps the tab configuration will be a future feature of Turbo C.

THE TURBO C LINK UTILITY

Turbo C includes its own link utility named **TLINK**. A link program is used to link various object files from C, assembly, and other language compilations into one executable module. Object files generated by Turbo C are compatible with the standard DOS LINK program, so Turbo C files can be linked with object libraries from other languages, including assembly language. The primary reason for using **TLINK** is speed; **TLINK** is much faster than the DOS LINK program.

The Turbo C Link program is a stand-alone program in the **tcc** command line compiler setup, and it is integrated into the Environment. When you build a program from the Environment, the link process is automatically invoked.

THE TURBO C PROJECT MAKE UTILITY

The Turbo C command line compiler has a conventional make utility similar to the UNIX make and that of other PC C compilers. The Environment has a unique make facility to associate source and object files with the executable program being developed. In this respect, it resembles the traditional make. It is, however, integrated with the Environment, and it uses a version of the make file—called a "project" file—that is easier to read and understand than that of the command line make utility. In a project file, you list the source modules that contribute to the program, one on each line. To the right of each module name, you enter the other files (headers, for example) on which the source file is dependent. These dependencies are in parentheses and separated by commas. Following is an example of a project file entry.

```
myprogram (keys.h, twindow.h)
```

If **myprogram.c** is newer than **myprogram.obj**, or either **keys.h** or **twindow.h** is newer than **myprogram.c**, **myprogram.c** is compiled into **myprogram.obj**. If **myprogram.obj** is newer than **myprogram.exe**, **myprogram.obj** is linked with the appropriate (depending on memory model) startup object file and run-time library.

The project make process becomes essential when the executable program is made up of numerous C source files dependent on various header files.

You can name object files and object libraries in a project make file. The Environment will include the object files without trying to compile them and will search the libraries to resolve external function calls.

THE COMPILER/LINKER ERROR TRAPS

When the Environment begins to build a project, it records all errors and warnings. When the build process is complete, the errors and warnings are listed in one window, and the source program is displayed in another window. You can step through the source files, moving forward and backward from error to error. The Environment displays each error message and places the cursor at the place on the offending line where the error was found. You can make corrections as you go, and you can restart the build at any time. The error-handler recognizes when you have added or deleted source lines and adjusts the cursor position accordingly.

LOW-LEVEL SOFTWARE SUPPORT

Turbo C includes several nonportable extensions to the C language that echo its Wizard heritage and are essential to the kind of software developed in this book. These extensions are aimed at the support of interrupt service routines and other machine-level operations.

The language adds the **interrupt** function type, which generates a far function that saves the 8086 registers when it is entered and initializes the data segment register to the data segment of the interrupt function. When the function returns, the registers are restored, and the return is the 8086 IRET instruction, which is used for returns from interrupts.

3 Turbo C

In-line assembly code is supported by the addition of the **asm** keyword. Anything following the asm keyword is passed directly to the Microsoft assembler, which you must have to use this feature. The in-line assembly code can use C variable names in scope when the assembly code is declared. This feature allows you to write assembly functions that are essentially independent of the memory model to be used. Programs without in-line assembly code are not passed to an assembler; they are compiled directly. Programs with in-line assembly code must be compiled from the **tcc** command-line compiler because the **tc** Environment compiler cannot execute the assembler program. Borland has tentative plans to change this limitation in future releases.

Several keywords are used as pseudo-variables to provide direct access to the machine registers. If you know what the registers contain and how they are used, some operations can be optimized. Use this feature with care. The best approach is to compile the function to assembly code with the -S feature of the **tcc** command line compiler and examine the compiled code to see if your intentions for the use of the registers are being realized. You should also be prepared to revisit any such usages when you convert to a future version of Turbo C. There is no assurance that Borland will not alter the way registers are used in compiled code, and this change could break your code.

INSTALLATION

The weakest area of the Turbo C documentation is in the area of installation. There are facts you need to know, and the organization of the manual does not lead you directly to the necessary information.

Both the command line compiler and the Environment run from files that specify the user's desired configuration, but these are two different files. The manual instructs you on the preparation of TURBOC.CFG, the configuration file for the command line compiler, but it is not as clear about TCCONFIG.TC, the configuration file for the Environment. After you have installed the environment, you should run it once to establish all your defaults, including the path specifications of where **tc** will expect to find libraries, startup code, include files, and itself. These options can be established from the Environment selection on the Options menu. When everything is as you want it, use the Store selection to build the TCCONFIG.TC file.

MEMORY MODELS

Turbo C supports six memory models: the tiny, small, medium, compact, large, and huge models. The user's guide includes a chapter on memory models that explains the 8086 segmented memory architecture and how it influences the various memory models. You are encouraged to read and understand that chapter because an understanding of the 8086 architecture will aid you in using and adding to the memory-resident utility software in this book.

LIBRARY SOURCE CODE

Turbo C is not distributed with source code for the run-time library functions, but a Turbo C user can purchase a license to use the source code, which Borland will provide.

SUMMARY

Chapter 4 begins the specification of a library of Turbo C functions. As this library grows in the chapters that follow, you will gain the software tools necessary to build pop-up video windows into your programs — programs that can later be built as memory-resident utilities. Until now, no C compiler has provided a support level for this kind of software equal to that of Turbo C.

CHAPTER 4

GENERAL-PURPOSE FUNCTIONS

4 General-purpose Functions

This is a book of software, and the following chapters contain a software tool collection that can be used to build applications systems. These tools are written in C language, compiled with the Turbo C compiler, and available for you to include in your programs. As software tools, they extend the C language by adding functions to the already expansive standard library with Turbo C extensions. This chapter presents the first level of functions to include when you build programs that use these libraries. The functions in this chapter are general-purpose, low-level operations (specific to the IBM PC and its hardware) that manage the screen display and keyboard.

You might find little reason to call some general-purpose functions from your programs. The purpose of these functions is to support the higher-level library functions in this book; they are useful, however, and you might find a purpose for them. Further, your understanding of the tools in this book can be enhanced by an understanding of *all* the code—even the functions you don't call from your programs.

As you read these function descriptions, refer to Listing 4.1, **ibmpc.c**, which follows the discussions.

void clear_screen()

This function clears the screen and positions the cursor in the upper left corner. The screen is cleared to blank characters, and the video attribute of the characters is taken from the character variable named **attrib**, declared in **ibmpc.c**. The value of that attribute corresponds to the video attribute byte that accompanies the ASCII character byte when a character is stored into video memory. This concept is more fully explained in Chapter 5. The **attrib** variable is initialized to a value that clears the screen to a black background with white characters. If you want a different attribute, you must change the value of this variable before you call **clear__screen**.

int vmode()

This function returns the current video mode; it is primarily used to determine if the software should address monochrome video memory or the text mode memory of the Color Graphics Adaptor or Enhanced Graphics Adaptor. These devices are more fully discussed in Chapter 5.

The **vmode** function returns a value of 7 if the PC is operating in the monochrome mode. Any other value is assumed to indicate CGA or EGA text mode.

void cursor(int x, int y)

This function positions the PC's cursor at the screen location specified by the **x** and **y** coordinates. The 0,0 coordinates are in the upper left corner of the screen. The **x** coordinate ranges from 0-79, and the **y** coordinate ranges from 0-24.

void curr_cursor(int *x, int *y)

This function reads the current cursor position and writes the **x** and **y** coordinates into the addresses pointed to by the pointers passed to the function.

int set_cursor_type(int t)

This function sets the current cursor size, interpreted by the software in this book as a **cursor type**. The size is specified by an integer that contains the starting scan line of the cursor in the upper byte of the integer and the ending scan line of the cursor in the lower byte of the integer.

The text editor and data entry programs in the following chapters use cursor size to indicate the setting of the Insert/Overwrite mode. A block cursor indicates that the insert mode is in effect and is specified by the value 0x0106, which generates a cursor that occupies scan lines 1 through 6 in the character box of the character where the cursor is positioned. The underline cursor indicates that the Overwrite mode is in effect and is specified by the value 0x0607. This value generates a cursor that occupies scan lines 6 and 7.

4 General-purpose Functions

int get_char()

This function is important; it serves several critical purposes for the software that calls it. **Get_char** reads a character from the keyboard by using the ROM-BIOS keyboard services of the PC. Its primary function is to provide unadorned, unechoed, single-character keyboard input while avoiding calls into DOS functions, and it also performs the following additional tasks.

While the system is waiting for a keystroke from the user, the **get_char** function generates software interrupts to vector 0x28, the **DOSOK** interrupt. This interrupt and its importance in a memory-resident utility are explained in Chapter 11.

When you press a function key, the PC's ROM-BIOS returns what appear to be two keystrokes. The first keystroke is a null value, indicating that the next character will represent a function key. The second value is a 7-bit ASCII code with a unique value for each function key. If you ignore the null character, the function keys resemble other keys with valid ASCII values, such as letters. The **get_char** function translates the two-key ROM-BIOS sequences into eight-bit values that are distinct from those of the non-function keys. It performs this translation by setting the most significant bit of the ASCII value that follows the null value. These values are defined as global symbols in the source file **keys.h** (see Listing 4.2).

The **get_char** function waits for the designated Help function key to be pressed. The Help function key value is defined in the global integer named **helpkey**. It is initialized to a null value, but the software that processes Help windows will set it to the value of a specified function key. When you press the Help function key, the **get_char** function looks at a global function pointer named **helpfunc**. If this pointer has a non-null value, the **get_char** function calls the designated help function through the **helpfunc** pointer.

General-purpose Functions 4

void vpoke(unsigned vseg, unsigned adr, unsigned chr)

int vpeek(unsigned vseg, unsigned adr)

These two functions read and write characters and video attributes from and into video memory. To understand how they are used, you must understand the nature of the PC's video memory and how video retrace works. Chapter 5 includes a more complete discussion of these topics.

The **vpoke** and **vpeek** functions use in-line assembly code. To compile these functions, you must have the Microsoft Macro Assembler (MASM) because it is used by Turbo C to implement in-line assembly code. This assembly code is required only if your programs are to be run on systems that use the IBM Color Graphics Adaptor or the equivalent. The reasons for this requirement are explained in Chapter 5. If this is not the case, and you want to use these functions without the MASM assembler, remove the functions from the **ibmpc.c** source module and insert the following statements into the source file named **twindow.h**, found in Chapter 6.

```
#define vpoke(vseg,adr,chr) poke(vseg,adr,chr)
#define vpeek(vseg,adr) peek(vseg,adr)
```

These macros will replace the **vpoke** and **vpeek** functions and will eliminate the requirement for the MASM program for the window functions in this book.

GENERAL-PURPOSE FUNCTIONS SOURCE LISTINGS

Listing 4.1 is **ibmpc.c**, the source file that contains the functions described in this chapter. Because the functions contain in-line assembly code, the source file must be compiled with the **tcc** command line compiler rather than from the **tc** environment.

To compile **ibmpc.c**, enter the following command (do not type the C> prompt):

```
C>tcc -c ibmpc
```

4 General-purpose Functions

Listing 4.1: ibmpc.c

```c
/* -------------- ibmpc.c -------------- */

/*
 * Low-level functions addressing BIOS & PC Hardware
 */

#pragma inline
#include <dos.h>
static union REGS rg;

/* ----------- position the cursor ------------- */
void cursor(int x, int y)
{
    rg.x.ax = 0x0200;
    rg.x.bx = 0;
    rg.x.dx = ((y << 8) & 0xff00) + x;
    int86(16, &rg, &rg);
}

/* ------------ return the cursor position ------------- */
void curr_cursor(int *x, int *y)
{
    rg.x.ax = 0x0300;
    rg.x.bx = 0;
    int86(16, &rg, &rg);
    *x = rg.h.dl;
    *y = rg.h.dh;
}

/* ----------- set cursor type --------------- */
void set_cursor_type(int t)
{
    rg.x.ax = 0x0100;
    rg.x.bx = 0;
    rg.x.cx = t;
    int86(16, &rg, &rg);
}
```

continued...

General-purpose Functions 4

...from previous page

```c
char attrib = 7;

/* ------------- clear the screen -------------- */
void clear_screen()
{
    cursor(0, 0);
    rg.h.al = ' ';
    rg.h.ah = 9;
    rg.x.bx = attrib;
    rg.x.cx = 2000;
    int86(16, &rg, &rg);
}

/* ----------- return the video mode ------------ */
int vmode()
{
    rg.h.ah = 15;
    int86(16, &rg, &rg);
    return rg.h.al;
}

/* -------- test for scroll lock -------- */
int scroll_lock()
{
    rg.x.ax = 0x0200;
    int86(0x16, &rg, &rg);
    return rg.h.al & 0x10;
}
```

continued...

4 General-purpose Functions

...from previous page

```c
void (*helpfunc)();
int helpkey = 0;
int helping = 0;

/* -------------- get a keyboard character ---------------- */
int get_char()
{
    int c;

    while (1)   {
        rg.h.ah = 1;
        int86(0x16, &rg, &rg);
        if (rg.x.flags & 0x40)   {
            int86(0x28, &rg, &rg);
            continue;
        }
        rg.h.ah = 0;
        int86(0x16, &rg, &rg);
        if (rg.h.al == 0)
            c = rg.h.ah | 128;
        else
            c = rg.h.al;
        if (c == helpkey && helpfunc)    {
            if (!helping)   {
                helping = 1;
                (*helpfunc)();
                helping = 0;
                continue;
            }
        }
        break;
    }
    return c;
}
```

continued...

...from previous page

```c
/* --- insert a character and attribute into video RAM --- */
void vpoke(unsigned vseg, unsigned adr, unsigned chr)
{
    if (vseg == 45056)          /* monochrome mode */
        poke(vseg, adr, chr);
    else    {
        _DI = adr;      /* offset of video character */
        _ES = vseg;     /* video segment */
        asm cld;
        _BX = chr;      /* the attribute and character */
        _DX = 986;      /* video status port */
        /* ------ wait for video retrace to start ----- */
        do
            asm in  al,dx;
        while (_AL & 1);
        /* ------ wait for video retrace to stop ----- */
        do
            asm in  al,dx;
        while (!(_AL & 1));
        _AL = _BL;
        asm stosb;      /* store character */
        /* ------ wait for video retrace to start ----- */
        do
            asm in  al,dx;
        while (_AL & 1);
        /* ------ wait for video retrace to stop ----- */
        do
            asm in  al,dx;
        while (!(_AL & 1));
        _AL = _BH;
        asm stosb;      /* store attribute */
    }
}
```

continued...

4 General-purpose Functions

...from previous page

```
/* ---- read a character and attribute from video RAM --- */
int vpeek(unsigned vseg, unsigned adr)
{
    int ch, at;

    if (vseg == 45056)                  /* monochrome mode */
        return peek(vseg, adr);
    asm push ds;
    _DX = 986;              /* video status port */
    _DS = vseg;             /* video segment address */
    _SI = adr;              /* video character offset */
    asm cld;
    /* ------ wait for video retrace to start ----- */
    do
        asm in  al,dx;
    while (_AL & 1);
    /* ------ wait for video retrace to stop ----- */
    do
        asm in  al,dx;
    while (!(_AL & 1));
    asm lodsb;              /* get the character */
    _BL = _AL;
    /* ------ wait for video retrace to start ----- */
    do
        asm in  al,dx;
    while (_AL & 1);
    /* ------ wait for video retrace to stop ----- */
    do
        asm in  al,dx;
    while (!(_AL & 1));
    asm lodsb;              /* get the attribute */
    _BH = _AL;
    _AX = _BX;
    asm pop ds;
    return _AX;
}
```

Listing 4.2 is **keys.h**, a header file included in many of the programs, and you may find it useful in your programs as well. The file contains global definitions of function key values returned by the **get_char** function.

Listing 4.2: keys.h

```
/* --------------------- keys.h -------------------------- */

#define HT          9
#define RUBOUT      8
#define BELL        7
#define ESC         27
#define SHIFT_HT    143
#define CTRL_T      20
#define CTRL_B      2
#define CTRL_D      4
#define ALT_D       160

#define F1          187
#define F2          188
#define F3          189
#define F4          190
#define F5          191
#define F6          192
#define F7          193
#define F8          194
#define F9          195
#define F10         196

#define HOME        199
#define UP          200
#define PGUP        201
#define BS          203
#define FWD         205
#define END         207
#define DN          208
#define PGDN        209
#define INS         210
#define DEL         211

#define CTRL_HOME   247
#define CTRL_BS     243
#define CTRL_FWD    244
#define CTRL_END    245
```

4 General-purpose Functions

SUMMARY

From this simple foundation of low-level functions, Chapter 5 will develop and explain the concept of **video windows**, which is the next level of a multi-layer function collection that comprises the software in this book.

CHAPTER 5

SCREEN WINDOWS

5 Screen Windows

This chapter discusses what **video windows** are and how they work. Chapter 6 explains how you can add windows to your Turbo C programs and includes a complete library of window management functions. Later chapters provide advanced library functions to support the use of windows for specific purposes, such as context-sensitive help, text editing, data entry, and menus.

As you read about video windows and their application and implementation, try to recall systems you have seen that use similar techniques. Also, think of past development projects in which programs you wrote might have benefitted from such a capability. Then, try to see if there are shortcomings in these functions that would make them more applicable to your experiences. You can almost always find some shortcomings, no matter what the program. With these functions, you have an advantage; the source code is included, and you can modify it to suit your requirements.

THE VIDEO WINDOW

A **window** is an area of the PC's video screen used for a specific purpose. A typical window is rectangular or square, and its boundaries are usually visually defined by a border of characters from the PC's graphics character set. Using windows has become a popular way to present information to the PC user in a manner that makes the most of the limited display space available on the screen while still appearing to support multiple, asynchronous tasks. Since video displays are generated in RAM memory space directly accessed by the processor (a technique called "memory-mapped video"), windows can be displayed rapidly, appearing instantly from nowhere and disappearing just as fast. With this capability, a program can use windows to manage the presentation of many different kinds of information.

Windows come and go; they appear on the screen when required, and they disappear when you no longer need to see information they contain. A program can display as many windows as the programmer wants to use, and the windows can be many different sizes, colors, and formats. You can place windows wherever they are needed. When you no longer need to display a window, and you delete it, it disappears, and you see whatever was under it before it was established.

Screen Windows 5

Anyone who has been near automated civilization in recent years has seen plenty of windows. The PC is everywhere; it dominates social and professional behavior, and wherever you find one, you also find **Sidekick**, the ubiquitous notepad, calculator, calendar, and dialer that pops up on the screen, performs its duty, and disappears without disturbing whatever was going on before it appeared. The software and marketing magic of Borland International (the folks who also brought you Turbo C) put the video window into universal use. If you have never seen a video window, put the book down, find a PC, and press the <Alt> and the <Ctrl> keys together. If you don't see a red-blue-aqua-white window (or a green and black window on a monochrome system), ask the PC owner why Sidekick isn't running. If you do see the little window, start playing with it. You can display other windows by selecting from the menu in the first window. You can move windows around by pressing the Scroll Lock key and then pressing the arrow keys. You can make windows disappear by pressing the <Esc> key. You can get help by pressing <F1>.

In this chapter, you will learn how such windows work, how they can overlap one another, how they can move around, and how you can incorporate them into your own Turbo C programs.

Windows are used to display menus, messages, notices, text files, data entry forms, and context-sensitive help displays. A system with window software can display each window as an individual, independent data presentation, unrelated to other windows and unconstrained by the amount of video space occupied by other windows. It is possible to have several windows in view even if each one uses most of the screen because windows can "pop up" on top of one another.

The pop-up characteristic of windows is often described by comparing a video screen to the surface of a desk. If you pass much paper across your desk, you might have a number of memos and documents on the desktop but be looking at only one, probably the most current one. Paper allows you do this, and so does the video screen. If the screen contains a window as shown in Figure 5.1, and the software needs to display a second window but does not need to erase the first, the display can appear as in Figure 5.2. Then, when the second window is no longer needed, it is erased, and the screen again looks like Figure 5.1.

5 Screen Windows

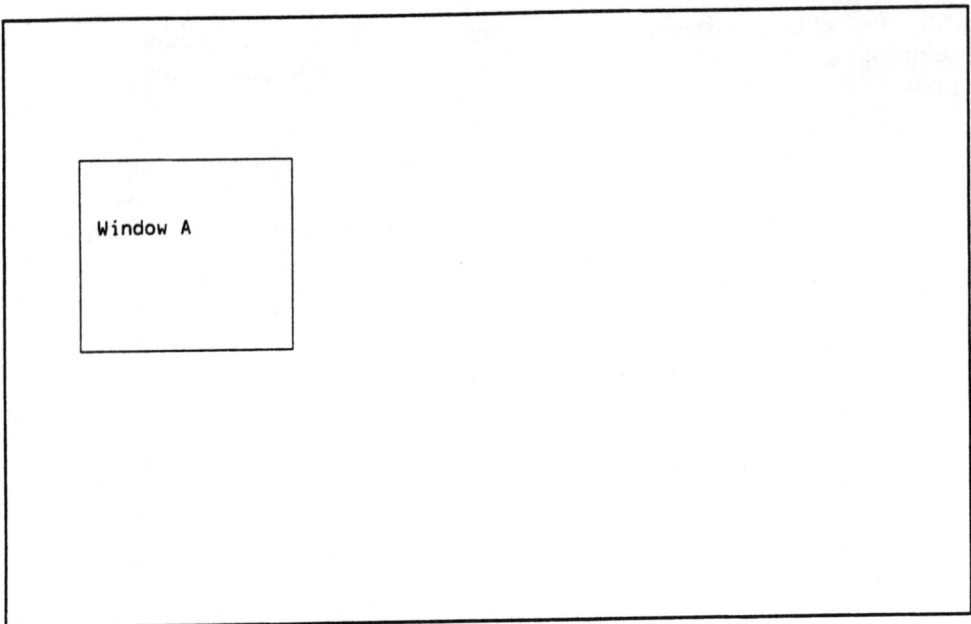

Figure 5.1 A Video Window

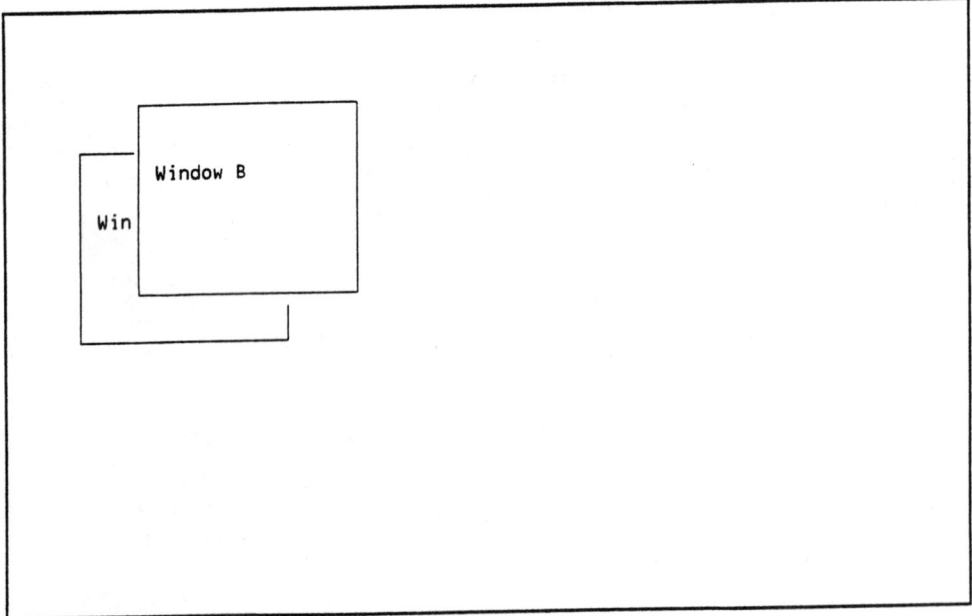

Figure 5.2 Overlapping Windows

Screen Windows 5

To understand how windows can be used in an application, it helps to know how windows work and how they are implemented. Remember that a window is a rectangular space on the video screen. A window has another property, however, that distinguishes it from just another screen display — the window can pop up and down.

When a window is about to be displayed (popped up), its rectangular screen space might contain some information that must survive the window. The window might cover all or any part of that information, and when the window is removed (popped down), that information must be restored. The display under a window can include other windows. Figure 5.3 shows a screen with several windows on it; each covers a part of the window under it.

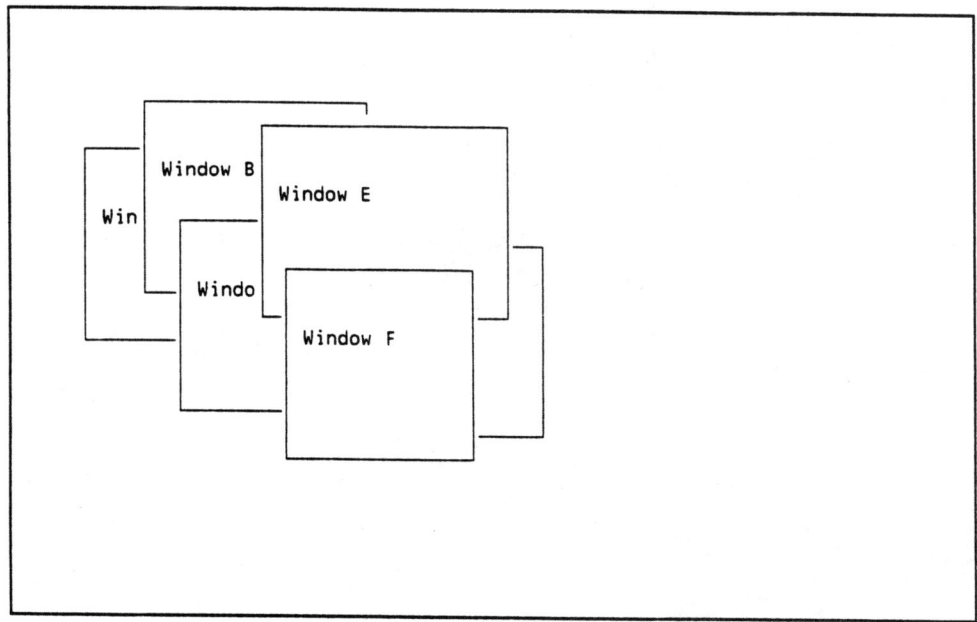

Figure 5.3 Many Overlapping Windows

5 Screen Windows

If every program had to manage window placement and when to restore the screen they covered, programs would be even more complex and difficult to write and maintain. This ability is not necessary; the properties and functions of windows are common from application to application, so a general-purpose library of window functions can be used. This book includes such a library; its functions are described in Chapter 6.

The basic window operations used in most programs are small in number and not very complicated. You need to establish a window, specifying its location and size. You might want to identify its colors, borders, and title. You must have a way to write text into the window. It might be necessary to move a window from one location to another. Finally, you must delete a window from the screen so that the previous screen image appears as it did before the window was established. With these window operations, you can develop a program that uses colorful and attractive video windows in the user interface. (Remember, using an effective library does not guarantee that the human factors in a program are of high quality. The programmer must use sound design techniques with windows as well as with any other software tool.)

To understand the management of video displays, you must understand the nature of video display memory. The following discussion is a basic introduction to video display memory architecture. For a comprehensive treatment of the subject, see *The Peter Norton Programmer's Guide to the IBM PC* (Peter Norton, Microsoft Press, 1985).

VIDEO MEMORY ARCHITECTURE

The video screen is an integral part of the PC. Earlier personal computers used video terminals connected to serial input/output ports, but the IBM PC uses a hardware architecture that includes the video electronics.

Screen displays are built from video refresh memory. The PC uses a portion of random access memory (RAM) for video displays. The video RAM can be read and written by the processor, and, therefore, by your programs. Since the video processor on the display adaptor is constantly generating display images from the contents of the video RAM, any new character written into RAM appears on the screen as soon as it is written. Since the video RAM is accessible to the microprocessor, changes to the display occur at speeds equivalent to memory transfer rates, and are, therefore, faster than display changes bound by the serial transfer rates of video terminals.

The location and characteristics of the video RAM device are standard throughout the PC product line, and, to ensure compatibility, all PC clones have the same configurations.

A PC can contain one of three video architectures, each of which uses a different kind of video monitor and, therefore, a different video display adaptor card inside the computer. The first device is the **Monochrome Adaptor** (MA), which supports a monochrome display monitor with text and no graphics. The second device is the **Color Graphics Adaptor** (CGA). The CGA connects to a color monitor that supports a text mode with eight foreground and background colors, two levels of foreground intensity, and, in a separate mode, low-resolution graphics (640×200 pixels) in a single color. The third device is the **Enhanced Graphics Adaptor** (EGA), which can be used in the same color text mode as the CGA and which supports multiple color graphics at higher resolution.

The software in this book works within the text modes of any of the three video devices. Since the CGA and EGA are functionally equivalent in this mode, the following discussions of the CGA apply to both devices.

Video RAM is organized into a two-dimensional array of character columns and rows. The memory is contiguous and consists of one 16-bit word for each character position. Each row contains 80 contiguous characters, and there are 25 contiguous rows. The word that represents a character consists of two eight-bit bytes—one for the ASCII value of the character and one for the video attributes the character will display. The ASCII character value is the least significant (right-most) of the two bytes.

The MA has one page of video RAM; the CGA has four pages. The software in this book uses the first page of the CGA video memory.

5 Screen Windows

Video memory is located in the upper regions of the processor's address space. The designers of the PC, faced with a maximum of one megabyte of addressable memory, decided to put the video RAM and the **Read Only Memory** (ROM) **Basic Input-Output System** (BIOS) in the upper reaches of this address space. To allow the MA and the CGA to coexist in the same machine, the designers assigned different segment addresses to the two video memories. Monochrome memory begins at the 0xb000 segment, and CGA memory begins at the 0xb800 segment. A program can determine which of the two displays is in use by calling a function in the ROM BIOS. The calling program can thus adjust itself to the appropriate video RAM segment address. Since the two video memory architectures are largely compatible, a program needs to do little else to adjust itself.

The video attribute byte consists of 2 three-bit color fields (one for the background color of the character and one for the foreground color), a foreground high/low intensity bit, and a bit that controls whether the character will blink when it is displayed. Figure 5.4 shows the configuration of the attribute byte.

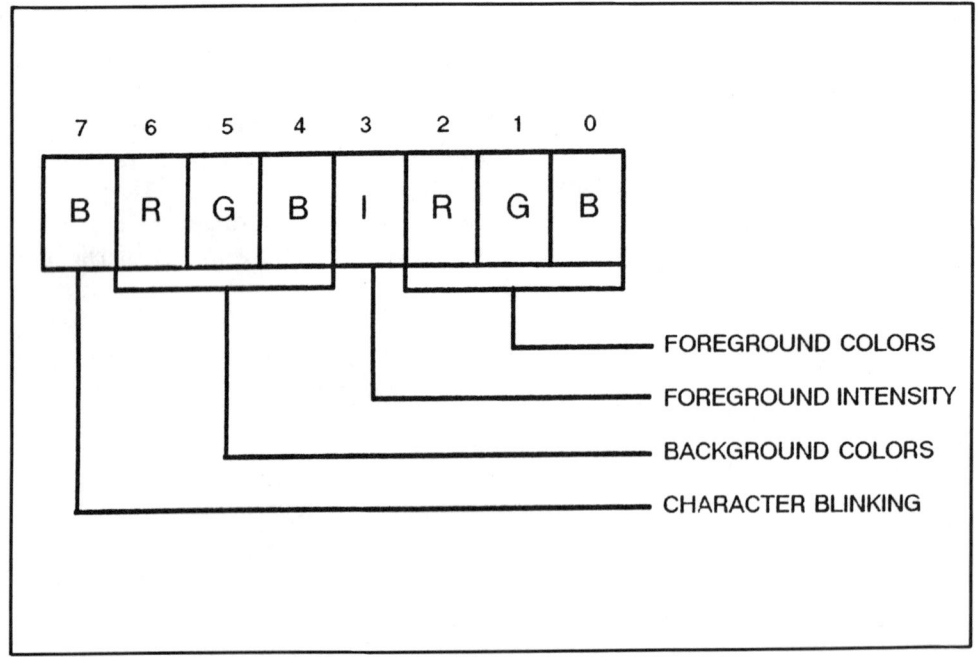

Figure 5.4 The Video Attribute Byte

The red, green, and blue components can be combined to provide eight distinct color settings that display white, red, green, blue, cyan, magenta, yellow, and black colors. The addition of the intensity bit for the foreground colors provides eight more values.

The values of the video attribute byte have slightly different meanings when the MA is used. Since color is not supported by the MA, only white on black and black on white have meaning to the MA. Other combinations produce either black on black or white on white, although the blue-foreground, black-background combination produces underlined characters, a feature unavailable on the CGA. The MA supports the same intensity and blinking character attributes as the CGA.

Once you determine where video memory is and what must go into it, you can experiment with **pokes** from your Turbo C library to change the video image. Listing 5.1 is a small program named **vidpoke.c** that writes a string directly into video memory. The program assumes that you have the CGA and combines the character value with a hex 7 attribute byte to display the string in white letters on a black background. If you are using the MA, change the **#define VSEG** from 0xb800 to 0xb000.

Listing 5.1: vidpoke.c

```
/* ---------- vidpoke.c ---------- */

#define VSEG 0xb800

char vdata [] = "What hath Kahn wrought?";

main()
{
    char *vp;
    int v;

    for (v = 0, vp = vdata; *vp; v += 2, vp++)
        poke(VSEG, v, 0x700 | *vp);
}
```

5 Screen Windows

SNOW AND VIDEO RETRACE

If you were to put the **vidpoke.exe** program into a loop or significantly increase the length of the string, you might see an annoying quantity of video "snow" when the program is run. You will see this snow only with a CGA or compatible product; the EGA and MA do not have this characteristic. The following discussion explains why you see snow and how software can eliminate it.

CGA snow results from the hardware architecture of the display device. Since the microprocessor and the CRT controller access the video memory, concurrent accesses must be coordinated. A CRT controller must operate in synchronization with the time base of the video sweep circuits. When it is time to paint a pixel on the screen, the CRT processor must have access to the memory location that contains the bit corresponding to the pixel. The processor cannot wait because it is working with the fixed dot clock of a raster video display device; therefore, if the CRT controller and the microprocessor both try to access the same memory location, the CRT controller should take precedence. A well-designed device will place a wait state on the microprocessor, gated through the microprocessor's request for video memory. The MA and EGA use such techniques, and you need not worry about memory access contention between the microprocessor and the CRT controller; however, the CGA does not perform this way in the text mode, and you must do something about it.

With the CGA, if the microprocessor wants to read or write the video memory, it is allowed to do so, and the CRT controller is denied access to the same memory. Since the CRT controller must adhere to a fixed time constant relative to the horizontal and vertical sweeps of the raster CRT, it simply paints random data in the absence of the real thing; therefore, while your program is changing the contents of video memory, you see a screen-wide scattering of snow.

Fortunately, the CGA provides a way to avoid this distracting flicker. To create an image, a **cathode ray tube** (CRT) has an electron gun that fires electrons at phosphor on the screen. If the voltage of the firing is high enough, the little dots of phosphor glow; otherwise, they are dark. A CRT paints a picture as a sequence of lines called **raster lines**. The CGA paints 200 of these lines. The electron gun sweeps from left to right and top to bottom. (Actually, three guns are used, one for each of the primary colors—red, green, and blue.) At the end of a line, the gun must sweep back to the left edge of the screen and down one line. This period is the **horizontal retrace sweep**. After the bottom-most line is displayed, the electron gun must sweep back to the top of the screen to repaint the first line, a procedure called the **vertical retrace sweep**. During these two time periods, the electron gun's voltage is low, and the CRT is not displaying pixels. At these times, no characters are displayed, and the CRT controller is not accessing video memory. The gun is not painting any pixels, so the display processor doesn't need to read video memory. The microprocessor has unlimited access to video memory when the retrace operations are in effect.

The CGA has a hardware register that indicates the status of the retrace circuits. By testing this register, a program can restrict its video memory accesses to times when retrace is occurring, thereby eliminating the flicker. The use of this register is time-sensitive; if you try to use it from a high-level language (C, for example), it won't work because the overhead of the language exceeds the retrace time, and the snow remains.

The problem is solved with assembly language. Assembly language functions can wait for retrace periods and have enough time during them to read or write a character, which is possible because assembly language code executes fast enough to deal with the strict constraints of a video time base.

Note that the MA and EGA do not need assembly language functions. Simple peeks and pokes of characters to and from video memory will work and will be faster, but for the CGA in text mode, the use of assembly language is necessary (unless you are willing to look at a lot of flicker).

5 Screen Windows

You should be aware that some so-called compatible video boards are not totally effective in a PC because of a problem with the retrace signal. The 4.77 Mhz processor speed of the 8088 is too slow, and the retrace status signal pulse width is too short. Programs that attempt to use these signals do not eliminate all of the flicker; however, these boards usually work properly in a computer with a faster processor clock, such as the IBM AT or a PC that has been souped up with accelerator hardware.

Following are descriptions of two functions found in the **ibmpc.c** source code module described in Chapter 4. These are C language functions, but they use the in-line assembly code feature of Turbo C, so you will need the MASM assembler program to use them. These functions work correctly with all video, and they eliminate snow when the CGA is in use.

You will not need to call these functions from your programs; they are used by the window programs in this chapter. You might, however, want to replace them with pokes and peeks if you are using the MA or EGA or if the MASM program is unavailable. If you are writing programs that will be used by an unknown consumer on an unknown hardware configuration, you should leave these functions unmodified and provide for their compilation by Turbo C through the MASM program.

vpoke(unsigned vseg, unsigned adr, unsigned chr)

This function inserts a character and video attribute byte into video RAM. The **adr** parameter is the byte offset from the beginning of the video segment: 0 is the first character, 2 is the second, and so on. The **chr** parameter contains the video attribute byte (most significant byte) and ASCII character. **Vseg** is the video segment (0xb800 = CGA, 0xb000 = MA). This function is the equivalent of a video poke, with tests for retrace where they are needed.

int vpeek(unsigned vseg, unsigned adr)

This function returns the video character and attribute (most significant byte) located at **vseg:adr**. It is the equivalent of a video peek, with tests for retrace where needed.

SUMMARY

From this explanation of the PC's video architecture and the basics of video windows, Chapter 6 describes and provides a library of window management functions in Turbo C source language. These functions relieve your programs of the responsibility of maintaining video displays. You can use the functions confidently, concentrating on problems specific to your application.

CHAPTER 6

THE WINDOWS FUNCTION LIBRARY

6 The Windows Function Library

The software programs in this chapter and the next several chapters provide a library of window functions that support a wide range of video window operations. The functions are divided into subsystems that, when used, will add menus, context-sensitive help, text editing, and formatted data entry to an applications system. These subsystems are supported by a general-purpose window library that can be used by the applications program as well as the subsystems. This chapter describes the general-purpose window function library.

The window functions described in this chapter can be built to support windows in one of two configurations: **stacked** and **layered**; one configuration is a subset of the other in the view of the program that uses it. Layered windows offer more features than stacked windows, but stacked windows are more efficient in that the stacked functions execute faster than their layered counterparts when windows are displayed and deleted. A program can be linked with either stacked window functions or layered window functions but not both.

You decide which of the window configurations you want to use when you compile the window functions themselves. A compile-time variable named **FASTWINDOWS** is defined for stacked windows, and it is removed for layered windows. An applications program can be linked with either library as long as it does not use the features that are supported only by layered windows. Those applications that use features exclusive to the layered windows must be linked with a window function library that was compiled without the **FASTWINDOWS** definition.

STACKED WINDOWS

A stacked window configuration assumes that any operation you perform on a window (write text into it, change its color, delete it, and so on) is done when the window is in full view by the user. Full view means that no part of the window is covered by another window and that the window has not been hidden by the **hide_window** function (explained later).

The Windows Function Library 6

When a stacked window is established, the window software builds a buffer to contain the prior contents of the video RAM that the window will occupy. The video RAM is saved in the buffer, and the window is written into the video RAM. When any operations are performed that modify the window, those changes are made directly to video RAM, and the software assumes that the entire window is in view. When a window is deleted, the contents of its save buffer are written back into video RAM, thereby restoring the video image to its condition prior to the establishment of the window.

You will usually address only the most recently established stacked window. If you establish window A first, then establish window B, which covers some of window A, and then write text to window A, chances are, some of the text will spill into the part of window B that covers window A. Further, if you delete window A before you delete window B, you will write some of window A's save buffer on top of part of window B.

Most commercial window packages support only stacked windows because most applications that use windows can operate successfully in the stacked window environment. It is common to have an application that always addresses the most recently opened window and that deletes windows in the reverse order in which they were established. Such an application should use stacked windows because of the performance advantage.

The window operations in this book allow you to establish one or more windows and then address various operations to one of the established windows. You can address a specific window, or you can use a null specification to tell the function being called that you intend the operation to be performed on the most recently established window. This convention is used for stacked as well as layered windows, but callers of stacked window functions should make sure that any window they address is either the most recently established window or is in full view by the user.

6 The Windows Function Library

LAYERED WINDOWS

Layered windows offer much more flexibility than stacked windows, and they include a few more features. Once a layered window is established, any window operation can be addressed to it regardless of its visibility or its proximity to other windows. In addition to the usual set of window operations, layered windows can be moved in their two-dimensional plane on the screen, and they can be promoted to the most current or least current window in the layers of established windows.

When a layered window is established, a save buffer is allocated for video contents, but the window is not displayed. The save buffer is initialized with the video values that the window would contain if it were visible. Any subsequent operations performed on this window while it is invisible are performed in the save buffer.

When the layered window is displayed, the contents of video RAM and the save buffer are exchanged. Then, any operations are performed on video RAM rather than the save buffer as long as the window is fully visible (not covered or partially covered by another window). When one or more other windows cover all or part of the window being addressed, the calculation of the area to be changed is more complex. For those parts of the window that are visible, the change is made to video RAM. But for those areas covered by other windows, the change is made to the save buffer of the covering window. Since a window can have different parts of it covered by different windows, the algorithm that computes where a change is to be made must proceed forward through all windows that are more recent than the one being addressed in order to determine if the change is occurring in an area covered by the next window in succession. If one is found, the change is written to that window's save buffer. If no windows cover the changed spot, the change is made to video RAM.

Observe Figure 6.1. The three windows are arranged so that a portion of window A is visible, a portion of it is covered by window B, and a portion of it is covered by window C. In the save buffers of each of the windows you can see the partial borders of the other windows that are covered.

The Windows Function Library 6

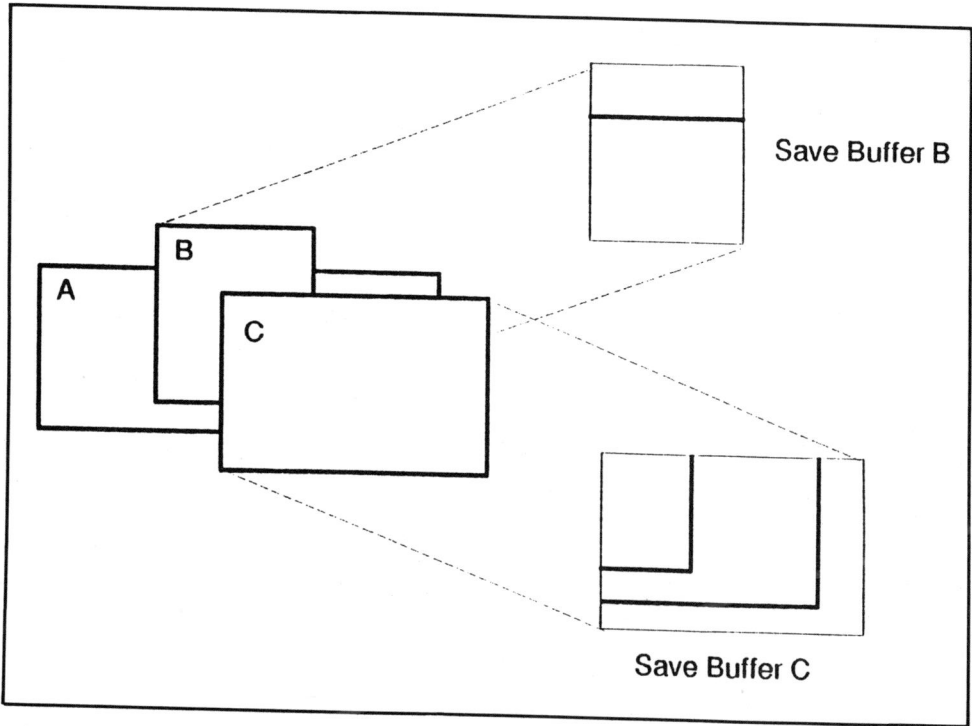

Figure 6.1   Three Layered, Overlapping Windows

If you write the text string "now is the time" into window A, the text will be directed into three different locations. This result is shown in Figure 6.2. Since the part of window A where "now" is to be written is visible, that word is written directly into video RAM, and the word can be read by the user. The words "is the" are in a part of window A that is covered by window B, so those words are written into the save buffer for window B. The word "time" goes to a part of window A that is covered by window C, so "time" is written into the save buffer for window C.

6 The Windows Function Library

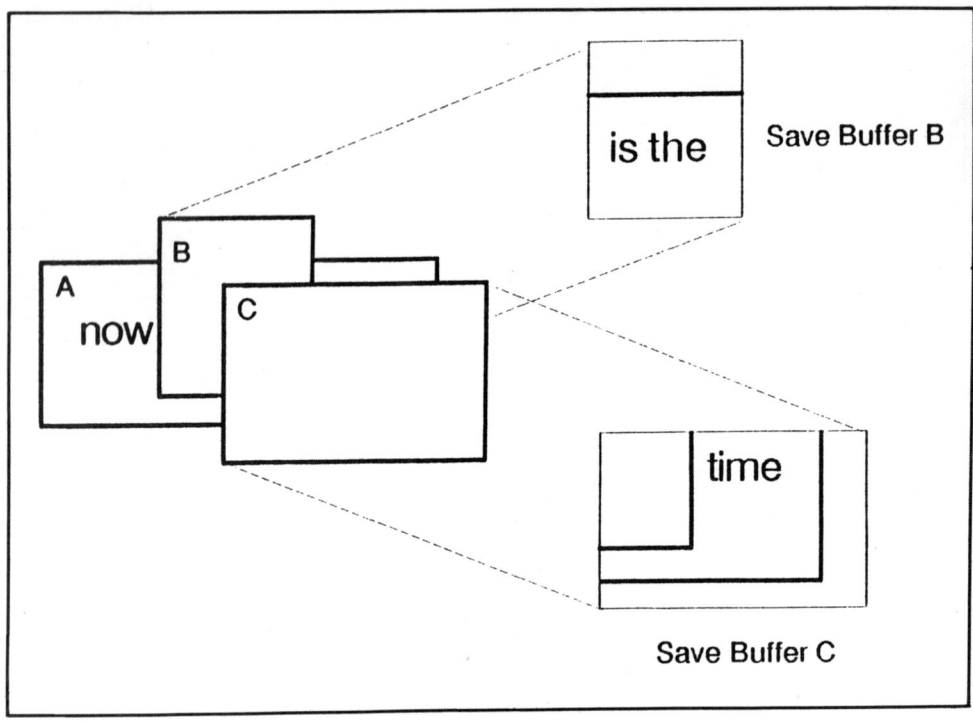

Figure 6.2 Layered Windows with Text

Figure 6.3 shows what happens if window B is deleted. A part of its save buffer goes to video RAM, and the word "is" can now be read by the user. But since part of window B was covered by window C, that part of window B's save buffer is copied into the save buffer of window C, so window C's save buffer now contains the words "the time."

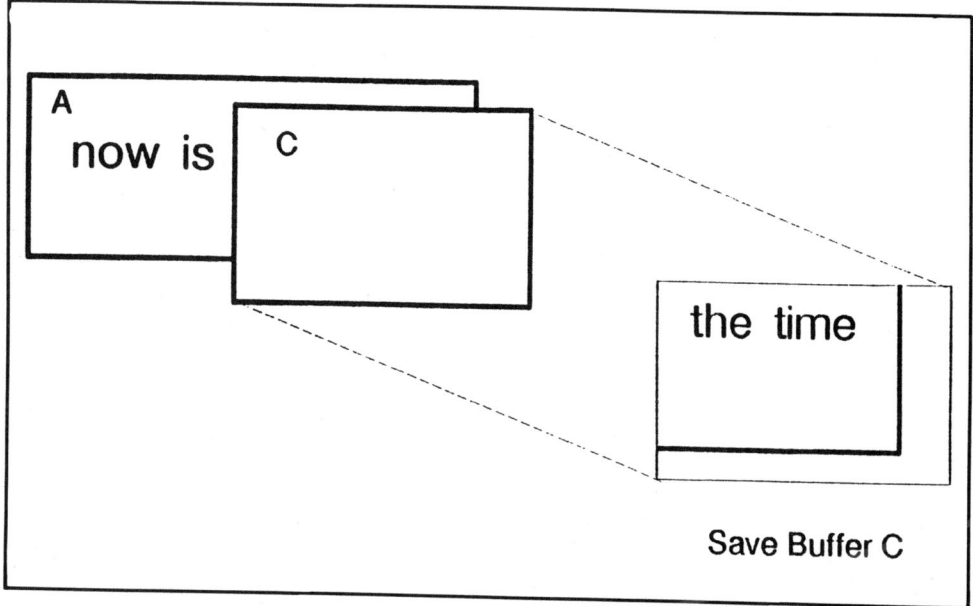

Figure 6.3 Deleting a Layered Window

Whether you use stacked or layered windows will depend on your system's requirements. Each approach has its advantages and disadvantages. If you begin with stacked windows and find later that you need the additional capabilities of a layered window architecture, you can make the change by recompiling the window functions without the FASTWINDOWS definition and relinking your programs.

WINDOW FUNCTIONS

These functions are included in the window library. Each function is described with its purpose and usage. Later, examples are provided for how these functions are used.

6 The Windows Function Library

WINDOW *establish_window(x, y, h, w)

This function establishes a window but does not display it. (Refer to the function named **display_window** to see how you can get the window displayed.) The parameters **x** and **y** are the coordinates for the upper left corner of the window. These parameters are expressed in screen character positions where the upper left coordinate of the screen itself is 0,0. The parameters **h** and **w** are the height and width of the window in character positions. This function will not allow any portion of a window to go off the screen. If you specify a window whose position and size would not allow it to be completely seen, the software will adjust the position so that the window is completely on the screen. If the width is greater than 80 or the height is greater than 25, the function changes the excessive dimension to its maximum value.

The window is established with default attributes. Its border consists of single lines; its color is bright white on a black background, and it has no title. These attributes may be modified by subsequent calls to other functions described later.

Windows exist in the reverse order in which they were established. The most recently established window is the top window on the screen and will (when displayed) overlap windows that were established earlier. This hierarchy is a function of the order in which windows are established, not the order in which they are displayed.

The **establish_window** function returns a pointer to the **WINDOW** structure, which is defined in the header file **twindow.h**. This pointer is used for subsequent calls to window functions to identify the window where the call is directed. Pass a **NULL** pointer to the other window functions if you want the functions to default to the most recently established window.

void set_border(WINDOW *wnd, int btype)

This function sets the border type for the window. The integer parameter **btype** must be one of the following:

- 0 = single lines (default)
- 1 = double lines
- 2 = single top & bottom, double sides
- 3 = double top & bottom, single sides
- 4 = special pop-down menu window, with single lines and the the t-bar as the upper left and right corners.

void set_colors(WINDOW *wnd, int area, int bg, int fg, int inten)

This function sets the colors for the window. The **area** parameter is one of the following:

- ALL
- BORDER
- TITLE
- ACCENT
- NORMAL

The parameter indicates the window area(s) affected. **ALL** affects all areas. **BORDER** sets the colors for the window's border, which occupies a character position around the window. **TITLE** sets the colors for the title, which is placed in the top border of the window. **ACCENT** is the area used for menu bars and other emphasized text, which appears as temporarily highlighted parts of the **NORMAL** area where text is displayed.

6   The Windows Function Library

The **bg** and **fg** integers specify the colors for the area's background and foreground. The colors can be one of the following:

- RED
- GREEN
- BLUE
- WHITE
- YELLOW
- AQUA
- MAGENTA
- BLACK

The **inten** integer specifies the intensity of the foreground characters and can be one of the following:

- BRIGHT
- DIM

All values are defined in the source file **twindow.h**, which is discussed later in this chapter.

void set_title(WINDOW *wnd, char *title)

This function sets the title value for the window. The string that you pass must remain in scope for the life of the window, so use a literal string constant or an external character array.

void set_intensity(WINDOW *wnd, int inten)

This function sets the foreground intensity for all areas of the window. The value in **inten** can be **BRIGHT** or **DIM**.

void display_window(WINDOW *wnd)

This function displays a window that has been previously established. To avoid visual confusion, call this function after all attributes have been set and, if possible, after the window is loaded with whatever text it is to initially display.

void delete_window(WINDOW *wnd)

This function deletes an established window. If the window is visible (has been displayed by **display_window**), it is erased, and the screen is restored to its former image.

void clear_window(WINDOW *wnd)

This function sets the text area of a window to spaces.

void hide_window(WINDOW *wnd)

This function erases a window that has been displayed, restoring the screen to its previous contents. The window still exists and may be modified in any way. A subsequent call to **display_window** will restore it to the screen in its proper proximity to the other windows on the screen.

void wcursor(WINDOW *wnd, int x, int y)

Each window has a logical cursor position that ranges from 0,0 (upper left corner of the text area of the window) to the outer dimensions of the window. This function repositions that cursor.

The **wputchar** and **wprintf** functions display text relative to this cursor position. They also modify the cursor position in a manner consistent with a console cursor. The newline character (\n) positions the cursor at row zero of the next line, scrolling the window's text up one line if the cursor is already on the bottom line of the window. The tab character (\t) moves the cursor to the next tab position in the window. Tabs are spaced four characters apart.

6 The Windows Function Library

void wprintf(WINDOW *wnd, char *fmt, ...)

This function is the window version of the standard C function **printf**. It uses the standard **sprintf** function to build a line to display in the window. Make sure that the resulting string is less than 100 characters, or modify the length of the **dlin** array in the **wprintf** function in the source file **twindow.c**.

void wputchar(WINDOW *wnd, int ch)

This function is the window version of **putchar**. It writes the character in **ch** into the window at the current window cursor location. The cursor location is advanced. If the character is a newline (\n), the cursor is advanced to the next line, column 0. If the character is a tab (\t), the cursor is advanced to the next window tab position. Window tab positions occur every four character positions in the window.

void reverse_video(WINDOW *wnd)

Following this call, all **wprintf** calls and **wputchar** calls will result in displays that use the **ACCENT** colors rather than the **NORMAL** colors.

void normal_video(WINDOW *wnd)

Following this call, all **wprintf** calls and **wputchar** calls will result in displays that use the **NORMAL** colors. This function is used to return to normal displays after **reverse__video** has been called.

void close_all()

This function deletes all established windows.

void move_window(WINDOW *wnd, int x, int y)

This function moves a window so that its upper left corner is positioned at character coordinates specified by **x** and **y**. This function may be used only when layered windows are in effect.

void rmove_window(WINDOW *wnd, int x, int y)

This function moves a window by adding the values in **x** and **y** to the present coordinates of the window's upper left corner coordinates. Use this function only with layered windows.

void forefront(WINDOW *wnd)

This function moves a window into the most recent position among the other windows. The window, if visible, is displayed on top of all others. Use this function only with layered windows.

void rear_window(WINDOW *wnd)

This function moves a window into the least recent position among the other windows. The window, if visible, is displayed under all others. Use this function only with layered windows.

int get_selection(WINDOW *wnd, int sel, char *keys)

This function allows you to use a window as a menu. You must establish the window and write some lines of text to it, perhaps with the **wprintf** function. You can use **set_colors** to establish **ACCENT** color values for the window (the default is black letters on a white background). Then you call **get_selection**. The function uses the window as a menu with each line of text representing a selection. The selections are highlighted by the ACCENT color. The integer value **sel** is used to initially place the accented menu cursor bar on one of the selections. The value 1 is the first selection, 2 is the second, and so on.

The user can move the menu bar up and down with the arrow keys and make a selection from the menu with the Enter key. The Esc key can be used to exit from the process.

The keys pointer points to a string of key values that can be used to select from the menu. Some menu systems allow the user to enter keystrokes as well as the cursor bar. To disable the feature, pass a NULL pointer.

6 The Windows Function Library

This function returns an integer value equal to the item selected from the menu. The value is relative to one. If the user presses the Esc key, the function returns zero. The function will also return the values **FWD** or **BS** if the user presses the right or left arrow keys. These values are defined in **keys.h**.

void error_message(char *s)

This function displays the error message pointed to by the **s** pointer and sounds the audible alarm. The message is displayed in a window in the lower right quadrant of the screen. The message remains on the screen when the function returns.

void clear_message()

This function clears an error message if one has been displayed by the **error__message** function.

WINDOW LISTINGS

These listings contain the window source files. Two listings are involved: **twindow.h** and **twindow.c**. Each listing is followed by a discussion of its code.

Source Listing: twindow.h

Listing 6.1, **twindow.h**, defines the window structures and contains the prototypes for the functions. You should include it in any source program that uses the window functions.

Listing 6.1: twindow.h

```c
/* ------------------ twindow.h ---------------------- */

/*      Uncomment this for stacked windows
 *      rather than layered windows.
 *
 * #define FASTWINDOWS
 *
 */

/* ------ window colors ---------- */
#define RED    4
#define GREEN  2
#define BLUE   1
#define WHITE (RED+GREEN+BLUE)
#define YELLOW (RED+GREEN)
#define AQUA (GREEN+BLUE)
#define MAGENTA (RED+BLUE)
#define BLACK 0
#define BRIGHT 8
#define DIM 0

#define BORDER 0
#define TITLE 1
#define ACCENT 2
#define NORMAL 3
#define ALL 4

#define TRUE 1
#define FALSE 0
#define ERROR -1
#define OK 0
```

continued...

6 The Windows Function Library

...from previous page

```c
/* ------------- window controller structures ----------- */
typedef struct field {   /* data entry field description */
    char *fmask;         /* field data entry mask         */
    int fprot;           /* field protection              */
    char *fbuff;         /* field buffer                  */
    int ftype;           /* field type                    */
    int frow;            /* field row                     */
    int fcol;            /* field column                  */
    void (*fhelp)();     /* field help function           */
    char *fhwin;         /* field help window             */
    int flx, fly;        /* help window location          */
    int (*fvalid)();     /* field validation function     */
    struct field *fnxt;  /* next field on template        */
    struct field *fprv;  /* previous field on template    */
} FIELD;
typedef struct _wnd {
    int _wv;             /* true if window is visible     */
    int _hd;             /* true if window was hidden     */
    char *_ws;           /* points to window save block   */
    char *_tl;           /* points to window title        */
    int _wx;             /* nw x coordinate               */
    int _wy;             /* nw y coordinate               */
    int _ww;             /* window width                  */
    int _wh;             /* window height                 */
    int _wsp;            /* scroll pointer                */
    int _sp;             /* selection pointer             */
    int _cr;             /* cursor x location             */
    int btype;           /* border type                   */
    int wcolor[4];       /* colors for window             */
    int _pn;             /* previous normal color         */
    struct _wnd *_nx;    /* points to next window         */
    struct _wnd *_pv;    /* points to previous window     */
    FIELD *_fh;          /* points to 1st data entry fld  */
    FIELD *_ft;          /* points to last data entry fld */
} WINDOW;
typedef struct w_menu {
    char *mname;
    char **mselcs;
    void (**func)();
} MENU;
```

continued...

The Windows Function Library 6

...from previous page

```
#define SAV      (wnd->_ws)
#define WTITLE   (wnd->_tl)
#define COL      (wnd->_wx)
#define ROW      (wnd->_wy)
#define WIDTH    (wnd->_ww)
#define HEIGHT   (wnd->_wh)
#define SCROLL   (wnd->_wsp)
#define SELECT   (wnd->_sp)
#define WCURS    (wnd->_cr)
#define WBORDER  (wnd->wcolor[BORDER])
#define WTITLEC  (wnd->wcolor[TITLE])
#define WACCENT  (wnd->wcolor[ACCENT])
#define WNORMAL  (wnd->wcolor[NORMAL])
#define PNORMAL  (wnd->_pn)
#define BTYPE    (wnd->btype)
#define NEXT     (wnd->_nx)
#define PREV     (wnd->_pv)
#define WCOLOR   (wnd->wcolor)
#define VISIBLE  (wnd->_wv)
#define HIDDEN   (wnd->_hd)
#define FHEAD    (wnd->_fh)
#define FTAIL    (wnd->_ft)

#define NW       (wcs[wnd->btype].nw)
#define NE       (wcs[wnd->btype].ne)
#define SE       (wcs[wnd->btype].se)
#define SW       (wcs[wnd->btype].sw)
#define SIDE     (wcs[wnd->btype].side)
#define LINE     (wcs[wnd->btype].line)
```

continued...

6 The Windows Function Library

...from previous page

```
/* -------- function prototypes and macros -------- */

/* ------ general-purpose functions and macros ----- */
void clear_screen(void);
int vmode(void);
void cursor(int, int);
void curr_cursor(int *, int *);
int cursor_type(void);
void set_cursor_type(int);
int get_char(void);
int scroll_lock(void);
void vpoke(unsigned, unsigned, unsigned);
int vpeek(unsigned, unsigned);

/* ----- window functions and macros ------- */
WINDOW *establish_window(int, int, int, int);
void set_border(WINDOW *, int);
void set_colors(WINDOW *, int, int, int, int);
void set_intensity(WINDOW *, int);
void set_title(WINDOW *, char *);
void display_window(WINDOW *);
void delete_window(WINDOW *);
void clear_window(WINDOW *);
void hide_window(WINDOW *);
void wprintf(WINDOW *, char *, ...);
void wputchar(WINDOW *, int);
void close_all(void);
void wcursor(WINDOW *, int x, int y);
void error_message(char *);
void clear_message(void);
int get_selection(WINDOW *, int, char *);

#define reverse_video(wnd) wnd->wcolor[3]=wnd->wcolor[2]
#define normal_video(wnd) wnd->wcolor[3]=wnd->_pn
#define rmove_window(wnd,x,y) repos_wnd(wnd, x, y, 0)
#define move_window(wnd,x,y) repos_wnd(wnd, COL-x, ROW-y, 0)
#define forefront(wnd) repos_wnd(wnd, 0, 0, 1)
#define rear_window(wnd) repos_wnd(wnd, 0, 0, -1)
```

continued...

...from previous page

```c
/* ----- internal to window processes ----- */
void accent(WINDOW *);
void deaccent(WINDOW *);
void scroll(WINDOW *, int);
void repos_wnd(WINDOW *, int, int, int);
void acline(WINDOW *, int);
#define accent(wnd) acline(wnd, WACCENT)
#define deaccent(wnd) acline(wnd, WNORMAL)
#define clr(bg,fg,in) ((fg)|(bg<<4)|(in))
#define vad(x,y) ((y)*160+(x)*2)
#ifdef FASTWINDOWS
#define cht(ch,at) (((ch)&255)|((at)<<8))
#define displ(w,x,y,c,a) vpoke(VSG,vad(x+COL,y+ROW),cht(c,a))
#define dget(w,x,y) vpeek(VSG,vad(x+COL,y+ROW))
#define verify_wnd(w) (*(w)=listtail)!=0
#else
void displ(WINDOW *wnd, int x, int y, int ch, int at);
#endif
/* ------ editor function ------- */
void text_editor(WINDOW *, char *, unsigned);
/* -------- menu function ------- */
void menu_select(char *name, MENU *mn);
/* ----- help functions ------- */
void load_help(char *);
void set_help(char *, int, int);
/* ----- data entry functions ---- */
void init_template(WINDOW *);
FIELD *establish_field(WINDOW *,int,int,char *,char *,int);
void clear_template(WINDOW *);
void field_tally(WINDOW *);
int data_entry(WINDOW *);
void wprompt(WINDOW *, int, int, char *);
void error_message(char *);
void clear_notice(void);
void field_window(FIELD *, char *, int, int);
#define field_protect(f,s)   f->fprot=s
#define field_help(f,h)      f->fhelp=h
#define field_validate(f,v) f->fvalid=v
```

6 The Windows Function Library

Program Description: twindow.h

The FASTWINDOWS global variable is a comment in the published code. Its purpose is to select the stacked window configuration. As published, the layered window configuration will be compiled. To compile the stacked window system, uncomment the **#define** statement.

The FIELD structure is used to define data entry fields within data entry template windows. This process is described in Chapter 8.

The WINDOW structure describes a window to the system. Each window is assigned one structure of this type.

The MENU structure is used by the window menu software in Chapter 10. There will be an array of MENU structures with one entry for each pop-down menu.

A list of **#define** statements is used to make the code in **twindow.c** more legible. The mnemonic names are equated to members of the WINDOW structure pointed to by a pointer named **wnd**. All the functions in **twindow.c** use that pointer name as a convention.

Twindow.h contains the prototypes for all the window functions that an applications program will call.

Source Listing: twindow.c

Listing 6.2 is **twindow.c**. It contains all the functions described previously in this chapter. You will compile it and link its object module with any program that uses windows. Since it calls functions in **ibmpc.c**, that object module must also be included in your links.

Listing 6.2: twindow.c

```c
/* ---------------------- twindow.c --------------------- */

#include <stdio.h>
#include <ctype.h>
#include <stdarg.h>
#include <dos.h>
#include <alloc.h>
#include <stdlib.h>
#include <string.h>
#include "twindow.h"
#include "keys.h"

#define TABS 4
#define SCRNHT 25
#define SCRNWIDTH 80
#define ON   1
#define OFF  0
#define ERROR -1

/* -------- local prototypes ---------- */
redraw(WINDOW *wnd);
wframe(WINDOW *wnd);
dtitle(WINDOW *wnd);
int *waddr(WINDOW *wnd, int x, int y);
vswap(WINDOW *wnd);
vsave(WINDOW *wnd);
vrstr(WINDOW *wnd);
add_list(WINDOW *wnd);
beg_list(WINDOW *wnd);
remove_list(WINDOW *wnd);
insert_list(WINDOW *w1, WINDOW *w2);
#ifndef FASTWINDOWS
int dget(WINDOW *wnd, int x, int y);
verify_wnd(WINDOW **w1);
#endif
```

continued...

6 The Windows Function Library

...from previous page

```
/* ---- array of border character sets ------ */
struct {
    int nw, ne, se, sw, side, line;
} wcs[] = {
    {218,191,217,192,179,196},   /* single line */
    {201,187,188,200,186,205},   /* double line */
    {214,183,189,211,186,196},   /* single top, double side */
    {213,184,190,212,179,205},   /* double top, single side */
    {194,194,217,192,179,196}    /* pop-down menu */
};

/* ---- window structure linked list head & tail ---- */
WINDOW *listhead = NULL;
WINDOW *listtail = NULL;
int VSG;        /* video segment address */

/* ----------- establish a new window -------------- */
WINDOW *establish_window(x, y, h, w)
{
    WINDOW *wnd;

    VSG = (vmode() == 7 ? 0xb000 : 0xb800);
    if ((wnd = (WINDOW *) malloc(sizeof (WINDOW))) == NULL)
        return NULL;
    /* ------- adjust for out-of bounds parameters ------- */
    WTITLE = "";
    HEIGHT = min(h, SCRNHT);
    WIDTH = min(w, SCRNWIDTH);
    COL = max(0, min(x, SCRNWIDTH-WIDTH));
    ROW = max(0, min(y, SCRNHT-HEIGHT));
    WCURS = 0;
    SCROLL = 0;
    SELECT = 1;
    BTYPE = 0;
    VISIBLE = HIDDEN = 0;
    PREV = NEXT = NULL;
    FHEAD = FTAIL = NULL;
    WBORDER=WNORMAL=PNORMAL=WTITLEC =
                clr(BLACK, WHITE, BRIGHT);
    WACCENT = clr(WHITE, BLACK, DIM);
```

continued...

...from previous page

```
    if ((SAV = malloc(WIDTH * HEIGHT * 2)) == (char *) 0)
        return NULL;
    add_list(wnd);
#ifndef FASTWINDOWS
    clear_window(wnd);
    wframe(wnd);
#endif
    return wnd;
}

/* ------ set the window's border --------- */
void set_border(WINDOW *wnd, int btype)
{
    if (verify_wnd(&wnd))    {
        BTYPE = btype;
        redraw(wnd);
    }
}

/* ------- set colors ----------- */
void set_colors(WINDOW *wnd,int area,int bg,int fg,int inten)
{
    if (vmode() == 7)    {
        if (bg != WHITE && bg != BLACK)
            return;
        if (fg != WHITE && fg != BLACK)
            return;
    }
    if (verify_wnd(&wnd))    {
        if (area == ALL)
            while (area)
                WCOLOR [--area] = clr(bg, fg, inten);
        else
            WCOLOR [area] = clr(bg, fg, inten);
        redraw(wnd);
    }
}
```

continued...

6 The Windows Function Library

...from previous page

```c
/* ----- set the intensity of a window ------ */
void set_intensity(WINDOW *wnd, int inten)
{
    int area = ALL;

    if (verify_wnd(&wnd))    {
        while (area)   {
            WCOLOR [--area] &= ~BRIGHT;
            WCOLOR [area] |= inten;
        }
        redraw(wnd);
    }
}

/* -------- set title ------------- */
void set_title(WINDOW *wnd, char *title)
{
    if (verify_wnd(&wnd))    {
        WTITLE = title;
        redraw(wnd);
    }
}

/* ------ redraw a window when an attribute changes ----- */
static redraw(WINDOW *wnd)
{
#ifndef FASTWINDOWS
    int x, y, chat, atr;

    for (y = 1; y < HEIGHT-1; y++)
        for (x = 1; x < WIDTH-1; x++)    {
            chat = dget(wnd, x, y);
            atr = (((chat>>8)&255) ==
                PNORMAL ? WNORMAL : WACCENT);
            displ(wnd, x, y, chat&255, atr);
        }
    wframe(wnd);
#endif
    PNORMAL = WNORMAL;
}
```

continued...

...from previous page

```
/* ------------ display an established window ------------ */
void display_window(WINDOW *wnd)
{
    if (verify_wnd(&wnd) && !VISIBLE)   {
        VISIBLE = 1;
#ifdef FASTWINDOWS
        if (HIDDEN) {
            HIDDEN = 0;
            vrstr(wnd);
        }
        else    {
            vsave(wnd);
            clear_window(wnd);
            wframe(wnd);
        }
#else
        vswap(wnd);
#endif
    }
}

/* ---------- close all windows -------------- */
void close_all()
{
    WINDOW *sav, *wnd = listtail;

    while (wnd) {
        sav = PREV;
        delete_window(wnd);
        wnd = sav;
    }
}
```

continued...

6 The Windows Function Library

...from previous page

```
/* ------------ remove a window ------------------ */
void delete_window(WINDOW *wnd)
{
    if (verify_wnd(&wnd))         {
        hide_window(wnd);
        free(SAV);
        remove_list(wnd);   /* remove window from list */
        free(wnd);
    }
}

/* ----------- hide a window --------------- */
void hide_window(WINDOW *wnd)
{
    if (verify_wnd(&wnd) && VISIBLE)     {
#ifndef FASTWINDOWS
        vswap(wnd);
#else
        vrstr(wnd);
#endif
        HIDDEN = 1;
        VISIBLE = 0;
    }
}
```

continued...

...from previous page

```
#ifndef FASTWINDOWS
/* ------ reposition the window in its 3-axis plane ------ */
void repos_wnd(WINDOW *wnd, int x, int y, int z)
{
    WINDOW *twnd;
    int x1, y1, chat;
    if (!verify_wnd(&wnd))
        return;
    twnd = establish_window(x+COL, y+ROW, HEIGHT, WIDTH);
    twnd->_tl = WTITLE;
    twnd->btype = BTYPE;
    twnd->wcolor[BORDER] = WBORDER;
    twnd->wcolor[TITLE] = WTITLEC;
    twnd->wcolor[ACCENT] = WACCENT;
    twnd->wcolor[NORMAL] = WNORMAL;
    twnd->_wsp = SCROLL;
    twnd->_cr = WCURS;
    if (z != 1) {
        remove_list(twnd);
        if (z == 0)
            insert_list(twnd, wnd);
        else
            beg_list(twnd);
    }
    for (y1 = 0; y1 < twnd->_wh; y1++)
        for (x1 = 0; x1 < twnd->_ww; x1++)  {
            chat = dget(wnd, x1, y1);
            displ(twnd, x1, y1, chat&255, (chat>>8)&255);
        }
    twnd->_wv = 1;
    vswap(twnd);
    hide_window(wnd);
    free(SAV);
    remove_list(wnd);
    *wnd = *twnd;
    insert_list(wnd, twnd);
    remove_list(twnd);
    free(twnd);
}
#endif
```

continued...

6   The Windows Function Library

...from previous page

```c
/* ----------- clear the window area -------------- */
void clear_window(WINDOW *wnd)
{
    register int x1, y1;

    if (verify_wnd(&wnd))
        for (y1 = 1; y1 < HEIGHT-1; y1++)
            for (x1 = 1; x1 < WIDTH-1; x1++)
                displ(wnd,x1, y1, ' ', WNORMAL);
}

/* ------------ draw the window frame --------------- */
static wframe(WINDOW *wnd)
{
    register int x1, y1;

    if (!verify_wnd(&wnd))
        return;
    /* --------- window title -------------- */
    displ(wnd,0, 0, NW, WBORDER);
    dtitle(wnd);
    displ(wnd,WIDTH-1, 0, NE, WBORDER);
    /* ------------ window sides ----------------- */
    for (y1 = 1; y1 < HEIGHT-1; y1++)   {
        displ(wnd,0, y1, SIDE, WBORDER);
        displ(wnd,WIDTH-1, y1, SIDE, WBORDER);
    }
    /* --------------- bottom of frame --------------- */
    displ(wnd,0, y1, SW, WBORDER);
    for (x1 = 1; x1 < WIDTH-1; x1++)
        displ(wnd,x1, y1, LINE, WBORDER);
    displ(wnd,x1, y1, SE, WBORDER);
}
```

continued...

...from previous page

```c
/* ------------- displ the window title -------------------- */
static dtitle(WINDOW *wnd)
{
    int x1 = 1, i, ln;
    char *s = WTITLE;

    if (!verify_wnd(&wnd))
        return;
    if (s)  {
        ln = strlen(s);
        if (ln > WIDTH-2)
            i = 0;
        else
            i = ((WIDTH-2-ln) / 2);
        if (i > 0)
            while (i--)
                displ(wnd, x1++, 0, LINE, WBORDER);
        while (*s && x1 < WIDTH-1)
            displ(wnd, x1++, 0, *s++, WTITLEC);
    }
    while (x1 < WIDTH-1)
        displ(wnd, x1++, 0, LINE, WBORDER);
}

/* ------------- window-oriented printf ---------------- */
void wprintf(WINDOW *wnd, char *ln, ...)
{
    char dlin [100], *dl = dlin;

    if (verify_wnd(&wnd))         {
        va_list ap;
        va_start(ap, ln);
        vsprintf(dlin, ln, ap);
        va_end(ap);
        while (*dl)
            wputchar(wnd, *dl++);
    }
}
```

continued...

6 The Windows Function Library

...from previous page

```c
/* ------------ write a character to the window ----------- */
void wputchar(WINDOW *wnd, int c)
{
    if (!verify_wnd(&wnd))
        return;
    switch (c)  {
        case '\n':
            if (SCROLL == HEIGHT-3)
                scroll(wnd, UP);
            else
                SCROLL++;
            WCURS = 0;
            break;
        case '\t':
            do displ(wnd,(WCURS++)+3,SCROLL+1,' ',WNORMAL);
                while ((WCURS%TABS) && (WCURS+1) < WIDTH-1);
            break;
        default:
            if ((WCURS+1) < WIDTH-1)    {
                displ(wnd, WCURS+1, SCROLL+1, c, WNORMAL);
                WCURS++;
            }
            break;
    }
}

/* ------- set window cursor --------- */
void wcursor(WINDOW *wnd, int x, int y)
{
    if (verify_wnd(&wnd) && x < WIDTH-1 && y < HEIGHT-1)    {
        WCURS = x;
        SCROLL = y;
        cursor(COL+x+1, ROW+y+1);
    }
}
```

continued...

...from previous page

```c
/* ------ allow the user to make a window selection ------ */
int get_selection(WINDOW *wnd, int s, char *keys)
{
    int c = 0, ky;
    if (!verify_wnd(&wnd))
        return 0;
    SELECT = s;
    while (c != ESC && c != '\r' && c != BS && c != FWD)    {
        accent(wnd);
        c = get_char();
        deaccent(wnd);
        switch (c)      {
            case UP:    if (SELECT >  1)
                            SELECT--;
                        else
                            SELECT = SCROLL+1;
                        break;
            case DN:    if (SELECT < SCROLL+1)
                            SELECT++;
                        else
                            SELECT = 1;
                        break;
            case '\r':
            case ESC:
            case FWD:
            case BS:    break;
            default:    if (keys)   {
                            ky = 0;
                            while (*(keys + ky))    {
                                if (*(keys+ky)==toupper(c) ||
                                    *(keys+ky)==tolower(c))
                                    return ky + 1;
                                ky++;
                            }
                        }
                        break;
        }
    }
    return  c == '\r' ? SELECT : c == ESC ? 0 : c;
}
```

continued...

6 The Windows Function Library

...from previous page

```c
union REGS rg;

/* ------- scroll a window's contents up or down --------- */
void scroll(WINDOW *wnd, int dir)
{
    int row = HEIGHT-1, col, chat;

    if (!verify_wnd(&wnd))
        return;
    if (NEXT == NULL && HEIGHT > 3 && VISIBLE)   {
        rg.h.ah = dir == UP ? 6 : 7;
        rg.h.al = 1;
        rg.h.bh = WNORMAL;
        rg.h.cl = COL + 1;
        rg.h.ch = ROW + 1;
        rg.h.dl = COL + WIDTH - 2;
        rg.h.dh = ROW + HEIGHT - 2;
        int86(16, &rg, &rg);
        return;
    }
    if (dir == UP) {
        for (row = 2; row < HEIGHT-1; row++)
            for (col = 1; col < WIDTH-1; col++) {
                chat = dget(wnd, col, row);
                displ(wnd,col,row-1,chat&255,(chat>>8)&255);
            }
        for (col = 1; col < WIDTH-1; col++)
            displ(wnd, col, row-1, ' ', WNORMAL);
    }
    else   {
        for (row = HEIGHT-2; row > 1; --row)
            for (col = 1; col < WIDTH-1; col++) {
                chat = dget(wnd, col, row-1);
                displ(wnd,col,row,chat&255,(chat>>8)&255);
            }
        for (col = 1; col < WIDTH-1; col++)
            displ(wnd, col, row, ' ', WNORMAL);
    }
}
```

continued...

...from previous page

```c
#ifndef FASTWINDOWS
/* --- compute address of a window's display character --- */
static int *waddr(WINDOW *wnd, int x, int y)
{
    WINDOW *nxt = NEXT;
    int *vp;

    if (!VISIBLE)
        return (int *) (SAV+y*(WIDTH*2)+x*2);
    x += COL;
    y += ROW;
    while (nxt) {
        if (nxt->_wv)
            if (x >= nxt->_wx && x <= nxt->_wx + nxt->_ww-1)
                if (y >= nxt->_wy &&
                        y <= nxt->_wy + nxt->_wh-1) {
                    x -= nxt->_wx;
                    y -= nxt->_wy;
                    vp = (int *)
                        ((nxt->_ws) +y*(nxt->_ww*2)+x*2);
                    return vp;
                }
        nxt = nxt->_nx;
    }
    return NULL;
}

/* ---------- display a character to a window --------- */
void displ(WINDOW *wnd, int x, int y, int ch, int at)
{
    int *vp;
    int vch = (ch&255)|(at<<8);

    if ((vp = waddr(wnd, x, y)) != NULL)
        *vp = vch;
    else
        vpoke(VSG,vad(x+COL,y+ROW),vch);
}
```

continued...

6 The Windows Function Library

...from previous page

```
/* ----- get a displayed character from a window ----- */
static int dget(WINDOW *wnd, int x, int y)
{
    int *vp;

    if ((vp = waddr(wnd, x, y)) != NULL)
        return *vp;
    return vpeek(VSG,vad(x+COL,y+ROW));
}

/* ------------- low-level video functions --------------- */

/* ------- swap the video image with the save buffer ----- */
static vswap(WINDOW *wnd)
{
    int x, y, chat;
    int *bf = (int *) SAV;

    for (y = 0; y < HEIGHT; y++)
        for (x = 0; x < WIDTH; x++) {
            chat = *bf;
            *bf++ = dget(wnd, x, y);
            displ(wnd, x, y, chat&255, (chat>>8)&255);
        }
}

#else

/* -------- save video memory into the save buffer ---- */
static vsave(WINDOW *wnd)
{
    int x, y;
    int *bf = (int *) SAV;

    for (y = 0; y < HEIGHT; y++)
        for (x = 0; x < WIDTH; x++)
            *bf++ = vpeek(VSG, vad(x+COL, y+ROW));
}
```

continued...

The Windows Function Library 6

...from previous page

```c
/* ----- restore video memory from the save buffer ----- */
static vrstr(WINDOW *wnd)
{
    int x, y;
    int *bf = (int *) SAV;

    for (y = 0; y < HEIGHT; y++)
        for (x = 0; x < WIDTH; x++)
            vpoke(VSG,vad(x+COL,y+ROW), *bf++);
}
#endif

/* ----- (de)accent the line where SELECT points ------- */
void acline(WINDOW *wnd, int set)
{
    int x, ch;

    if (!verify_wnd(&wnd))
        return;
    for (x = 1; x < WIDTH - 1; x++) {
        ch = dget(wnd, x, SELECT) & 255;
        displ(wnd, x, SELECT, ch, set);
    }
}

/* ---------- linked list functions --------- */

/* ----- add a window to the end of the list ------ */
static add_list(WINDOW *wnd)
{
    if (listtail)   {
        PREV = listtail;
        listtail->_nx = wnd;
    }
    listtail = wnd;
    if (!listhead)
        listhead = wnd;
}
```

continued...

6 The Windows Function Library

...from previous page

```c
/* ----- add a window to the beginning of the list ------ */
static beg_list(WINDOW *wnd)
{
    if (listhead)   {
        NEXT = listhead;
        listhead->_pv = wnd;
    }
    listhead = wnd;
    if (!listtail)
        listtail = wnd;
}

/* --------- remove a window from the list -------- */
static remove_list(WINDOW *wnd)
{
    if (NEXT)
        NEXT->_pv = PREV;
    if (PREV)
        PREV->_nx = NEXT;
    if (listhead == wnd)
        listhead = NEXT;
    if (listtail == wnd)
        listtail = PREV;
    NEXT = PREV = NULL;
}

/* ----- insert w1 after w2 ------ */
static insert_list(WINDOW *w1, WINDOW *w2)
{
    w1->_pv = w2;
    w1->_nx = w2->_nx;
    w2->_nx = w1;
    if (w1->_nx == NULL)
        listtail = w1;
    else
        w1->_nx->_pv = w1;
}
```

continued...

...from previous page

```
#ifndef FASTWINDOWS
/* ---- verify the presence of a window in the list ----- */
static verify_wnd(WINDOW **w1)
{
    WINDOW *wnd;

    wnd = listhead;
    if (*w1 == NULL)
        *w1 = listtail;
    else    {
        while (wnd != NULL) {
            if (*w1 == wnd)
                break;
            wnd = NEXT;
        }
    }
    return wnd != NULL;
}
#endif

WINDOW *ewnd = NULL;

/* ------- error messages ------- */
void error_message(char *s)
{
    ewnd = establish_window(50, 22, 3, max(10, strlen(s)+2));
    set_colors(ewnd, ALL, RED, YELLOW, BRIGHT);
    set_title(ewnd, " ERROR! ");
    display_window(ewnd);
    wprintf(ewnd, s);
    putchar(BELL);
}

void clear_message()
{
    if (ewnd)
        delete_window(ewnd);
    ewnd = NULL;
}
```

6 The Windows Function Library

Program Description: twindow.c

Following is a description of the **twindow.c** source program. Each function is described in terms of what it does and how it works. A programmer can use this narrative to understand the code.

The external data declarations in **twindow.c** include the prototypes for the functions that are local to the source file, an array of structures that define the five border types that windows can have, and the list head and tail pointers for the linked list of WINDOW structures.

The border of a window is controlled by a member in the WINDOW structure that represents the window. That member is an integer offset into the border type table. The entry that the offset points to contains six values, each one representing one of the sides or corners of a window. The first value represents the upper left, or northwest corner. The variable name (**nw**, **ne**, **se**, **sw**) will tell you which corner is represented. The integer named **side** is for the vertical sides of a border; the integer named **line** is for the top and bottom horizontal lines of a border. The values correspond to characters in the PC's graphics character set.

The two WINDOW pointers named **listhead** and **listtail** are the head and tail pointers for the linked list of windows. As windows are established, they are added to this linked list. Initially, these two pointers are NULL. When the first window is established, memory is allocated for a WINDOW structure, and its address is copied into both pointers. The linked list approach has the list head pointing to the first window in the list and the list tail pointing to the last. When a second window is established, its address is copied to the list tail pointer. Additionally, the address of the second window is written to the **__nx** pointer in the WINDOW structure of the first, and the address of the first is written to the **__pv** pointer of the second. The list head points to the first window, which points to the second window, and so on. The list tail points to the last window. Each window also points to the one ahead of it in the chain, so the linked list is a bi-directional data structure called a **doubly linked list**. (See *C Development Tools for the IBM PC*, also by the author, Brady, 1986, for a discussion of linked list data structures.)

The **establish_window** function initializes the VSG variable to the segment address of video RAM. The function allocates memory for a WINDOW structure and initializes that structure with the default window characteristics and the size and coordinates specified by the caller to the function. It allocates memory for a video RAM save buffer and writes that buffer's address into the WINDOW structure. With the structure thus initialized, the function calls **add_list** to add the structure to the linked list of windows. The window text area is cleared, and the window frame is drawn if layered windows are being processed. These functions operate on the save buffer since the window has not been displayed yet. The **establish_window** function returns the address of the WINDOW structure to the caller.

The **set_border**, **set_colors**, **set_intensity**, and **set_title** functions all modify the characteristics of an established window. First, they call **verify_wnd** to ensure that the caller is passing the address of an established window. Then, they modify the specified attribute. Finally, they call the **redraw** function so that the change can be recorded on the screen.

The **redraw** function redraws a window if layered windows are being processed.

The **display_window** function operates differently for stacked and layered windows. In either case, it does nothing if the window is visible to the user. If the window is not visible, by calling the **vswap** function, **display_window** swaps video memory with the window's save buffer if layered windows are in effect. For stacked windows, a test is made to see if the window has been hidden. If so, the window's save buffer is written to video RAM by a call to **vrstr**. If the window has not been hidden, it has never been displayed, so **vsave** is called to save the current contents of video RAM, and **clear_window** and **wframe** are called to display the empty window.

The **close_all** function deletes all windows by navigating the linked list of WINDOW structures and calling **delete_window**.

The **delete_window** function removes a window from the system by hiding it, freeing the memory that its save buffer occupied, removing the WINDOW structure from the linked list, and freeing the memory that contained the WINDOW structure.

6 The Windows Function Library

The **hide_window** function calls **vswap** to swap the save buffer with video RAM for a layered window and calls **vrstr** to restore video RAM for a stacked window.

The **repos_window** function exists only for layered windows. It is invoked by one of the macros, **move_window**, **rmove_window**, **rear_window**, and **forefront**. It changes a window's position by establishing a temporary window, locating the temporary window in the linked list in a position consistent with the macro's intention, writing the original window's contents into the save buffer of the temporary window, displaying the temporary window, and hiding the original.

Clear_window writes blanks to the window's data area, and **wframe** and **dtitle** draw the window frame with the title at the top. These functions use the **displ** function to write values to the window.

The **wprintf** function is an example of the new ANSI proposed standard for functions with a variable number of parameters. In the past, most compilers have managed **printf** with assembly language to parse the variable number of parameters from the stack. The proposed standard uses ellipses (...) in the function's parameter list to indicate the presence of a variable number of parameters with varying data types. The special array type **va_list** is used to declare the list, and **va_start** establishes the beginning and end of the list. The **vsprintf** function is a version of **sprintf** that will accept a **va_list** parameter. In this use, the parameters passed to **wprintf** are processed by **vsprintf** into a string named **dlin**. Then the string is displayed in the window one character at a time with calls to **wputchar**. If you will ever have a **wprintf** call that will result in a string greater than 100 characters, you must increase the length of the **dlin** array.

The **wputchar** function displays a character in a window at its current cursor location. The window cursor location is a function of the two members of the WINDOW structure that are referenced by the macros named **WCURS** (column) and **SCROLL** (row). The function reacts to the newline (\n) and tab (\t) characters in the following ways. For a newline, if the SCROLL variable is at the bottom of the window, the window is scrolled up one line; otherwise, the SCROLL variable is incremented. In either case, the WCURS variable is set to column 0. When the tab character is sent to **wputchar**, the WCURS variable is advanced to the next tab stop in the window. Other characters are displayed in the window, and the WCURS variable is incremented. Strings that exceed the width of the window are not wrapped; they are truncated.

The **wcursor** function sets the WCURS and SCROLL variables to the coordinates specified by the caller. It also positions the video cursor to the screen location relative to the window cursor.

The **get_selection** function establishes a cursor bar in a window and lets the user move the bar up and down and make a selection by pressing the Enter key. The SELECT macro refers to a variable in the WINDOW structure and is used to track the location of the cursor bar in the window. The **accent** and **deaccent** functions are used to turn the cursor bar on and off by changing the video attribute of the line to ACCENT and NORMAL. As the user presses the up and down arrow keys, the function alters the value of the SELECT variable. The caller may also pass the address of a character array that contains a list of keystrokes that can be used to select from the window. If the user presses one of these keys, the corresponding selection is made just as if the cursor bar was on the proper line and the Enter key was pressed.

The **scroll** function scrolls the text portion of the window up or down one line. If the window is the latest one and it is visible, the ROM-BIOS scroll function is used because it is faster than a software scroll. The ROM-BIOS function is bypassed if the window has only one line of text because of a bug in the IBM PC and some AT clones. That bug causes odd video results when you try to scroll a single line. The bug was fixed by IBM in the AT BIOS, but some clones who cloned the bug failed to clone the fix. If the window is not the latest one, or if it has a single line of text, the text area is scrolled with software using the **dget** and **displ** functions to read and write text characters from and to the window.

The **waddr** function operates only on layered windows. It returns the integer address relative to a position within a window where a character and attribute are stored. If the window is not visible, the function returns the address in the save buffer as computed from the **x** and **y** coordinates. If the window is visible, the linked list is scanned for each window that is more current than the window being addressed. If a more current window covers the character position being addressed, the relative address of that window's save address is returned. If no more current window covers the character position, a NULL pointer is returned to tell the caller to address video RAM.

The **displ** function and the **dget** function are called to display and retrieve a video character and attribute to and from a layered window. These functions call **waddr** to see if the character should be read from or written to a save area. If not, video RAM is addressed.

6   The Windows Function Library

The **vswap** function exchanges the contents of a layered window's save buffer and video RAM or, possibly, the save buffers of more current windows that cover the window being addressed. The function uses **displ** and **dget** to make the exchange.

The **vsave** and **vrstr** functions work on stacked windows. **Vsave** copies the contents of video RAM into the window's save buffer, and **vrstr** copies the save buffer to video RAM.

The **acline** function is called by the macros **accent** and **deaccent** to change a selected line in a window to the ACCENT color configuration or the NORMAL color configuration.

The **add__list** function adds a WINDOW structure to the end of the linked list.

The **beg__list** function adds a WINDOW structure to the beginning of the linked list.

The **remove__list** function removes a WINDOW structure from the linked list.

The **insert__list** function inserts a WINDOW structure into the linked list after another specified WINDOW structure.

The **verify__wnd** function searches the linked list for a specified WINDOW structure address. It returns a true or false value reflecting the presence or absence of the WINDOW structure in the list. If the specified WINDOW pointer is NULL, the function returns the address of the most current (last) WINDOW structure in the list.

The **error__message** function establishes a window to display a specified error message. The message is written into the window with a **wprintf** call, and the audible alarm is sounded.

The **clear__message** function clears the latest error message.

WINDOW EXAMPLES

Following are discussions of the window library's features. These discussions are accompanied by example programs, each of which illustrates the feature being discussed. The examples consist of a small driver program with a main function that calls the example function for the feature being demonstrated. The example function contains the calls to the previously described window library functions and serves as an illustration of how to use the library functions. Each example program includes a project (**.prj**) file that Turbo C uses to build the executable program.

Later, these same example functions will be integrated into a single executable module that demonstrates the menu windows, which is why they are written without their own **main** functions.

Moving a Window

With layered windows, you have functions that allow you to move a window to an absolute or relative screen location. Note that these functions — **move__window** and **rmove__window** — are not available with stacked windows.

The program that illustrates window movement is shown in Listings 6.3, 6.4, and 6.5. Listing 6.3 is the small driver program, and Listing 6.5 is the project make file. Refer to Listing 6.4, **testmove.c**, as you read this explanation.

To run the example, type the following command:

C>move

(In all the examples that follow, it is assumed that C is your system drive. Do *not* type the C> prompt.)

6 The Windows Function Library

Besides illustrating window movement, **testmove.c** also shows you how to establish windows, set their colors, display them, and write text into them. The program establishes three windows, gives each of them their own colors, displays them, and writes a quote into the second of the three windows. This example illustrates how you can write text into a window that is partially covered by another window. When you run the program, you will see the display shown in Figure 6.4.

Figure 6.4 Moving Layered Windows

The program now waits for you to enter a keystroke. The program is specifically watching for one of the cursor arrow keys or the Esc key. Each press of an arrow key causes the middle window to be moved one character position in the direction of the arrow. The function **rmove_window** is used to move the window. Note how the center window moves between the other two.

When you press the Esc key, the first window opened is deleted. Another keypress causes the top window to be deleted. A final keypress deletes the middle window with the quotation and exits the program.

Moving a window illustrates the use of the window save buffers programmed into the library. Because of the amount of processing required to examine each buffer when a character is written to a window, the performance of the functions degrades as the windows get bigger and as more windows are established. Moving a large, layered window can seem to take forever when the processor is one of the older, slower PCs.

Listing 6.3: move.c

```
/* ------ move.c ------ */

void testmove(void);

main()
{
    testmove();
}
```

6 The Windows Function Library

Listing 6.4: testmove.c

```c
/* ------------ testmove.c ------------ */

#include "twindow.h"
#include "keys.h"

void testmove()
{
    WINDOW *wndA, *wndB, *wndC;
    int c;

    wndA = establish_window(5, 5, 9, 19);
    wndB = establish_window(10, 3, 9, 23);
    wndC = establish_window(13, 8, 9, 12);
    set_colors(wndA, ALL, RED, YELLOW, BRIGHT);
    set_colors(wndB, ALL, AQUA, YELLOW, BRIGHT);
    set_colors(wndC, ALL, WHITE, YELLOW, BRIGHT);
    display_window(wndA);
    display_window(wndB);
    display_window(wndC);
    wprintf(wndB, "\n I wouldn't care who");
    wprintf(wndB, "\n wrote the laws if I");
    wprintf(wndB, "\n could write the");
    wprintf(wndB, "\n ballads.");
    wprintf(wndB, "\n\n    Thomas Jefferson");
    do  {
        int x = 0, y = 0;
        c = get_char();
        switch (c)  {
            case FWD:   x++;
                        break;
            case BS:    --x;
                        break;
            case UP:    --y;
                        break;
            case DN:    y++;
            default:    break;
        }
        if (x || y)
            rmove_window(wndB, x, y);
    } while (c != ESC);
```

continued...

...from previous page

```
    delete_window(wndA);
    get_char();
    delete_window(wndC);
    get_char();
    delete_window(wndB);
}
```

Listing 6.5: move.prj

```
move
testmove (twindow.h, keys.h)
twindow (twindow.h, keys.h)
ibmpc.obj
```

Promoting and Demoting Windows

With the **forefront** and **rear_window** functions, you can **promote** a window into the most current position, placing it on top of all others, and you can **demote** a window into the least current position, placing it under all others. This feature is valuable in a program that has numerous windows and where the user selects one of them for some purpose while sending the others temporarily to the background. This feature is useful in any application where the user frequently changes from window to window.

The program that illustrates window promotions and demotions is shown in Listings 6.6, 6.7, and 6.8. Listing 6.6 is the small driver program, and Listing 6.8 is the project make file. Refer to Listing 6.7, **promote.c**, as you read this explanation.

To run the example, type the following command:

```
C>prom
```

6 The Windows Function Library

The **promote.c** program uses the same pattern of three windows used by the **testmove.c** program. This time, all three windows have text written into them, each with its name—Window A, Window B, and Window C. Figure 6.5 shows the screen as it is initially displayed.

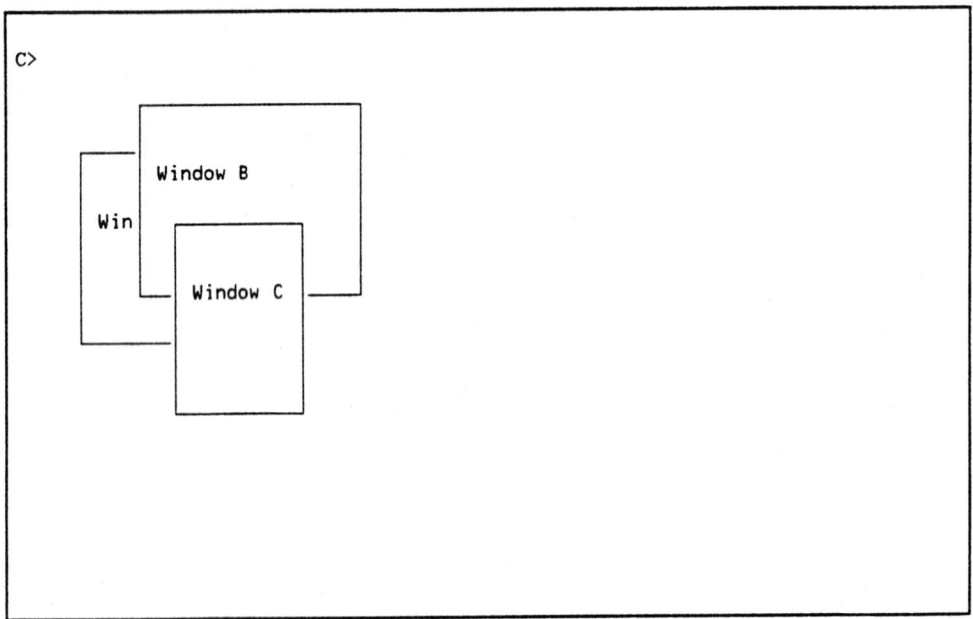

Figure 6.5 Promoting Layered Windows

You use the keyboard to promote and demote windows. Use the lowercase a, b, and c keystrokes to promote the windows named by those letters. Use their uppercase keystrokes to demote them. This process continues until you press the Esc key when one of the windows is deleted. Two more keystrokes will delete the other two windows, and the program will exit.

Listing 6.6: prom.c

```
/* ------ prom.c ------ */

void promote(void);

main()
{
    promote();
}
```

6 The Windows Function Library

Listing 6.7: promote.c

```c
/* ------------ promote.c ------------ */

#include "twindow.h"
#include "keys.h"

void promote()
{
    WINDOW *wndA, *wndB, *wndC;
    int c;

    wndA = establish_window(5, 5, 9, 19);
    wndB = establish_window(10, 3, 9, 20);
    wndC = establish_window(13, 8, 9, 12);
    set_colors(wndA, ALL, RED, YELLOW, BRIGHT);
    set_colors(wndB, ALL, AQUA, YELLOW, BRIGHT);
    set_colors(wndC, ALL, WHITE, YELLOW, BRIGHT);
    display_window(wndA);
    display_window(wndB);
    display_window(wndC);
    wprintf(wndA, "\n\n Window A");
    wprintf(wndB, "\n\n Window B");
    wprintf(wndC, "\n\n Window C");
    do {
        c = get_char();
        switch (c) {
            case 'a':   forefront(wndA);
                        break;
            case 'b':   forefront(wndB);
                        break;
            case 'c':   forefront(wndC);
                        break;
            case 'A':   rear_window(wndA);
                        break;
            case 'B':   rear_window(wndB);
                        break;
            case 'C':   rear_window(wndC);
                        break;
            default:    break;
        }
    } while (c != ESC);
```

continued...

...from previous page

```
    delete_window(wndA);
    get_char();
    delete_window(wndC);
    get_char();
    delete_window(wndB);
}
```

Listing 6.8: prom.prj

```
prom
promote (twindow.h, keys.h)
twindow (twindow.h, keys.h)
ibmpc.obj
```

Assigning Titles and Changing Window Colors

When a window has been established, you can assign a title to it, as well as a set of foreground and background colors.

The program that illustrates window titles and colors is shown in Listings 6.9, 6.10, and 6.11. Listing 6.9 is the small driver program, and Listing 6.11 is the project make file. Refer to Listing 6.10, **ccolor.c**, as you read this explanation.

To run the example, type the following command:

```
C>color
```

Once again, three windows are displayed. Each of them has a different color (if you have a color monitor), and none of them has a title. The windows are in the same location and are the same size as those used for the earlier examples. The program waits for a keystroke and is looking for one of the letters, r, g, or b. It will use these letters to change the title of the middle window to "RED," "GREEN," or "BLUE," and it will change the color of the middle window to the color that corresponds to its new title. Figure 6.6 shows the screen after you select a red window.

6 The Windows Function Library

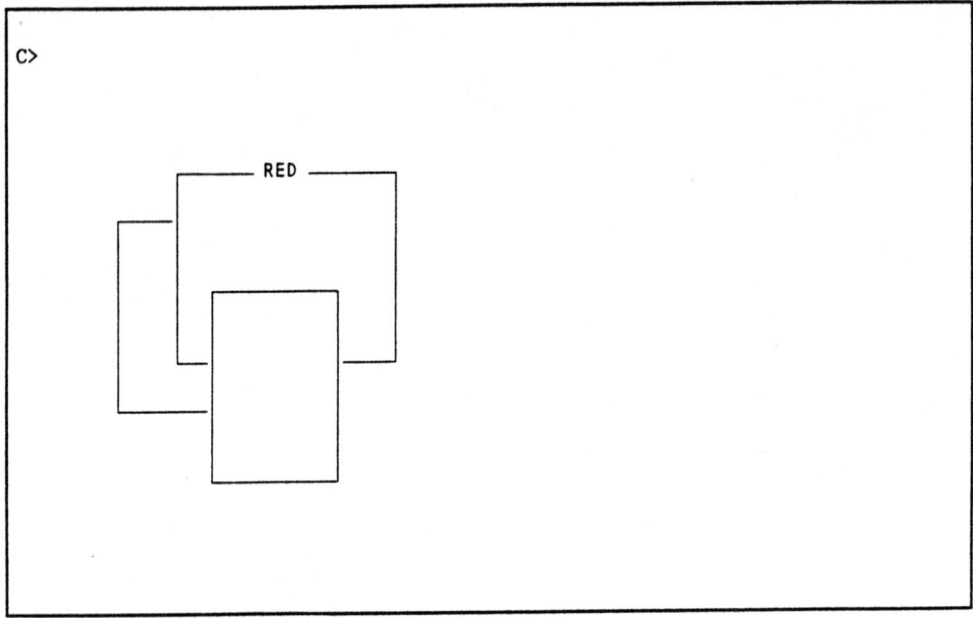

Figure 6.6 Changing Colors and Titles

Press the Esc key to break out and delete a window, and press any two other keys to delete the other two windows and exit the program.

Listing 6.9: color.c

```
/* -------- color.c ------- */

void ccolor(void);

main()
{
    ccolor();
}
```

Listing 6.10: ccolor.c

```c
/* ------------ ccolor.c ------------ */

#include "twindow.h"
#include "keys.h"

void ccolor()
{
    WINDOW *wndA, *wndB, *wndC;
    int c;

    wndA = establish_window(8, 8, 9, 19);
    wndB = establish_window(13, 6, 9, 20);
    wndC = establish_window(16, 11, 9, 12);
    set_colors(wndA, ALL, RED, YELLOW, BRIGHT);
    set_colors(wndB, ALL, AQUA, YELLOW, BRIGHT);
    set_colors(wndC, ALL, WHITE, YELLOW, BRIGHT);
    display_window(wndA);
    display_window(wndB);
    display_window(wndC);
    do  {
        c = get_char();
        switch (c)  {
            case 'r':
                set_title(wndB, " RED ");
                set_colors(wndB, ALL, RED, WHITE, BRIGHT);
                break;
            case 'b':
                set_title(wndB, " BLUE ");
                set_colors(wndB, ALL, BLUE, WHITE, BRIGHT);
                break;
            case 'g':
                set_title(wndB, " GREEN ");
                set_colors(wndB, ALL, GREEN, WHITE, BRIGHT);
                break;
            default:
                break;
        }
    } while (c != ESC);
    delete_window(wndA);
    get_char();
```

continued...

6 The Windows Function Library

...from previous page

```
    delete_window(wndC);
    get_char();
    delete_window(wndB);
}
```

Listing 6.11: color.prj

```
color
ccolor (twindow.h, keys.h)
twindow (twindow.h, keys.h)
ibmpc.obj
```

Comparing Stacked and Layered Windows

The program that accompanies this discussion is meant to compare the performance of stacked and layered windows. You can compile it with a window library that has been compiled for either kind of window.

The program that illustrates the differences between stacked and layered windows is shown in Listings 6.12, 6.13, and 6.14. Listing 6.12 is the small driver program, and Listing 6.14 is the project make file. Refer to Listing 6.13, **fast.c**, as you read this explanation.

To run the example, type the following command:

```
C>fast
```

Remember that the program does not show a comparison by itself. You must build two versions of it, one with a stacked window library and one with a layered window library, and compare the performance of the two programs.

When you run the program, it will establish and display fifteen windows in succession, as shown in Figure 6.7. When you press any key, it will delete each of the windows in reverse order. You can compare the relative speed of the processes when the program is compiled into the two environments.

The Windows Function Library 6

Figure 6.7 Comparing Layered and Stacked Windows

Listing 6.12: fast.c

```
/* ------- fast.c ------- */

void fasttest(void);

main()
{
    fasttest();
}
```

6 The Windows Function Library

Listing 6.13: fasttest.c

```c
/* ------------ fasttest.c ------------ */

#include <stdio.h>
#include "twindow.h"

void fasttest()
{
    int row, col;

    for (row = 0, col = 0; col < 15; row += 3, col++)   {
        establish_window(row, col, 10, 30);
        set_colors(NULL, ALL, RED, YELLOW, BRIGHT);
        display_window(NULL);
        wprintf(NULL,"\n\n\n   Hello, Dolly # %d", col);
    }
    get_char();
    while (col--)
        delete_window(NULL);
}
```

Listing 6.14: fast.prj

```
fast
fasttest (twindow.h)
twindow (twindow.h, keys.h)
ibmpc.obj
```

The Windows Function Library 6

Moving, Promoting, Hiding, Intensity, and Menus

This next example combines several of the features already shown and gives examples of two more features: the use of **get_selection** to process a simple menu and the use of **set_intensity** to change the foreground intensity of windows.

The program that illustrates these features is shown in Listings 6.15, 6.16, and 6.17. Listing 6.15 is the small driver program, and Listing 6.17 is the project make file. Refer to Listing 6.16, **poems.c**, as you read this explanation.

To run the example, type the following command:

C>poetry

This program displays five different poems on the screen and allows you to select one of them, move it around, promote it to the front, demote it to the back, and delete it. The program begins with a window menu that lists each of the poems. You can move the cursor bar up and down and select one by pressing the Enter key, or you can press one of the numbers 1 to 5, selecting the number that is associated with the poem. Whichever poem you select will be displayed. Figure 6.8 shows the poem menu.

6 The Windows Function Library

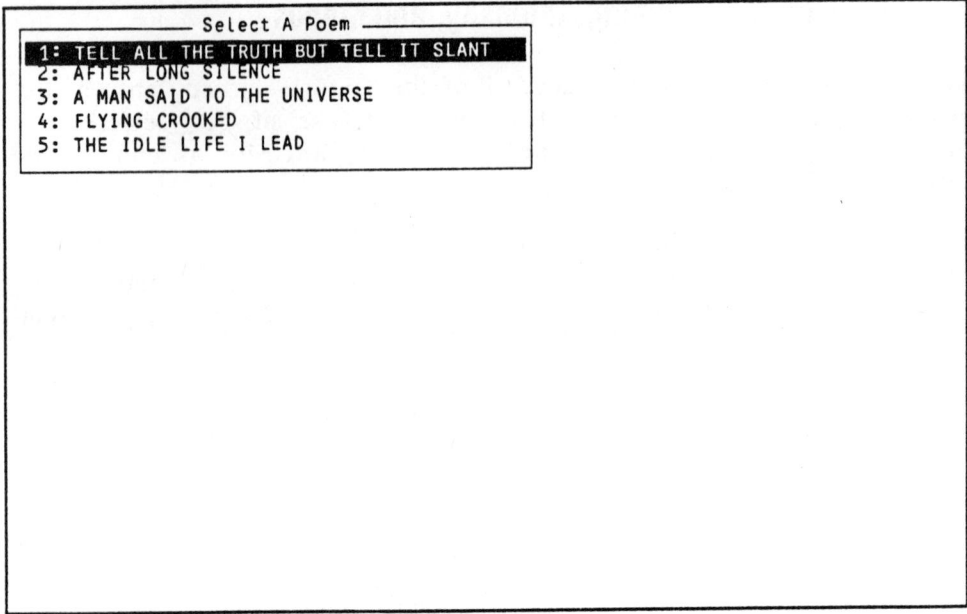

Figure 6.8   The Poem Menu

After a poem is selected, you can move it around with the arrow keys, return to the menu by pressing the Esc key, or select another poem by pressing the associated number key. The currently selected poem is displayed with the bright intensity, and all others are dim. If you select a poem that is dim, it becomes bright and the others become dim. To bring a poem to the foreground, press the plus (+) key; to send it to the background, press the minus (-) key. To delete the current poem, press the Del key. You can retrieve it by pressing its number key. When you are done, press the Esc key to return to the menu, and press the Esc key again to exit from the program.

Figure 6.9 shows the poems scattered about the screen in various locations.

The Windows Function Library 6

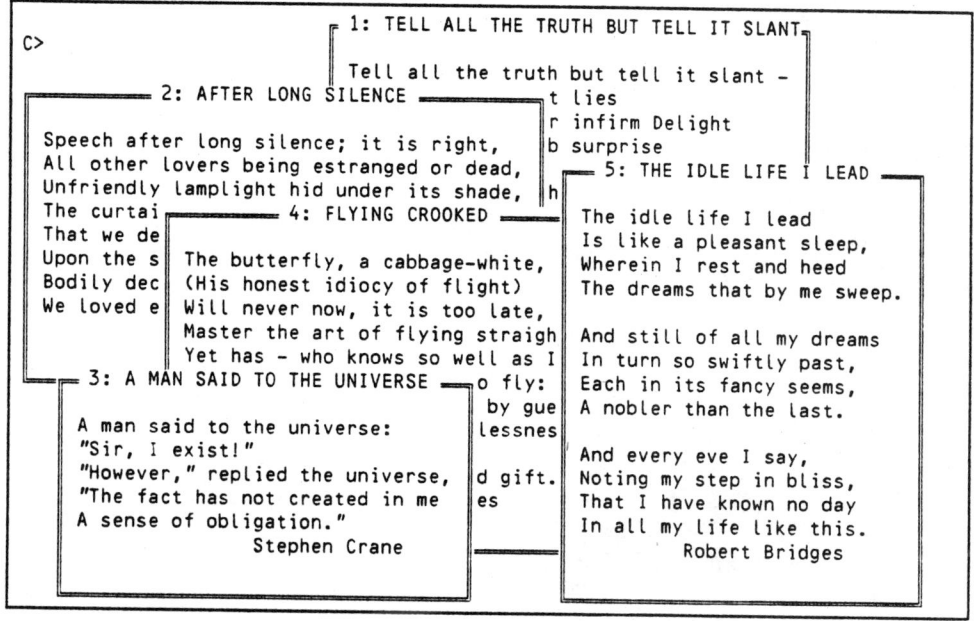

Figure 6.9   Poems

Listing 6.15: poetry.c

```
/* ---- poetry.c ------ */

#include "twindow.h"
void poems(void);

main()
{
    load_help("tcprogs.hlp");
    poems();
}
```

6 The Windows Function Library

Listing 6.16: poems.c

```c
/* --------------- poems.c ---------------- */

#include <stdio.h>
#include <string.h>
#include <stdlib.h>
#include "twindow.h"
#include "keys.h"

/* -------- local prototypes ----------- */
void get_poem(int s);
int ht (char **tb);
int wd (char **tb);
char *titles [] = {
    " 1: TELL ALL THE TRUTH BUT TELL IT SLANT ",
    " 2: AFTER LONG SILENCE ",
    " 3: A MAN SAID TO THE UNIVERSE ",
    " 4: FLYING CROOKED ",
    " 5: THE IDLE LIFE I LEAD ",0
};
WINDOW *pno [] = {0, 0, 0, 0, 0};
static int x [] = {20, 15, 29, 10, 17};
static int y [] = {5, 10, 13, 18, 6};
static int wcl [] [2] = {    {BLUE, WHITE},
                             {MAGENTA, WHITE},
                             {RED, WHITE},
                             {GREEN, WHITE},
                             {AQUA, WHITE}   };
char *poem1 [] = {
    "Tell all the truth but tell it slant -",
    "Success in Circuit lies",
    "Too bright for our infirm Delight",
    "The Truth's superb surprise",
    "",
    "As Lightning to the Children eased",
    "With explanation kind",
    "The Truth must dazzle gradually",
    "Or every man be blind -",
    "             Emily Dickenson",
    0
};
```

continued...

...from previous page

```c
char *poem2 [] = {
    "Speech after long silence; it is right,",
    "All other lovers being estranged or dead,",
    "Unfriendly lamplight hid under its shade,",
    "The curtains drawn upon unfriendly night,",
    "That we descant and yet again descant",
    "Upon the supreme theme of Art and Song:",
    "Bodily decrepitude is wisdom; young",
    "We loved each other and were ignorant.",
    "            William Butler Yeats",
    0
};

char *poem3 [] = {
    "A man said to the universe:",
    "\"Sir, I exist!\"",
    "\"However,\" replied the universe,",
    "\"The fact has not created in me",
    "A sense of obligation.\"",
    "            Stephen Crane",
    0
};

char *poem4 [] = {
    "The butterfly, a cabbage-white,",
    "(His honest idiocy of flight)",
    "Will never now, it is too late,",
    "Master the art of flying straight,",
    "Yet has - who knows so well as I? -",
    "A just sense of how not to fly:",
    "He lurches here and there by guess",
    "And God and hope and hopelessness.",
    "Even the aerobatic swift",
    "Has not his flying-crooked gift.",
    "            Robert Graves",
    0
};
```

continued...

6 The Windows Function Library

...from previous page

```c
char *poem5 [] = {
    "The idle life I lead",
    "Is like a pleasant sleep,",
    "Wherein I rest and heed",
    "The dreams that by me sweep.",
    "",
    "And still of all my dreams",
    "In turn so swiftly past,",
    "Each in its fancy seems,",
    "A nobler than the last.",
    "",
    "And every eve I say,",
    "Noting my step in bliss,",
    "That I have known no day",
    "In all my life like this.",
    "           Robert Bridges",
    0
};
char **poem [] = {poem1,poem2,poem3,poem4,poem5,0};

void poems()
{
    int s = 0, i, c;
    WINDOW *mn;
    char **cp;

    cursor(0, 25);
    mn = establish_window(0, 0, 7, 45);
    set_title(mn, " Select A Poem ");
    set_colors(mn, ALL, BLUE, GREEN, BRIGHT);
    set_colors(mn, ACCENT, GREEN, WHITE, BRIGHT);
    display_window(mn);
    cp = titles;
    while (*cp)
        wprintf(mn, "\n%s", *cp++);
    while (1)   {
        set_help("poemmenu", 40, 10);
        s = get_selection(mn, s+1, "12345");
        if (s == 0)
            break;
```

continued...

...from previous page
```
        if (s == FWD || s == BS)      {
            s = 0;
            continue;
        }
        hide_window(mn);
        get_poem(--s);
        c = 0;
        set_help("poems    ", 5, 15);
        while (c != ESC)     {
            c = get_char();
            switch (c)   {
                case FWD:   rmove_window(pno[s], 1, 0);
                            break;
                case BS:    rmove_window(pno[s], -1, 0);
                            break;
                case UP:    rmove_window(pno[s], 0, -1);
                            break;
                case DN:    rmove_window(pno[s], 0, 1);
                            break;
                case DEL:   delete_window(pno[s]);
                            pno[s] = NULL;
                            break;
                case '+':   forefront(pno[s]);
                            break;
                case '-':   rear_window(pno[s]);
                default:    break;
            }
            if (c > '0' && c < '6')
                get_poem(s = c - '1');
        }
        forefront(mn);
        display_window(mn);
    }
    close_all();
    for (i = 0; i < 5; i++)
        pno[i] = NULL;
}
```
continued...

6 The Windows Function Library

...from previous page

```c
/* --- activate a poem by number ---- */
static void get_poem(int s)
{
    char **cp;
    static int lastp = -1;
    if (lastp != -1)
        set_intensity(pno[lastp], DIM);
    lastp = s;
    if (pno [s])
        set_intensity(pno[s], BRIGHT);
    else   {
        pno [s] = establish_window
            (x[s], y[s], ht(poem[s]), wd(poem[s]));
        set_title(pno[s], titles[s]);
        set_colors(pno[s],ALL,wcl[s][0],wcl[s][1],BRIGHT);
        set_border(pno[s], 1);
        display_window(pno[s]);
        cp = poem[s];
        while (*cp)
            wprintf(pno[s], "\n %s", *cp++);
    }
}
/* ------- compute height of a window display table ---- */
static int ht(char **tb)
{
    int h = 0;
    while (*(tb + h++)) ;
    return h + 3;
}
/* ------- compute width of a window display table ------- */
static int wd(char **tb)
{
    int w = 0;
    while (*tb)    {
        w = max(w, strlen(*tb));
        tb++;
    }
    return w + 4;
}
```

Listing 6.17: poetry.prj

```
poetry
poems (twindow.h, keys.h)
thelp (twindow.h, keys.h)
twindow (twindow.h, keys.h)
ibmpc.obj
```

In the poetry program, the F1 key is used as a context-sensitive help function key. When you press F1, a window appears with a help message related to what you are currently doing. Chapter 7 will explain how this feature is included.

SUMMARY

Now you have the basis for a window software toolset. With these functions, you can add windows to your software, and you can display text in the windows. But the application of windows can be further defined into more higher-level features that are common to many applications systems. The next several chapters add those features to your window library. Chapter 7 introduces the use of windows to add context-sensitive user help to your programs.

CHAPTER 7

CONTEXT-SENSITIVE HELP WINDOWS

7 Context-sensitive Help Windows

When a new program is started, the first problem usually encountered is the unfamiliarity of the program and its user language. What key should be pressed? What process comes next? What does that menu item do? No matter how much effort is put into the development of a self-explanatory user language, users will always have questions because the language of a new system is always a foreign tongue. Not only do users not know the language, but often they are not even aware of what the system can and cannot do. Traditionally, this problem is addressed with a printed user's manual and, perhaps, an automated tutorial. The disadvantage of these solutions is that the user must divert attention from the system to read the manual or run the tutorial.

If screens were big enough, a system could maintain a constant display of the user manual. Whenever a user wanted information, the manual would be available. This solution would wear out its welcome before long; once a user knows the system, the helpful information is unnecessary and unwanted. Valued information to a novice user is screen clutter to a veteran.

Most interactive systems have a common characteristic: when a user needs help, he or she is looking at the screen and wondering what key to press. It seems only natural that the keystrokes a system will recognize at any time should include a Help function key. Press the correct applications key, and the program will do your bidding; press the Help function key, and the program will tell you something about what keys it expects and what will happen when you press them.

Because interactive systems use the screen for routine user language and data displays, a Help message is prime material for a pop-up window. The pop-up nature of a window delivers help without disturbing the application's use of the screen. Such a window is called the **context-sensitive Help window**, a window that pops up to help the user when he or she presses the designated Help function key. (The software industry has recognized <F1> as a standard for the Help function key, but many software packages use other keys.) A Help window contains text that explains some part of the program. As users operate the program and move from feature to feature, the content and location of Help windows change to reflect the current context. These changes are not seen; they occur within the software. When a user presses the Help function key, the appropriate Help message is displayed in a pop-up window.

Because the Help message is related to the current location in the program, the Help window is said to be context-sensitive. Experienced users can ignore the Help features of a program; novices can press the Help function key with every change in the program's condition and receive hints, reminders, or detailed instructions.

The system designer decides how much and what kind of help a system will provide to the user. Some systems offer several help levels, depending on the user's experience. The WordStar word-processing program has employed such a technique for years. Help levels range from simple "press Esc to return to ..." messages to complete on-line user manuals. Many software developers prefer to distribute the user manual in this manner rather than as expensive, bound documents. This procedure has two drawbacks: users have come to associate extravagant manuals with quality software, and expensive books tend to discourage software pirates.

Nonetheless, users have also come to expect systems that require minimal use of a user's manual. Users want on-line help.

PROGRAMMING FOR HELP WINDOWS

The Help functions in this book support the concept of context-sensitive help by using the window functions, a text file, and function calls from the application program. Each application program tells the Help functions which Help file to use and which Help window is current. The Help file contains the text for each Help window. The Help functions watch the keyboard and display the current Help window when the Help function key is pressed.

A program that uses Help software must provide the following interfaces to Help functions:

- a function call to specify the name of the help text file
- a value for the help function key
- function calls to identify the current help window
- the use of the **get_char** keyboard input function for all keyboard input (**get_char** is described in Chapter 4)

7 Context-sensitive Help Windows

The last of these four requirements might need some justification. While a program is running, Help software intercepts each keyboard character to see if the Help function key has been pressed. If so, the Help window process takes over. If not, the keystroke value is sent to the software function waiting for it. Help software can manage this intercept only if you use the **get_char** function for keyboard input. As explained previously, **get_char** monitors the keyboard for the Help function key. If you use other means to read characters from the keyboard, the Help function key intercept will not be made.

There are other methods for watching the keyboard for the Help function key. Some of these methods involve attaching interceptor software to the keyboard interrupt vector or the keyboard BIOS vector. For several reasons, it was decided that these methods would not be used. First, the software in this book provides a user environment that includes windows for menus, data entry, and text entry. All the keyboard input a program needs can be managed by one of these features, and they all use the **get_char** function. You might never again need to code any keyboard input. Next, if a program attaches itself to an interrupt vector, strange things happen when the program is abnormally terminated; usually, the computer must be restarted. Finally, programs you develop with this software can be **memory-resident**. Memory-resident programs are often attached to the keyboard for other purposes.

You will learn more about memory-resident programs, interrupt vectors, and how to attach one to the other in Chapter 11. For now, have your software read the keyboard with the **get_char** function. This way, the keyboard vectors are left alone, and the system is well-behaved regardless of resident programs, program aborts during testing, or unexpected program terminations in a production system.

The required use of **get_char** costs you three standard C capabilities:

- You will be unable to use the standard library functions **scanf** or **getchar**, since neither of these functions uses the **get_char** function.

- You will be unable to use the unadorned console input function (**getch**) provided by Turbo C.

- You be unable to use the **stdin** logical device for keyboard input, which means that your program cannot redirect files or pipes in place of the keyboard.

Context-sensitive Help Windows 7

The loss of the **scanf** and **getchar** functions is no great loss to the on-line programmer. These functions are useless in an interactive environment. They are buffered input functions that require pressing the Enter key to terminate an input character or string, and they are insensitive to cursor location and field length. These functions echo their inputs, watching for DOS command line conventions, and they will echo dual-character displays when a control character is typed. If the Ctrl/C key combination is typed, the functions might abort the program. The functions do not work well with function or cursor keys. Turbo C includes them to retain UNIX compatibility. Their origins are in computer systems with Teletype-like terminals.

It might seem that you are losing a capability when you eliminate the **stdin** device, but this device is intended for programs that can take their input from files and output of other programs as well as from the keyboard. Those programs—or at least the **stdin** inputs to those programs—are not usually meant to be run in an interactive environment.

THE HELP WINDOW TEXT FILE

The Help windows displayed when a user presses the Help function key are described in a text file. The Help text file is an ASCII file that you can build with your Turbo C editor or any other editor that can produce ASCII files.

Help windows are described by a mnemonic identifier that is used by the Help software to identify and locate the text. The lines following the identifier contain text, the number and length of which define the height and width of the Help window. Figure 7.1 shows a small Help file that describes two Help windows.

7 Context-sensitive Help Windows

```
<name    >
Enter the name of the
employee as last name,
comma, first name, middle
initial. Example:
Hart, William S
<emplnumb>
Enter the employee number
with from 1 to five digits.
Example: 12345
<end>
```

Figure 7.1   An Example of a Help File

The Help window identifier is exactly eight characters long and is surrounded by angle brackets, as shown in Figure 7.1. Each identifier appears on its own line. The last line in the file must be the token entry. Figure 7.2 shows the two Help windows that would be displayed as the result of these descriptions.

Context-sensitive Help Windows 7

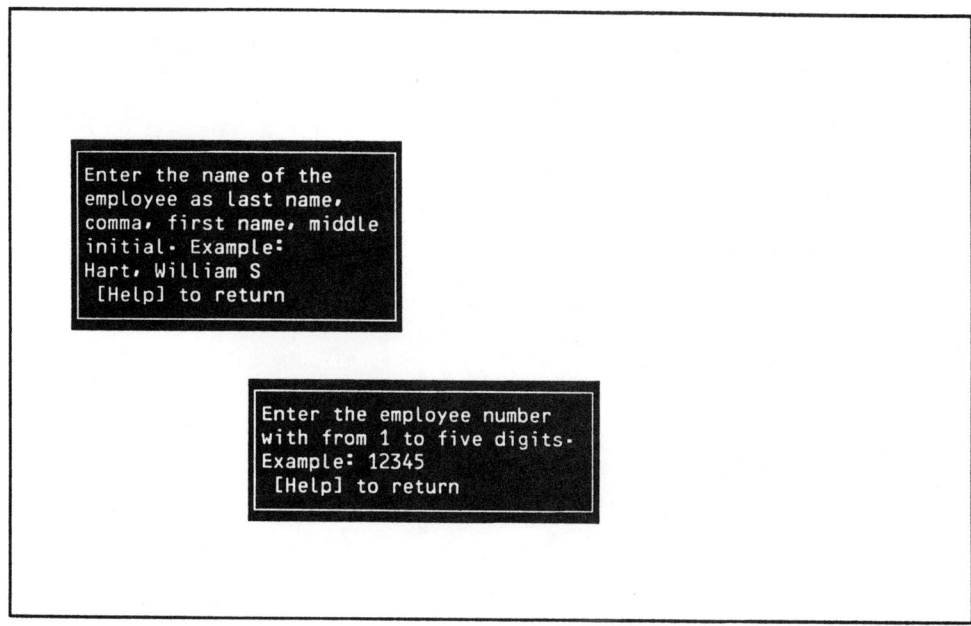

Figure 7.2 Example Help Windows

All example programs that follow in this and later chapters use the Help software. Following is a simple example to illustrate Help itself, but the rest of the examples use Help for its intended purpose—to provide users with on-line, context-sensitive help. For this reason, one Help file is provided for all the programs. It is called **tcprogs.hlp** and is shown in Listing 7.1.

7 Context-sensitive Help Windows

Listing 7.1: tcprogs.hlp

```
<maxims  >
 Press 1, 2, or 3
 for a pithy maxim.
<menu    >
 Use arrow keys to move the cursor bars.
 Use Enter to make the selection.
<poemmenu>
 Arrows move the cursor bar.
 Enter will select the poem
 under the cursor bar.
 Press a digit (1-5) to
 select any other poem.
<poems   >
 Move poem with arrow keys
 Select poem with 1 - 5
 Use + to bring poem forward
 Use - to push poem back
<name    >
 Enter the name of the person
 who is placing the order.
<address >
 Enter the address of the
 person who is placing the
 order.
<state   >
 The State may be one of these:
 VA, NC, SC, GA, FL
<phone   >
 Enter the phone number
 of the person who is
 placing the order
<amount  >
 Enter the amount
 of the order
<notepad >
 -------Cursor Movement-----  --------Page Movement--------
 arrows   = move text cursor  Ctrl-Home = Beginning of File
 Ctrl-T   = Top of Window     Ctrl-End  = End of File
 Ctrl-B   = Bottom of Window  PgUp      = Previous Page
 Ctrl ->  = Next Word         PgDn      = Next Page
```

continued...

...from previous page

```
Ctrl <- = Previous Word
Home    = Beginning of Line  --------Editor Control-------
End     = End of Line        Scroll Lock = No Auto Reform

--------Block Controls-----  --------Edit Commands--------
F4  = Form Paragraph         F2 or Esc = Done
F5  = Mark Block Beginning   F3        = Erase File
F6  = Mark Block End         Ins       = Toggle Insert Mode
F7  = Move Block             Del       = Delete Char
F8  = Copy Block             <--       = Rubout
F9  = Delete Block           Ctrl-D    = Delete Word
F10 = Unmark Block           Alt-D     = Delete Line
<end>
```

HELP FUNCTIONS

To install context-sensitive Help windows into your software, you must add two function calls to your programs, which are calls to functions in the source file **thelp.c**, shown later as Listing 7.2.

void load_help(char *filename)

Call this function to load the Help file or change to a different Help file. The function opens the Help file and scans it for Help messages, building a table of Help window identifiers, their sizes, and their locations in the Help file.

void set_help(char *helpname, int x, int y)

This function specifies the current Help window with an eight-character array matching the window's mnemonic in the Help file. The mnemonic is surrounded by angle brackets in the Help file, but the array does not include them. The **x** and **y** integers specify the upper left screen coordinates (in character positions) of the Help window, which allows users to use the same window for different contexts but in different locations on the screen.

7 Context-sensitive Help Windows

CHANGING THE HELP FUNCTION KEY

If you want to specify a function key value other than <F1> (the default), you must change the value of the global integer named **helpkey**. That variable is declared in **ibmpc.c** in Chapter 4. You can include the source file named **keys.h** (see Chapter 4) in your program and use one of the defined key values given in that file. The following code will change the Help function key to <F2>.

```
#include "keys.h"
extern int helpkey;
helpkey = F2;
```

CHANGING THE HELP FUNCTION

The file named **ibmpc.c** in Chapter 4 includes a function pointer named **helpfunc**. Normally, that pointer contains the NULL value. When the Help functions are used, the pointer is initialized with the address of a function appropriately named **help**. If you want to use a different function, say, ahead of the standard **help** function, you can change the value of the **helpfunc** pointer. To cause the Help function key to call your function, use the following code:

```
extern void (*helpfunc)();
void yourfunc();
helpfunc = yourfunc;
```

You can point **helpfunc** back to the standard Help function with the following code:

```
extern void (*helpfunc)();
extern void help();
helpfunc = help;
```

DISABLING HELP

There are three ways to turn Help off: you can set the Help function key value to 0; you can set the Help function pointer to NULL; and you can call **set_help**, passing it a pointer to a zero-length string. To re-enable Help, you must reverse the action you have chosen.

SOURCE LISTING: thelp.c

Immediately following is Listing 7.2, **thelp.c**. This file is the source code for the functions that support context-sensitive Help windows.

(Listing 7.2 on next page)

7 Context-sensitive Help Windows

Listing 7.2: thelp.c

```c
/* --------- thelp.c ----------- */

#include <stdio.h>
#include <string.h>
#include <stdlib.h>
#include "twindow.h"
#include "keys.h"

#define MAXHELPS 25
#define HBG WHITE
#define HFG BLACK
#define HINT DIM

#define TRUE 1
#define FALSE 0

static struct helps {
    char hname [9];
    int h, w;
    long hptr;
} hps [MAXHELPS+1];

static int hp = 0;
static int ch = 0;
static int hx, hy;
FILE *helpfp = NULL;
long ftell();
char *fgets();
void help();
char helpname[64];
void getline(char *lineh);
```

continued...

Context-sensitive Help Windows 7

...from previous page

```c
/* ----------- load the HELP! definition file ------------ */
void load_help(char *hn)
{
    extern void (*helpfunc)();
    extern int helpkey;
    char lineh [80];

    if (strcmp(helpname, hn) == 0)
        return;
    helpfunc = help;
    helpkey = F1;
    hp = 0;
    strcpy(helpname, hn);
    if ((helpfp = fopen(helpname, "r")) == NULL)
        return;
    getline(lineh);
    while (1)   {
        if (hp == MAXHELPS)
            break;
        if (strncmp(lineh, "<end>", 5) == 0)
            break;
        if (*lineh != '<')
            continue;
        hps[hp].h = 3;
        hps[hp].w = 18;
        strncpy(hps[hp].hname, lineh+1, 8);
        hps[hp].hptr = ftell(helpfp);
        getline(lineh);
        while (*lineh != '<')   {
            hps[hp].h++;
            hps[hp].w = max(hps[hp].w, strlen(lineh)+2);
            getline(lineh);
        }
        hp++;
    }
}
```

continued...

7 Context-sensitive Help Windows

...from previous page

```c
/* -------- get a line of text from the help file -------- */
static void getline(char *lineh)
{
    if (fgets(lineh, 80, helpfp) == NULL)
        strcpy(lineh, "<end>");
}
/* -------- set the current active help screen ----------- */
void set_help(char *s, int x, int y)
{
    for (ch = 0; ch < hp; ch++)
        if (strncmp(s, hps[ch].hname, 8) == 0)
            break;
    hx = x;
    hy = y;
}
/* ---------- display the current help window ----------- */
void help()
{
    char ln [80];
    int i, xx, yy;
    WINDOW *wnd;
    extern int helpkey;
    if (hp && ch != hp) {
        curr_cursor(&xx, &yy);
        cursor(0, 25);
        wnd = establish_window(hx, hy, hps[ch].h, hps[ch].w);
        set_colors(wnd, ALL, HBG, HFG, HINT);
        display_window(wnd);
        fseek(helpfp, hps[ch].hptr, 0);
        for (i = 0; i < hps[ch].h-3; i++)    {
            getline(ln);
            wprintf(wnd, ln);
        }
        wprintf(wnd, " [Help] to return");
        while (get_char() != helpkey)
            putchar(BELL);
        delete_window(wnd);
        cursor(xx, yy);
    }
}
```

PROGRAM DESCRIPTION: thelp.c

Thelp.c contains four **#define** symbols that establish global parameters for the Help system. MAXHELPS is set to the maximum number of Help windows that the program can support at one time. HBG, HFG, and HINT are the background and foreground colors and intensity of Help windows.

The **helps** structure describes a Help window. It contains the window's mnemonic name, its height and width, and the character offset of the window description in the text file that contains Help windows. The **hps** array of **helps** structures contains one entry for each window in the text file and is built by the **load_help** function.

The **load_help** function reads the Help text file specified by the caller and builds the **hps** array. It keys on the angle bracket that identifies each window's name, copying the name and the file character offset into the structure. Then, it reads the text for the window to calculate the window's length and width. The length is a function of the number of lines of text, and the width is a function of the length of the longest line in the window's text.

The **set_help** function searches the array for a match on the window name passed by the caller. The **ch** integer variable, which is used to subscript through the array until a match is found, will be a subscript to the current window when the Help function key is pressed. The **hx** and **hy** variables are set to the values passed by the caller. This procedure establishes the position of the window.

The **help** function is called by the **get_char** function in **ibmpc.c** when the designated Help function key is pressed. The **help** function saves the current cursor location and positions the cursor to an off-screen location. A Help window is established with the coordinates and dimensions recorded in the array entry subscripted by the **ch** variable. The current character position of the text file is moved to the location stored in the array entry. Each line of text is read and written into the window. The last line is written, instructing the user to press the Help key a second time to clear the Help window and return. The program waits for the Help key to be pressed, deletes the window, and restores the cursor to the position it held before the Help key was initially pressed.

7 Context-sensitive Help Windows

AN EXAMPLE OF CONTEXT-SENSITIVE HELP

The programs in Listings 7.3, 7.4, and 7.5 provide an example of how to use the Help software. Listing 7.3, **sayings.c**, provides a **main** function to call the example function, **maxims.c**, shown in Listing 7.4. Listing 7.5 is the project make file that Turbo C uses to build this example.

To run the program, enter the following command:

```
C>sayings
```

Sayings.c loads the **tcprogs.hlp** file with a call to **load_help** and then calls the function named **maxims**. This sequence was chosen so that **maxims.c** could be integrated into later programs that provide examples of menu processing and memory-resident utilities.

Maxims.c shows how to use **set_help** and **get_char** in your programs. Only one Help window is used. **Maxims.c** opens a window and waits for a keystroke. If you press 1, 2, or 3, one of three dusty old maxims is displayed in the window. Figure 7.3 shows the window with one of the maxims displayed. If you press <Esc>, the program exits. If you press <F1>, the Help window shown in Figure 7.4 is displayed.

Context-sensitive Help Windows 7

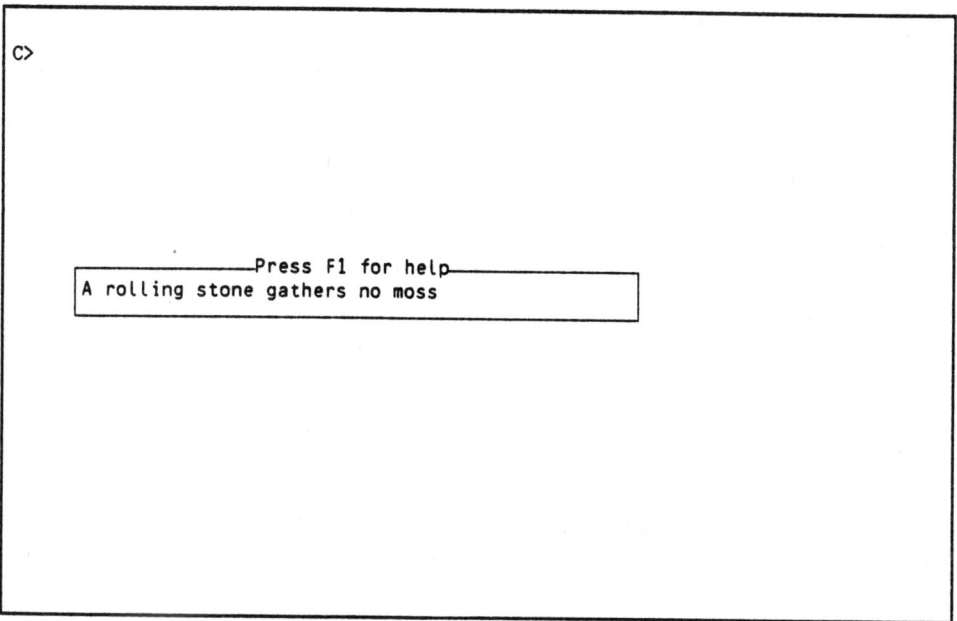

Figure 7.3 A Pithy Maxim

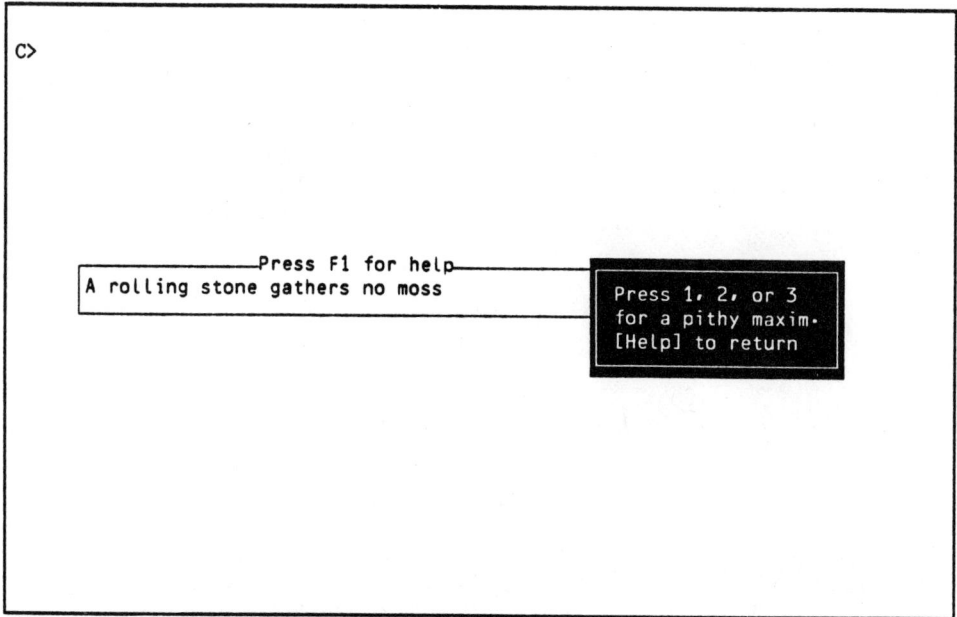

Figure 7.4 Help for the Maxims

135

Listing 7.3: sayings.c

```c
/* ------ sayings.c ------ */

#include "twindow.h"
void maxims(void);

main()
{
    load_help("tcprogs.hlp");
    maxims();
}
```

Listing 7.4: maxims.c

```c
/* ------ maxims.c --------- */

#include "twindow.h"
#include "keys.h"

void maxims()
{
    int c;
    WINDOW *wnd;

    set_help("maxims  ", 50, 10);
    wnd = establish_window(5, 10, 3, 50);
    set_title(wnd, "Press F1 for help");
    set_colors(wnd, ALL, RED, WHITE, DIM);
    display_window(wnd);
    while ((c = get_char()) != ESC) {
        switch (c)       {
            case '1':
                wprintf(wnd, "\nA stitch in time \
saves nine   ");
                break;
            case '2':
                wprintf(wnd, "\nA rolling stone \
gathers no moss");
                break;
            case '3':
                wprintf(wnd, "\nA penny saved \
is a penny earned");
                break;
            default:
                break;
        }
    }
    delete_window(wnd);
}
```

7 Context-sensitive Help Windows

Listing 7.5: sayings.prj

```
sayings
maxims (twindow.h, keys.h)
thelp (twindow.h, keys.h)
twindow (twindow.h, keys.h)
ibmpc.obj
```

SUMMARY

Your window tools now include the context-sensitive Help feature. The following chapters add more features to window processing and provide examples of these features. Each of the examples uses context-sensitive Help windows, so your understanding of the Help feature is reinforced with each added capability. This lesson is valuable because, as a general rule, interactive programs should provide on-line help to the user.

The next addition to the use of windows in an interactive program is presented in Chapter 8, which describes the use of windows as data entry forms. Chapter 8 includes functions that allow you to describe the content and format of a data entry form, and it provides the software for the collection of data elements the user enters onto the form.

CHAPTER 8

DATA ENTRY WINDOWS

8 Data Entry Windows

Interactive programs process data values that the user types into the computer. These data values take many forms, so the programs can use many different techniques for the entry of data values. A word processor uses free-form text entry. A spreadsheet uses the familiar row and column format with a bar cursor. (But be careful of copying the "look and feel" of someone else's program—too much familiarity breeds litigation.)

Many interactive programs accept data values in ways that resemble the manual entry of data onto a printed form. Everyone is familiar with paper forms—the Internal Revenue Service has seen to that. In a forms-oriented interactive program, the screen emulates a paper form with fields of data values and descriptive text to explain each field. As the user keys data values into the field positions, the software validates those values and manages the placement of the cursor. In this chapter, a forms-oriented data entry capability is implemented by using the window as the template for the data entry form. A data entry template consists of a window along with its associated descriptions of data entry fields and text prompts.

DATA ENTRY TEMPLATE

To use the data entry window feature, you must open a window, assign attributes to it that are appropriate for a **data entry template** in the application, and describe the text prompts and data entry fields. Once the template is established, you can call a data entry function, which manages the input of all the data elements on the template. When the function returns, the data element values are in your buffers, validated, properly formatted, and ready for any subsequent processing that your program will do.

Data Entry Field

A **data entry field** is, simply, a data element. It can be a date, an amount, a name, or an earned run average. It has these properties: it has a definable length and format, and it must fit on one line in the window. The data entry field is the traditional data base data element.

Data Entry Windows 8

As you describe the fields for a template, you specify the position, attribute, collection buffer, validation function, help information, and a data entry mask for each field. These components of a field's description are discussed in the following sections.

Position

A field's **position** is expressed in column and row character coordinates relative to the text area of the template window. The use of window coordinates rather than screen coordinates is beneficial; if you decide later to change the position of the window, the field position descriptions do not need to be changed.

Attribute

A field's **attribute** declares that the field is one of several generic data element types. These types are described in detail later in this chapter, but for now, you should know that you can specify a field that is a date, nomenclature, currency, or a number. The field attribute controls the manner in which data values may be entered into the field.

Buffer

Each field is assigned a **data collection buffer,** which is the address of the character array into which the data value is to be collected. Your program provides this space and passes its address to the data entry software.

Validation

Your program provides the address of a **validation** function if one is to be used. The data entry software will call your function after a data value has been entered into the field. The software does some basic validation as a result of the field's attribute, but you can do more extensive checking in a custom validation routine.

8   Data Entry Windows

Help

You can specify a **Help window mnemonic** (as described in Chapter 7) for each field, and you can specify a Help function for those fields where the help you want to give cannot be described in a constant text window. The Help window comes from a Help file, and the Help function must be included in your program. If an overriding Help function is specified, it replaces the standard Help function and is called when the user presses the Help function key. These Help specifications are in effect while the user is entering data into the field to which those specifications are assigned.

Data Entry Mask

When you define a field, you must provide a **data entry mask**. This mask is specified in a character array that contains underline characters and punctuation. The underline characters correspond to the positions in the mask where characters may be entered, and the punctuation can be any other displayable ASCII characters. The length of the data element itself is described by the number of underline characters, and your data entry buffer must be at least equal to this length plus one. Punctuation characters are not transferred to the buffer. The data entry mask for a phone number with area code and extension could look like the following:

```
char phone_mask [] = "(___)___-____ ext:____";
```

Field Prompts

Each field should have a **prompt**, which is text that tells the user what the field means and what information is expected to be entered. Prompts are literal strings that cannot be changed by the user. You specify their values and position. A prompt must fit on one line in the window.

DATA ENTRY

When the data entry function is executed, it processes the fields on the template in the sequence in which they were defined (without regard to position), and performs simple validations (valid date, digits only, etc.). It will call the defined custom function for further validation or the function that provides custom help to the user. The entry process uses the ACCENT color attributes of the window to highlight the field where entry is presently expected. The PC's cursor is positioned in this field. As the user moves the data entry activity from field to field, both the highlighted accent and the cursor also move.

DATA COLLECTION FUNCTIONS

These functions are the library functions that your program calls to use a window as a data entry template. Remember that you must have established a window before you use these functions.

void init_template(WINDOW *wnd)

This function initializes a window for use as a data entry template. It establishes a linked list of **FIELD** structures, first clearing any existing descriptions. A **FIELD** structure describes the characteristics of a data entry field and is defined in **twindow.h** (see Chapter 6). The **init_template** function serves two purposes. If it finds any fields already established for the window, they are deleted; therefore, you should use this function when a window template is no longer needed because the **FIELD** structures must be deallocated.

8 Data Entry Windows

FIELD *establish_field

(WINDOW *wnd,int x,int y,char *msk,char *bf,int t)

This function establishes a data entry field in a window that has been initialized by **init_template** as a data entry template. The **x** and **y** character coordinates specify the location of the field's entry mask and are relative to the window rather than the screen. The **bf** pointer points to the caller-defined collection buffer. The **t** integer is a field type that can be one of the following:

```
A = alphanumeric
N = numeric, space-filled
Z = numeric, zero-filled
C = currency
D = date
```

The **msk** pointer points to a character mask that defines the field length and allows for punctuation that appears on the screen but is not copied into the field collection buffer. The mask can contain any characters. The underscore character represents the character positions where data characters may be entered. The **bf** array must include as many characters as the mask has underscores, plus one for the null terminator.

A currency field may have any number of digits to the left of the decimal point and must have two digits to the right.

Dates are validated in "mmddyy" format. If the user keys in an invalid date, the program displays an error message and requires the user to correct the entry.

Establish_field returns a pointer to a **FIELD** structure as defined in **twindow.h**. You use this pointer when you call **field_window**, **field_help**, **field_protect**, and **field_validate**, which are described later.

void wprompt(WINDOW *wnd, int x, int y, char *s)

This function writes a literal prompt to a window. The prompt in string **s** is written, beginning at the window coordinates **x**, **y**.

void field_tally(WINDOW *wnd)

When you call this function, data values in the buffers for all fields on a template are displayed. You might use this function after you have loaded your buffers with values from a data base record.

void field_window(FIELD *fld, char *helpname, int x, int y)

This function establishes a context-sensitive Help window for a field. The **helpname** string must match a Help window mnemonic in the current Help file as specified by the most recent call to **load_help** (see Chapter 7). As the **data_entry** function moves from field to field, it calls **set_help** for those fields that have Help windows assigned to them. The **x** and **y** parameters specify where the Help windows will be displayed.

Note that this function and the three that follow do not require a **WINDOW** pointer. The specification of the **FIELD** pointer is sufficient because **FIELD** pointers are chained in a linked list that is attached to a window. These functions modify the field definition without regard to the window template that owns it.

void clear_template(WINDOW *wnd)

This function sets the collection buffers of all fields in a template to null-terminated strings of spaces and displays all fields.

8 Data Entry Windows

void field_validate(FIELD *fld, int (*validfn)())

This function is implemented as a macro. It is used to provide the address of a custom validation function for a given string. The standard field validation routines might not provide sufficient error checking for a particular field. In that case, you need to write a custom validation function. The **data_entry** function will call your validation function after its generic validations have been passed. When it does so, it will pass the address of the collection buffer so that your function can examine the value entered by the user. Your validation function can call the **error_message** function (see Chapter 6) if the entry is found to be invalid. The function must return **OK** or **ERROR** as defined in **twindow.h**. If the function returns **OK**, the **data_entry** function will proceed with the next field on the template. If the function returns **ERROR**, the **data_entry** function will remain in the field where the error occurred.

void field_protect(FIELD *fld, int prot)

This function is implemented as a macro. It sets the protect characteristic of a field to a true or false value, depending on the value of the **prot** parameter. A protected field is bypassed by the **data_entry** function. By using the **field_protect** function, you can selectively toggle the user's write permission to a field on the template.

This function can be used along with the **field_validate**, **clear_template**, and **field_tally** functions to control changes to a data base record where the record's data elements are shown on the template.

Data Entry Windows 8

To understand how to develop code that uses **field_protect**, consider the template in Figure 8.1. Assume that this template represents fields in an employee record in a data base file. The template is used to retrieve and change records in the file. Before data entry is begun, your program can call **field_protect** to protect all fields except the employee number. Then, you can call the **field_validate** function to point to a custom validation function. When the user types the employee number, the **data_entry** function (described later) calls the custom validation function, which retrieves the matching employee record. The validation function loads the field collection buffers with the data elements from the record, calls **field_tally** to display the data element values, calls **field_protect** to turn protection on for the employee number, and calls **field_protect** to turn protection off for the rest of the fields. The validation function then returns to the **data_entry** function, and the user may proceed to change data element values at will. When the user is finished with the record, the system returns to the application function that called **data_entry**. This function can rewrite the record to the file, clear the buffers and the template by calling the **clear_template** function, reprotect the record fields, unprotect the employee number, and start the process over again.

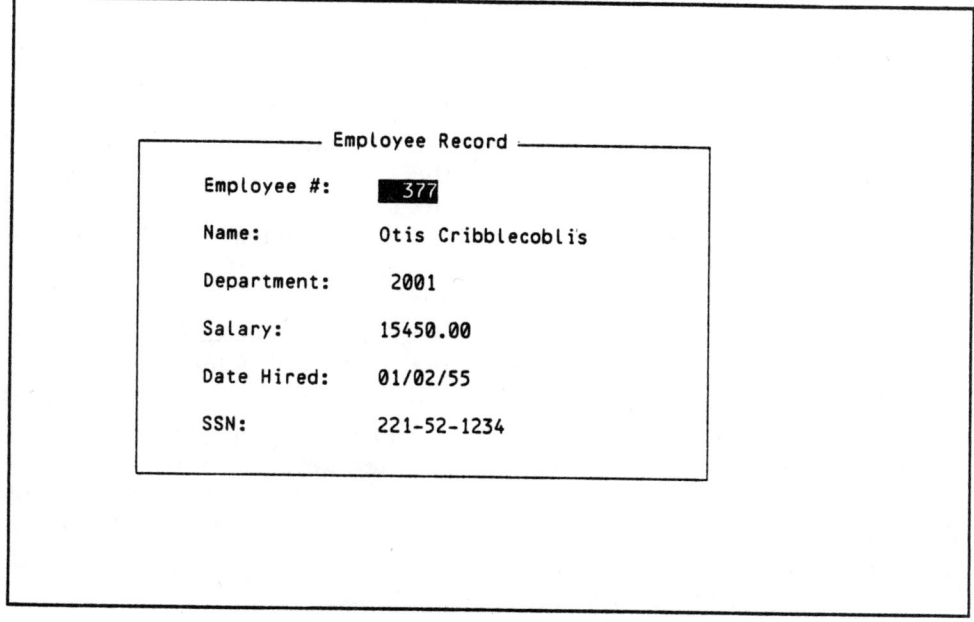

Figure 8.1 An Example of a Data Entry Template

147

8 Data Entry Windows

void field_help(FIELD *fld, int (*helpfn)())

This function is implemented as a macro. It allows you to install a custom Help function to be called in place of the standard Help function. It is used for fields when the user requires more help than can be provided in a constant text window.

When the user is entering data into the field in question and presses the Help function key, the custom Help function is called. The **data_entry** function passes the address of the field's data entry collection buffer, which allows the custom Help function to insert a value into the field.

This feature is useful when the application contains a list of possible values from which the user can select. You might open another window from your custom Help function, load it with these values, and use **get_selection** (see Chapter 6) for the user to choose a value. You might, as is done in the example that appears later in this chapter, write the current date into the field's collection buffer. You might provide a query into a data base. Perhaps in the example discussed previously for the employee record, your Help function for the employee number would provide a list of employee numbers and names taken from the employee file itself.

int data_entry(WINDOW *wnd)

This function processes data entry for a template. The user is shown the template with all fields displaying the current values in their collection buffers. The user enters data into the fields in the sequence in which the fields were established by the **establish_field** function, without regard to the position of the fields on the template.

The user is then shown the first field with its complete data space, including punctuation, highlighted with the ACCENT color values of the window. The cursor is positioned in the first location of the field, and the function waits for a keystroke. The user can begin typing characters or move to another field by using the Enter key, the Tab key, or the arrow keys. The Esc key, PgUp, PgDn, Home, End, and any function key (F1 through F10, except the Help function key) will terminate the data entry and return to the caller of **data_entry**. This applies regardless of which field the user is currently editing.

When the user types the last character of a field, the highlight and the cursor move to the next field. Before they do so, however, the **data_entry** function calls its own generic validation functions followed by the caller's custom validation function if one is installed. These functions must return OK, or the **data_entry** function will not move the cursor to the next field.

If the user presses the Help function key, the **data_entry** function will call the custom Help function if one is installed for the current field, passing it the address of the field's data collection buffer. If no Help function is installed, and a Help window was installed for the field, the Help functions from Chapter 7 will display the Help window. If neither a Help window nor a Help function is installed, nothing happens when the user presses the Help function key unless, of course, the program is using the Help functions outside the context of the data entry window.

When the **data_entry** function returns to its caller, all field buffers contain the data values that were entered by the user. This function returns the keystroke that ended the template entry. Recall that pressing the Esc key, a page key, or a function key will terminate the entry. An application program can use the terminating keystroke value to determine the user's intentions. A function key could be used for normal completion. Pressing the Esc key might mean "Ignore my changes, return me to the prior values of the template." The PGUP or PGDN values (as defined in **keys.h**) might be used to retrieve the previous or next record in the data base. When the user terminates the entry, the terminating code is returned to the program for its use.

SOURCE LISTING: entry.c

Listing 8.1 is the source code for **entry.c**, the file containing the library functions that support window data entry templates.

8 Data Entry Windows

Listing 8.1: entry.c

```c
/* --------- entry.c ---------- */

#include <stdio.h>
#include <ctype.h>
#include <stdlib.h>
#include <alloc.h>
#include <mem.h>
#include <string.h>
#include "twindow.h"
#include "keys.h"

#define FIELDCHAR '_'
int insert_mode = FALSE;        /* insert mode, TRUE/FALSE */
extern int helpkey;

/* -------- local prototypes -------- */
void addfield(WINDOW *wnd, FIELD *fld);
void disp_field(WINDOW *wnd, char *bf, char *msk);
void data_value(WINDOW *wnd, FIELD *fld);
void insert_status(void);
int read_field(WINDOW *wnd, FIELD *fld);
void right_justify(char *s);
void right_justify_zero_fill(char *s);
int validate_date(char *s);
int endstroke(int c);
int spaces(char *c);

/* -------- initialize a template --------- */
void init_template(WINDOW *wnd)
{
    FIELD *fld, *fl;

    fld = FHEAD;
    while (fld) {
        fl = fld->fnxt;
        free(fld);
        fld = fl;
    }
    FHEAD = NULL;
}
```

continued...

...from previous page

```
/* ------ establish a field in a template ------- */
FIELD *establish_field(wnd, cl, rw, msk, bf, ty)
WINDOW *wnd;
int rw;
int cl;
char *msk;
char *bf;
int ty;
{
    FIELD *fld;

    if ( (fld = malloc(sizeof(FIELD))) == NULL)
        return NULL;
    fld->fmask = msk;
    fld->frow = rw;
    fld->fcol = cl;
    fld->fbuff = bf;
    fld->ftype = ty;
    fld->fprot = 0;
    fld->fnxt = fld->fprv = NULL;
    fld->fvalid = NULL;
    fld->fhelp = NULL;
    fld->fhwin = NULL;
    fld->flx = fld->fly = 0;
    addfield(wnd, fld);
    return fld;
}

/* ----- add a field to the end of the list ------ */
static void addfield(WINDOW *wnd, FIELD *fld)
{
    if (FTAIL)  {
        fld->fprv = FTAIL;
        FTAIL->fnxt = fld;
    }
    FTAIL = fld;
    if (!FHEAD)
        FHEAD = fld;
}
```

continued...

8 Data Entry Windows

...from previous page

```c
/* -------- display a data field ------ */
static void disp_field(WINDOW *wnd, char *bf, char *msk)
{
    while (*msk)    {
        wputchar(wnd, *msk != FIELDCHAR ? *msk : *bf++);
        msk++;
    }
}

/* ------- display the data value in a field ------ */
static void data_value(WINDOW *wnd, FIELD *fld)
{
    wcursor(wnd, fld->fcol, fld->frow);
    disp_field(wnd, fld->fbuff, fld->fmask);
}

/* ------ display all the fields in a window ------- */
void field_tally(WINDOW *wnd)
{
    FIELD *fld;

    fld = FHEAD;
    while (fld != NULL) {
        data_value(wnd, fld);
        fld = fld->fnxt;
    }
}

/* ----- set a field's help window ------- */
void field_window(FIELD *fld, char *hwin, int x, int y)
{
    fld->fhwin=hwin;
    fld->flx = x;
    fld->fly = y;
}
```

continued...

Data Entry Windows 8

...from previous page

```
/* ------- clear a template to all blanks ------ */
void clear_template(WINDOW *wnd)
{
    FIELD *fld;
    char *bf, *msk;

    fld = FHEAD;
    while (fld != NULL) {
        bf = fld->fbuff;
        msk = fld->fmask;
        while (*msk)    {
            if (*msk == FIELDCHAR)
                *bf++ = ' ';
            msk++;
        }
        fld = fld->fnxt;
    }
    field_tally(wnd);
}

/* ---------- set insert/exchange cursor shape ----------- */
static void insert_status()
{
    set_cursor_type(insert_mode ? 0x0106 : 0x0607);
}
```

continued...

8 Data Entry Windows

...from previous page

```c
/* -------- read a field from the keyboard ------------- */
static int read_field(WINDOW *wnd, FIELD *fld)
{
    char *mask = fld->fmask, *buff = fld->fbuff;
    int done = FALSE, c, column;

    column = fld->fcol;
    while (*mask != FIELDCHAR)  {
        column++;
        mask++;
    }
    while (TRUE)    {
        wcursor(wnd, column, fld->frow);
        c = get_char();
        if (fld->ftype == 'A')
            c = toupper(c);
        clear_message();
        switch (c)  {
            case '\b':
            case BS:
                if (buff == fld->fbuff) {
                    done = c == BS;
                    break;
                }
                --buff;
                do  {
                    --mask;
                    --column;
                } while (*mask != FIELDCHAR);
                if (c == BS)
                    break;
            case DEL:
                movmem(buff+1, buff, strlen(buff));
                *(buff+strlen(buff)) = ' ';
                wcursor(wnd, column, fld->frow);
                disp_field(wnd, buff, mask);
                break;
            case FWD:
                do  {
                    column++;
```

continued...

Data Entry Windows 8

...from previous page

```
                mask++;
        } while (*mask && *mask != FIELDCHAR);
        buff++;
        break;
    case INS:
        insert_mode ^= TRUE;
        insert_status();
        break;
    case '.':
        if (fld->ftype == 'C')  {
            if (*mask++ && *buff == ' ')    {
                *buff++ = '0';
                if (*mask++ && *buff == ' ')
                    *buff++ = '0';
            }
            right_justify(fld->fbuff);
            wcursor(wnd, fld->fcol, fld->frow);
            disp_field(wnd, fld->fbuff, fld->fmask);
            column = fld->fcol+strlen(fld->fmask)-2;
            mask = fld->fmask+strlen(fld->fmask)-2;
            buff = fld->fbuff+strlen(fld->fbuff)-2;
            break;
        }
    default:
        if (endstroke(c))   {
            done = TRUE;
            break;
        }
        if (toupper(fld->ftype)!='A'&&!isdigit(c))  {
            error_message("Numbers only");
            break;
        }
        if (insert_mode)    {
            movmem(buff, buff+1, strlen(buff)-1);
            disp_field(wnd, buff, mask);
            wcursor(wnd, column, fld->frow);
        }
        *buff++ = c;
        wputchar(wnd, c);
        do  {
```

continued...

8 Data Entry Windows

...from previous page

```
                    column++;
                    mask++;
            } while (*mask && *mask != FIELDCHAR);
            if (!*mask)
                    c = FWD;
            break;
        }
        if (!*mask)
            done = TRUE;
        if (done)   {
            if (fld->ftype == 'D' &&
                    c != ESC &&
                        validate_date(fld->fbuff) != OK)
                return ERROR;
            break;
        }
    }
    if (c != ESC && toupper(fld->ftype) != 'A') {
        if (fld->ftype == 'C')  {
            if (*mask++ && *buff == ' ')       {
                *buff++ = '0';
                if (*mask++ && *buff == ' ')
                    *buff++ = '0';
            }
        }
        if (fld->ftype == 'Z' || fld->ftype == 'D')
            right_justify_zero_fill(fld->fbuff);
        else
            right_justify(fld->fbuff);
        wcursor(wnd, fld->fcol, fld->frow);
        disp_field(wnd, fld->fbuff, fld->fmask);
    }
    return c;
}
```

continued...

Data Entry Windows 8

...from previous page

```
/* ---------- test c for an ending keystroke ---------- */
static int endstroke(int c)
{
    switch (c)  {
        case '\r':
        case '\n':
        case '\t':
        case ESC:
        case F1:
        case F2:
        case F3:
        case F4:
        case F5:
        case F6:
        case F7:
        case F8:
        case F9:
        case F10:
        case PGUP:
        case PGDN:
        case HOME:
        case END:
        case UP:
        case DN:
            return TRUE;
        default:
            return FALSE;
    }
}
```

continued...

8 Data Entry Windows

...from previous page

```c
/* ------- right justify, space fill -------- */
static void right_justify(char *s)
{
    int len;

    len = strlen(s);
    while (*s == ' ' || *s == '0' && len)    {
        len--;
        *s++ = ' ';
    }
    if (len)
        while (*(s+(len-1)) == ' ') {
            movmem(s, s+1, len-1);
            *s = ' ';
        }
}

/* ---------- right justify, zero fill ---------------- */
static void right_justify_zero_fill(char *s)
{
    int len;

    if (spaces(s))
        return;
    len = strlen(s);
    while (*(s + len - 1) == ' ')   {
        movmem(s, s + 1, len-1);
        *s = '0';
    }
}

/* ----------- test for spaces -------- */
int spaces(char *c)
{
    while (*c == ' ')
        c++;
    return !*c;
}
```

continued...

Data Entry Windows 8

...from previous page

```c
/* -------------- validate a date ---------------- */
static int validate_date(char *s)
{
    static int days [] =
        { 31,28,31,30,31,30,31,31,30,31,30,31 };
    char date [7];
    int mo;

    strcpy(date, s);
    if (spaces(date))
        return OK;
    days[1] = (atoi(date+4)%4) ? 28 : 29;
    *(date + 4) = '\0';
    mo = atoi(date+2);
    *(date+2) = '\0';
    if (mo && mo<13 && atoi(date) && atoi(date)<=days[mo-1])
        return OK;
    error_message("Invalid date");
    return ERROR;
}

/* ----- Process data entry for a screen template. ---- */
int data_entry(WINDOW *wnd)
{
    FIELD *fld;
    int exitcode, isvalid, done=FALSE, oldhelpkey=helpkey;
    field_tally(wnd);
    fld = FHEAD;
    /* ---- collect data from keyboard into screen ---- */
    while (fld != NULL && done == FALSE)    {
        set_help(fld->fhwin, fld->flx, fld->fly);
        helpkey = (fld->fhelp) ? 0 : oldhelpkey;
        wcursor(wnd, fld->fcol, fld->frow);
        if (fld->fprot == FALSE)    {
            reverse_video(wnd);
            data_value(wnd, fld);
            wcursor(wnd, fld->fcol, fld->frow);
            exitcode = read_field(wnd, fld);
            isvalid = (exitcode != ESC && fld->fvalid) ?
                        (*(fld->fvalid))(fld->fbuff) : OK;
```

continued...

8 Data Entry Windows

...from previous page

```
            }
        else    {
            exitcode = FWD;
            isvalid = OK;
        }
        if (isvalid == OK)  {
            normal_video(wnd);
            data_value(wnd, fld);
            switch (exitcode)   {          /* passed edit */
                case F1:   if (fld->fhelp) {
                                (*(fld->fhelp))(fld->fbuff);
                                data_value(wnd, fld);
                           }
                           break;
                case DN:
                case '\r':
                case '\t':
                case FWD:  fld = fld->fnxt;
                           if (fld == NULL)
                                fld = FHEAD;
                           break;
                case UP:
                case BS:   fld = fld->fprv;
                           if (fld == NULL)
                                fld = FTAIL;
                           break;
                default:   done = endstroke(exitcode);
                           break;
            }
        }
    }
    helpkey = oldhelpkey;
    return (exitcode);
}
/* --------- display a window prompt -------- */
void wprompt(WINDOW *wnd, int x, int y, char *s)
{
    wcursor(wnd, x, y);
    wprintf(wnd, s);
}
```

Data Entry Windows **8**

PROGRAM DESCRIPTION: entry.c

The FIELDCHAR macro in **entry.c** identifies the special character that is used in a field's character mask to represent the data bytes. This character cannot, therefore, be used as a punctuation character in a mask. As published, the FIELDCHAR is an underline. You can change the definition of FIELDCHAR to use a different character.

Fields are assigned to windows in a doubly linked list. The list head and list tail are in the WINDOW structure for the field. Each field is represented by a FIELD structure that is allocated when the field is established.

The **init_template** function is used to initialize a window as a data entry template. It traces the FIELD linked list and frees any previously allocated FIELDs.

The **establish_field** function allocates a FIELD buffer and initializes it with values passed by the caller and other default initial values. The mask, position, buffer address, and data type of the field are passed by the caller. The FIELD is added to the FIELD linked list of the specified WINDOW, and a pointer to the FIELD is returned to the caller.

The **addfield** function is called to add a FIELD to the linked list of a specified WINDOW.

The **disp_field** function is used to display the data value in a field's buffer on the screen. A mask is passed by the caller to be used in displaying the field. This function is called with a WINDOW, a buffer pointer, and a mask pointer. It is assumed that the window's cursor is already positioned at the field's beginning position. Characters are displayed from the buffer, with punctuation characters inserted from the mask.

The **data_value** function is called to display the current value of a field in a window. The function positions the window's cursor at the field's first character position and calls **disp_field**, passing the WINDOW address and the field's buffer and mask addresses.

The **field_tally** function is called to display all fields on a screen template. It walks down the FIELD linked list and calls **data_value** for each field on the template.

8 Data Entry Windows

The **field__window** function is called to establish a Help window for a field. The caller's Help window name and screen coordinates are copied into the specified FIELD structure.

The **clear__template** structure walks down the FIELD linked list, looking for the specified window. The function sets the buffer for each field in the template to a null-terminated, space-filled string by using the mask to determine the field's length. When all fields are cleared, **field__tally** is called.

The data entry program works in Insert or Overstrike mode. The Ins key is used to toggle this mode, and the **insert__mode** variable indicates the current mode setting. The **insert__status** function changes the cursor type, depending on the value of the **insert__mode** variable. Insert mode is represented by a box cursor, and Overstrike mode is represented by an underline cursor. The function **set__cursor__type** in **ibmpc.c** (see Chapter 4) is used to change the shape of the cursor.

The **read__field** function is called to read a field's data entry from the user. It positions the cursor at the beginning of the field and begins to read keystrokes. Two local pointers are used to track the data entry. The **mask** pointer maintains the current position within the mask, and the **buff** pointer maintains the current position within the buffer. As the user moves the cursor, deletes characters, and types characters, these pointers are adjusted.

For the character delete operations, the Turbo C **movmem** function is used to shift characters in the buffer, and the **disp__field** function is used to display the results.

The Ins key toggles the Insert/Overwrite mode.

If the period (.) is entered for a currency field, the field is zero-filled for the two right-most positions and right-justified, and the pointers and cursor are positioned at the most significant pennies position.

Data Entry Windows 8

If the user types a key that ends the entry, as tested by the **endstroke** function, the entry is terminated; otherwise, the character is to be written into the buffer. First, non-alphanumeric field types are tested to be sure the user entered a digit. If a digit was not entered, an error message is displayed, and the keystroke is rejected. If the insert mode is in effect, the buffer is shifted one character position to the right, and the field is displayed with **disp_field**. The character is written into the buffer and displayed on the screen. The pointers are advanced, with the mask pointer jumping over punctuation characters. When the last character is entered, the entry for the field is terminated.

When the entry is terminated, dates are validated, dates and numeric fields are justified, the cursor is positioned, and the field is displayed.

The **endstroke** function tests a key for a value that should end data entry.

Two functions justify fields. One, **right_justify**, right-justifies and space-fills a field. The other, **right_justify_zero_fill** right-justifies and zero-fills a field.

The **spaces** function tests a field for all space characters.

The **validate_date** function tests for a valid date.

The **data_entry** function is called to process all the fields on a template. The function calls **field_tally** to display all the data values in the buffers for the field. Then, the function walks down the linked list of FIELD structures and manages data entries for each field.

First, the **set_help** function is called to establish the assigned Help window for this field. Then, the **helpkey** external variable is assigned. If this field has a custom Help function, the helpkey is disabled because **data_entry** will intercept the Help function key itself.

If the field is not protected, the **reverse_video** function is called so that the field will be displayed with the ACCENT color configuration. The **data_value** function is called to display the current field value in the ACCENT colors, and **read_field** is called to get the user's input. The value returned from **read_field** is the ending keystroke for the field's data entry. If the field has a validation function, that function is called.

8 Data Entry Windows

If all validations are passed for the field, the **normal_video** function resets the window to the NORMAL colors, and the **data_value** function redisplays the field in these NORMAL colors. Then, the ending keystroke is tested. If data entry was terminated by the Help function key, the custom Help function is called. Since that function has the opportunity to change the field's buffered data, the **data_value** function is called again to redisplay the field.

The ending keystroke can be a forward-moving key (down arrow, Enter, tab) or a backward-moving key (up arrow, left arrow). The next field is chosen from the FIELD linked list for the WINDOW on the basis of this value. Either the next or the prior field in the list is chosen, and data entry continues.

If the ending keystroke was one of those tested by the **endstroke** function and not one of those already tested here, data entry for the window template is completed, and the **data_entry** function returns to the caller.

AN EXAMPLE: ORDER ENTRY

The source files shown in Listings 8.2, 8.3, and 8.4 provide an example of the use of a data entry template window. Listing 8.2, **order.c**, is the main function that calls the example function, **ordent.c**. Ordent.c will be integrated into the menu example in Chapter 10 and the memory-resident utility in Chapter 12. Listing 8.4 is **order.prj**, the project make file used by Turbo C to build the program.

To run the example program, enter the following command:

```
C>order
```

The window shown in Figure 8.2 will pop up on your screen. Refer to Listing 8.3, **ordent.c**, as you read this explanation and run the program.

Data Entry Windows 8

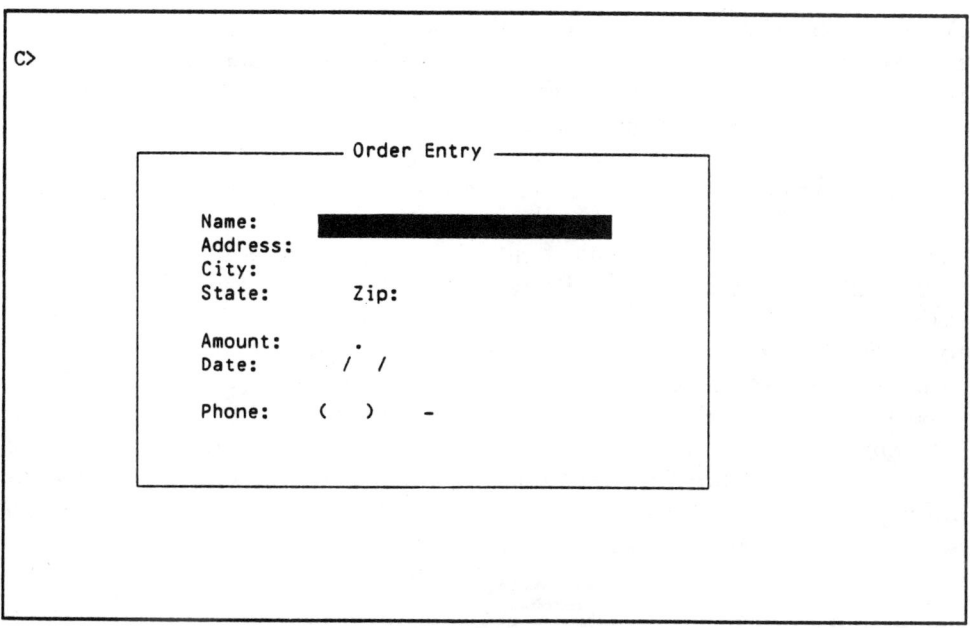

Figure 8.2 The Order Entry Data Entry Template

The example program begins by establishing a window and giving it a title and colors. The window is displayed, and prompts are added to the template. After **init_template** is called, each field is established with a call to **establish_field** followed by a call to **field_window** to identify the help window that explains the field. The last field established in this example does not use a Help window. Instead, the function **field_help** is used to identify a custom Help function for this field. Notice that one field, the state data element, will be validated by a custom function as specified by the call to **field_validate.**

The program calls **clear_template** to establish an empty template, and then it calls **data_entry** to allow data values to be entered into the template. When this function returns, the program deletes the window. At this point in a real program, you would do something with the data values that were entered. This example program simply exits.

165

8 Data Entry Windows

As you run the program, observe how the characters you enter are placed into the fields and see how the cursor is managed. The insert/overwrite mode is controlled by the Ins key and is indicated by the shape of the cursor. When the cursor is a flat, blinking underscore, the entry process is in overwrite mode. When you press the Ins key, the cursor becomes a blinking box, and you are in insert mode.

Press <F1> for help on each field. Figure 8.3 shows the template with some data values and a Help window displayed. Observe the valid states as shown by the Help window for the state data element, and try to enter a different one, which will demonstrate how a custom validation function works, and how it can use the **error_message** function to report an entry error. Figure 8.4 shows the screen in this configuration. The custom Help function for the date field demonstrates how you can provide a data value from outside the **data_entry** function. In this example, it reads the current date by using the Turbo C **getdate** function and writes the current date into the date field's buffer.

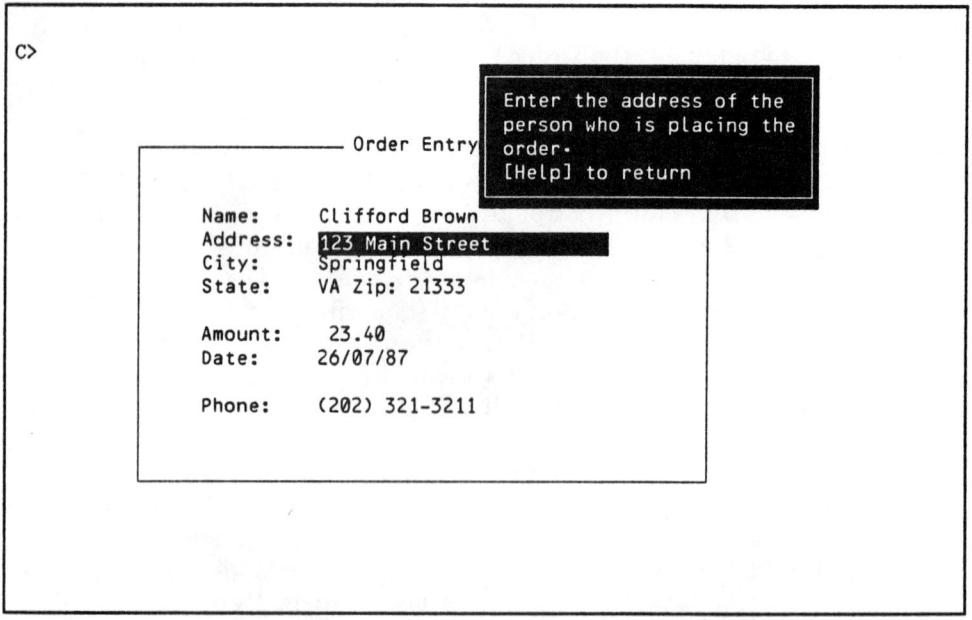

Figure 8.3 The Order Entry Template with Data and Help

Data Entry Windows **8**

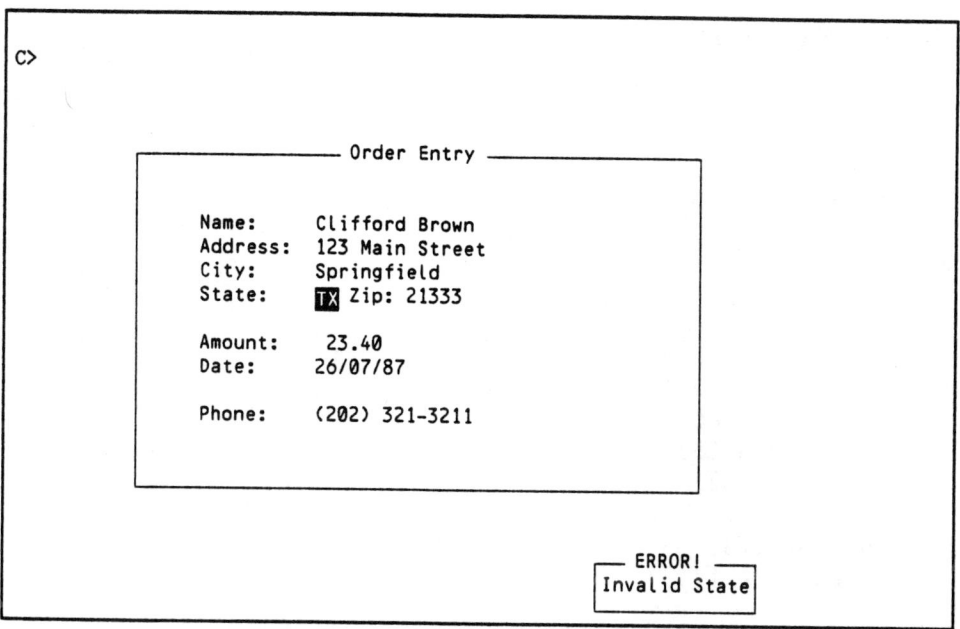

Figure 8.4   Data Entry Validation Errors

Listing 8.2: order.c

```
/* ----- order.c ------ */

#include "twindow.h"
void ordent(void);

main()
{
    load_help("tcprogs.hlp");
    ordent();
}
```

8 Data Entry Windows

Listing 8.3: ordent.c

```c
/* ---------- ordent.c ----------- */

#include <dos.h>
#include <stdio.h>
#include <string.h>
#include "twindow.h"

struct {
    char name [26];
    char addr [26];
    char city [26];
    char state [3];
    char zip [6];
    char amt [6];
    char dt [7];
    char phone [11];
} rcd;

char msk25 []       = "_____";
char mskamt []      = "___.__";
char mskdate []     = "__/__/__";
char mskphone []    = "(___) ___-____";
#define mskst msk25+23
#define mskzip msk25+20

int validate_state(char *, int);
void help_date(char *);
```

continued...

Data Entry Windows 8

...from previous page

```
void ordent()
{
    WINDOW *wnd;
    FIELD *fld;

    wnd = establish_window(10, 5, 15, 50);
    set_title(wnd, " Order Entry ");
    set_colors(wnd, ALL, BLUE, AQUA, BRIGHT);
    set_colors(wnd, ACCENT, WHITE, BLACK, DIM);
    display_window(wnd);
    wprompt(wnd, 5, 2, "Name:");
    wprompt(wnd, 5, 3, "Address:");
    wprompt(wnd, 5, 4, "City:");
    wprompt(wnd, 5, 5, "State:");
    wprompt(wnd, 18, 5, "Zip:");
    wprompt(wnd, 5, 10, "Phone:");
    wprompt(wnd, 5, 7, "Amount:");
    wprompt(wnd, 5, 8, "Date:");
    init_template(wnd);
    fld = establish_field(wnd, 15, 2, msk25, rcd.name, 'a');
    field_window(fld,"name     ", 40, 1);
    fld = establish_field(wnd, 15, 3, msk25, rcd.addr, 'a');
    field_window(fld,"address  ", 40, 2);
    fld = establish_field(wnd, 15, 4, msk25, rcd.city, 'a');
    field_window(fld,"address  ", 40, 3);
    fld = establish_field(wnd, 15, 5, mskst, rcd.state, 'A');
    field_validate(fld, validate_state);
    field_window(fld,"state    ", 40, 4);
    fld = establish_field(wnd, 23, 5, mskzip, rcd.zip, 'Z');
    field_window(fld,"address  ", 40, 4);
    fld = establish_field(wnd,15,10,mskphone,rcd.phone, 'N');
    field_window(fld,"phone    ", 40, 9);
    fld = establish_field(wnd, 15, 7, mskamt, rcd.amt, 'C');
    field_window(fld,"amount   ", 40, 8);
    fld = establish_field(wnd, 15, 8, mskdate, rcd.dt, 'D');
    field_help(fld, help_date);
    clear_template(wnd);
    data_entry(wnd);
    delete_window(wnd);
}
```

continued...

8 Data Entry Windows

...from previous page

```c
/* ----- validate the state that is entered ------ */
int validate_state(bf, key)
char *bf;
{
    static char *states [] =
        {"  ","VA","NC","SC","GA","FL",0};
    char **st = states;

    while (*st)
        if (strcmp(*st++, bf) == 0)
            return OK;
    error_message("Invalid State");
    return ERROR;
}

/* ----- provide today's date -------- */
void help_date(bf)
char *bf;
{
    struct date dat;

    getdate(&dat);
    sprintf(bf, "%02d%02d%02d",
            dat.da_day, dat.da_mon, dat.da_year % 100);
}
```

Listing 8.4: order.prj

```
order
ordent (twindow.h)
entry (twindow.h, keys.h)
thelp (twindow.h, keys.h)
twindow (twindow.h, keys.h)
ibmpc.obj
```

Data Entry Windows 8

SUMMARY

The window library now has context-sensitive help and support for formatted data entry. With these capabilities, you can build a basic interactive data entry system. Data entry templates support fixed-format data element entry. In Chapter 9, a text editor function is added, one that uses a window for the entry and modification of free-form text.

CHAPTER 9

THE WINDOW TEXT EDITOR

9 The Window Text Editor

Chapter 8 discussed using a video window for entering data fields into a forms-oriented template. Not all data fields, however, have a defined, fixed format. Some fields and files consist of free-flowing text such as words in a book or comments on a loan application. Word processors and text editors allow you to build files of text without regard to format, but to integrate the entry of text into an application, you need an editor function that you can call from your programs.

This chapter introduces the **window text editor**, which uses a video window for entering and modifying text, much like a programmer's editor or word processor. This feature is used for applications that involve entering free-form text. The Sidekick notepad is such an application, and the example program included in this chapter implements a similar notepad. The window text editor can also be used in data entry applications that require multiple-line, free-form text. An application such as the order entry program in Chapter 8 might require a field of descriptive text, and a text window can serve this purpose. Many data base applications call for data elements characterized as remarks, comments, descriptions, or nomenclature. These fields can be supported with the window text editor. You might even write a program to use the window text editor to compose the context-sensitive Help window text files described in Chapter 7.

To use the text editor, a program establishes a window and provides a buffer where text data will be entered and edited by the user. The text buffer is an array containing enough space for a fixed number of lines that are each the width of the window's text area. For example, if you establish a window that is 42 characters wide, the text area is 40 characters wide (the window border occupies two character positions). If you then provide a buffer that is 4000 characters long, the editor will allow up to 100 lines of text because the buffer can contain 100 lines of 40 characters each. As the user enters text, it is collected in this array without new lines or tab characters.

If the text buffer already contains text when the editor function is first called, that text is displayed in the fixed-length line format just described.

9 The Window Text Editor

TEXT EDITOR COMMANDS

The text editor contains a full set of editing commands. The commands are summarized in the screen display in Figure 9.1. The example notepad program shown later includes a Help window that is displayed by pressing <F1> and that uses the display in Figure 9.1 to show the editor's command set. Most of the editing commands use function keys, although a few use <Alt> or <Ctrl> key combinations. Following is a discussion of each of the window editor commands.

```
-------Cursor Movement-----    --------Page Movement--------
arrows   = move text cursor    Ctrl-Home = Beginning of File
Ctrl-T   = Top of Window       Ctrl-End  = End of File
Ctrl-B   = Bottom of Window    PgUp      = Previous Page
Ctrl ->  = Next Word           PgDn      = Next Page
Ctrl <-  = Previous Word
Home     = Beginning of Line   --------Editor Control--------
End      = End of Line         Scroll Lock = No Auto Reform

---------Block Controls-----   ---------Edit Commands--------
F4  = Form Paragraph           F2 or Esc = Done
F5  = Mark Block Beginning     F3        = Erase File
F6  = Mark Block End           Ins       = Toggle Insert Mode
F7  = Move Block               Del       = Delete Char
F8  = Copy Block               <--       = Rubout
F9  = Delete Block             Ctrl-D    = Delete Word
F10 = Unmark Block             Alt-D     = Delete Line
    [Help] to return
```

Figure 9.1 Text Editor Commands

175

9 The Window Text Editor

Cursor Movement

Use the arrow keys to move the cursor around the screen. If you move the cursor to the top or bottom of the screen and continue to press the Up arrow key at the top or the Down arrow key at the bottom, the screen will scroll until the cursor reaches the beginning or end of the buffer.

- <Ctrl/T> and <Ctrl/B> move the cursor to the top or bottom of the screen.

- <Ctrl/Right arrow> moves the cursor to the beginning of the next word in the text buffer.

- <Ctrl/Left arrow> moves the cursor to the beginning of the previous word in the text buffer.

- <Home> positions the cursor at the beginning of the current line.

- <End> positions the cursor at the end of the current line.

- <Tab> advances the cursor to the next tab stop.
  <Shift/Tab> moves the cursor to the previous tab stop.

Page Movement

- <PgUp> and <PgDn> move the text page backward and forward.

- <Ctrl/Home> moves the text page to the first page in the buffer and positions the cursor at the beginning of the first line.

- <Ctrl/End> moves the text page to the last page in the buffer and positions the cursor in the first column of the line following the last line in the buffer.

Text Block Commands

The text editor contains a number of text block commands. These commands operate on blocks of text that are defined on line boundaries.

- <F4> forms a paragraph from the text lines marked as a block.

- <F5> marks the first line in a block. The line the cursor occupies will become the first line in the block. Blocks are displayed in the ACCENT colors of the window.

- <F6> marks the last line in a block.

- <F7> moves a block to the line where the cursor is positioned. The move is non-destructive; space is opened for the block.

- <F8> copies a block to the current line. The difference between this command and the Move command is that the original block remains in place.

- <F9> deletes the block. The lines following the deleted block are moved up next to those lines preceding it.

- <F10> unmarks a block.

9 The Window Text Editor

Editing Commands

As you enter text and move the cursor, the editor automatically reformats the paragraph. The editor defines a paragraph as a group of lines of text, up to the first blank line. Reformatting of the paragraphs can be suppressed by placing the keyboard into Scroll Lock mode.

- <F3> erases all text in the buffer after confirmation.

- <Ins> toggles the Insert/Overwrite mode and changes the shape of the cursor to indicate the mode.

- <Del> deletes the character under the cursor and moves all following text on the line one position to the left.

- <Backspace> (the big arrow pointing left in the upper right corner of the keyboard) deletes the character to the left of the cursor, moves the cursor one position to the left, and moves all following text on the line one position to the left.

- <Ctrl/D> deletes the word on which the cursor is presently positioned.

- <Alt/D> deletes the line where the cursor is presently positioned.

- <F2> or <Esc> causes the text editor function to return to the applications function.

THE TEXT EDITOR FUNCTION

Text editing has one function for your program to call. To use the function, you must establish a window into which text data entry will be processed.

The Window Text Editor 9

void text_editor(WINDOW *wnd, char *bf, unsigned bsize)

This function processes window text data entry with the text editor. The **wnd** pointer specifies the previously established window. The **bf** pointer points to the text buffer, and the **bsize** integer specifies the size of the buffer. The number of lines in the buffer is a function of the size of the buffer and the width of the window as set when the window was established.

When the function is called, it displays the text in the first page of the buffer and allows text entry and text editor commands to proceed from the keyboard. When the function returns, the buffer contains the text as entered and modified by the user.

SOURCE LISTING: editor.c

Listing 9.1 is **editor.c**, the source file that contains the window text editor.

(Listing 9.1 on next page)

9 The Window Text Editor

Listing 9.1: editor.c

```c
/* ---------------------- editor.c ---------------------- */
#include <stdio.h>
#include <ctype.h>
#include <mem.h>
#include <conio.h>
#include <alloc.h>
#include "twindow.h"
#include "keys.h"

#define TRUE 1
#define FALSE 0
#define TAB 4
#define NEXTTAB (TAB-(x%TAB))
#define LASTTAB (((wwd-1)/TAB)*TAB)
#define PREVTAB (((x-1)%TAB)+1)
#define curr(x,y) (bfptr+(y)*wwd+(x))
#define lineno(y) ((int)(bfptr-topptr)/wwd+(y))

extern int VSG;
int last_x, last_y;
static int wht;
static int wwd;
static int wsz;
static char *topptr;
static char *bfptr;
static char *lstptr;
static int lines;
static char *endptr;
static int blkbeg;
static int blkend;
static int inserting;
static WINDOW *wnd;
static int do_display_text = 1;
```

continued...

...from previous page

```c
/* ---------- local function prototypes ---------- */
void erase_buffer(int *x, int *y);
int lastword(int x, int y);
void last_char(int *x, int *y);
void test_para(int x, int y);
int trailing_spaces(int y);
int first_wordlen(int y);
void paraform(int x, int y);
int blankline(int line);
void delete_word(int x, int y);
void delete_line(int y);
void delete_block(void);
void copy_block(int y);
void move_block(int y);
void mvblock(int y, int moving);
void findlast(void);
void find_end(int *x, int *y);
void carrtn(int *x, int *y, int insert);
void backspace(int *x, int *y);
void fore_word(int *x, int *y, char *bf);
int spaceup(int *x, int *y, char **bf);
void back_word(int *x, int *y, char *bf);
int spacedn(int *x, int *y, char **bf);
void forward(int *x, int *y);
int downward(int *y);
void upward(int *y);
void display_text(void);
void disp_line(int y);
void insert_line(void);
```

continued...

9 The Window Text Editor

...from previous page

```c
/* ----- Process text entry for a window. ---- */
void text_editor(WINDOW *wnd1, char *bf, unsigned bsize)
{
    char *b, *buff;
    int depart = FALSE, i, c;
    int x, y, svx, svlw, tx, tabctr = 0;

    wnd = wnd1;
    wht = HEIGHT-2;
    wwd = WIDTH-2;
    wsz = wwd * wht;
    topptr = bfptr = bf;
    lines = bsize / wwd;
    endptr = bf + wwd * lines;
    blkbeg = 0;
    blkend = 0;
    inserting = FALSE;
    x = 0;
    y = 0;
    display_text();
    /* --------- read in text from the keyboard ---------- */
    findlast();
    while (TRUE)    {
        last_x = COL + 1 + x;
        last_y = ROW + 1 + y;
        cursor(last_x, last_y);
        buff = curr(x, y);
        if (tabctr) {
            --tabctr;
            c = ' ';
        }
        else    {
            c = get_char();
            clear_message();
        }
        switch (c)  {
            case '\r':  carrtn(&x, &y, inserting);
                        break;
            case DN:    downward(&y);
                        break;
```

continued...

...from previous page

```
         case PGUP:   y = 0;
                      for (i = 0; i < wht; i++)
                          upward(&y);
                      break;
         case PGDN:   y = HEIGHT - 2;
                      for (i = 0; i < wht; i++)
                          downward(&y);
                      y = 0;
                      break;
         case '\t':   if (x + NEXTTAB < wwd)  {
                          if (inserting)
                              tabctr = NEXTTAB;
                          else
                              x += NEXTTAB;
                      }
                      else
                          carrtn(&x, &y, inserting);
                      break;
         case SHIFT_HT:
                      if (x < TAB)     {
                          upward(&y);
                          x = LASTTAB;
                      }
                      else
                          x -= PREVTAB;
                      break;
         case CTRL_FWD:
                      fore_word(&x, &y, buff);
                      break;
         case CTRL_BS:
                      back_word(&x, &y, buff);
                      break;
         case CTRL_B:
                      y = wht - 1;
                      break;
         case CTRL_T:
                      y = 0;
                      break;
         case CTRL_HOME:
                      x = y = 0;
```

continued...

9 The Window Text Editor

...from previous page

```
                bfptr = topptr;
                display_text();
                break;
    case HOME:  x = 0;
                break;
    case CTRL_END:
                find_end(&x, &y);
                display_text();
                break;
    case END:   last_char(&x, &y);
                break;
    case UP:    upward(&y);
                break;
    case F2:
    case ESC:   depart = TRUE;
                break;
    case '\b':
    case BS:    if (curr(x, y) == topptr)
                    break;
                backspace(&x, &y);
                if (x == wwd - 1)
                    last_char(&x, &y);
                if (c == BS)
                    break;
                buff = curr(x, y);
    case DEL:   movmem(buff+1, buff, wwd-1-x);
                *(buff+wwd-1-x) = ' ';
                disp_line(y);
                test_para(x+1, y);
                break;
    case ALT_D: delete_line(y);
                break;
    case CTRL_D:delete_word(x, y);
                test_para(x, y);
                break;
    case INS:   inserting ^= TRUE;
                insert_line();
                break;
    case F3:    erase_buffer(&x, &y);
                break;
```

continued...

...from previous page

```
case F4:    paraform(0, y);
            break;
case F5:    blkbeg = lineno(y) + 1;
            if (blkbeg > blkend)
                blkend = lines;
            display_text();
            break;
case F6:    blkend = lineno(y) + 1;
            if (blkend < blkbeg)
                blkbeg = 1;
            display_text();
            break;
case F7:    move_block(y);
            break;
case F8:    copy_block(y);
            break;
case F9:    delete_block();
            break;
case F10:   blkbeg = blkend = 0;
            display_text();
            break;
case FWD:   forward(&x, &y);
            break;
default:    if (!isprint(c))
                break;
            if (curr(x, y) == endptr-1 ||
                (lineno(y)+1 >= lines && inserting
                    && *curr(wwd-2, y) != ' ')) {
                error_message(" End of Buffer ");
                break;
            }
            if (inserting) {
                buff = curr(x, y);
                movmem(buff, buff + 1, wwd-1-x);
            }
            buff = curr(x, y);
            if (buff < endptr) {
                if (buff >= lstptr)
                    lstptr = buff + 1;
                *buff = c;
```

continued...

9 The Window Text Editor

...from previous page

```
                            disp_line(y);
                        }
                        buff = curr(wwd-1, y);
                        if (endptr && *buff != ' ') {
                            for (b = buff+1; b < endptr; b++)
                                if (*b==' ' && *(b + 1)==' ')
                                    break;
                            movmem(buff+1, buff+2, b-buff-1);
                            *(buff+1) = ' ';
                            svx = x;
                            svlw = lastword(x, y);
                            x = wwd-1;
                            if (*(buff-1) != ' ')
                                back_word(&x, &y, buff);
                            tx = x;
                            carrtn(&x, &y, TRUE);
                            if (svlw)
                                x = svx-tx;
                            else    {
                                x = svx;
                                --y;
                            }
                        }
                        forward(&x, &y);
                        break;
            }
            if (depart)
                break;
        }
        inserting = FALSE;
        insert_line();
}
```

continued...

...from previous page

```
/* -------- erase the buffer --------------- */
static void erase_buffer(int *x, int *y)
{
    int c = 0;
    WINDOW *sur;

    sur = establish_window(28, 11, 4, 24);
    set_colors(sur, ALL, RED, YELLOW, BRIGHT);
    display_window(sur);
    wprintf(sur, " Erase text window\n Are you sure? (y/n)");
    while (c != 'y' && c != 'n')    {
        c = get_char();
        c = tolower(c);
        if (c == 'y')    {
            lstptr = bfptr = topptr;
            *x = *y = 0;
            setmem(bfptr, lines * wwd, ' ');
            blkbeg = blkend = 0;
            display_text();
        }
    }
    delete_window(sur);
}

/* ----- see if a word is the last word on the line ------ */
static int lastword(int x, int y)
{
    char *bf = curr(x, y);

    while (x++ < wwd-1)
        if (*bf++ == ' ')
            return 0;
    return 1;
}
```

continued...

9 The Window Text Editor

...from previous page

```c
/* --- go to last displayable character on the line --- */
static void last_char(int *x, int *y)
{
    char *bf;

    *x = wwd-1;
    bf = curr(0, *y);
    while (*x && *(bf + *x) == ' ')
        --(*x);
    if (*x && *x < wwd - 1)
        (*x)++;
}

/* ----- test to see if paragraph should be reformed ----- */
static void test_para(int x, int y)
{
    int ts, fw;

    if (!scroll_lock() && y < lines)     {
        ts = trailing_spaces(y);
        fw = first_wordlen(y+1);
        if (fw && ts > fw)
            paraform(x, y);
    }
}

/* ---- count the trailing spaces on a line ----- */
static int trailing_spaces(int y)
{
    int x = wwd-1, ct = 0;
    char *bf = curr(0, y);

    while (x >= 0)  {
        if (*(bf + x) != ' ')
            break;
        --x;
        ct++;
    }
    return ct;
}
```

continued...

...from previous page

```
/* ----- count the length of the first word on a line --- */
static int first_wordlen(int y)
{
    int ct = 0, x = 0;
    char *bf = curr(0, y);

    while (x < wwd-1 && *(bf+x) == ' ')
        x++;
    while (x+ct < wwd-1 && *(bf+x+ct) != ' ')
        ct++;
    return ct;
}


/* ------------ form a paragraph -------------- */
static void paraform(int x, int y)
{
    char *cp1, *cp2, *cpend, *svcp;
    int x1;

    if (blankline(lineno(y)+1))
        return;
    if (!blkbeg)    {
        blkbeg = blkend = lineno(y)+1;
        blkend++;
        while (blkend < lines)  {
            if (blankline(blkend))
                break;
            blkend++;
        }
        --blkend;
    }
    if (lineno(y) != blkbeg-1)
        x = 0;
    x1 = x;
    cp1 = cp2 = topptr + (blkbeg - 1) * wwd + x;
    cpend = topptr + blkend * wwd;
    while (cp2 < cpend) {
        while (*cp2 == ' ' && cp2 < cpend)
            cp2++;
```

continued...

9 The Window Text Editor

...from previous page

```
            if (cp2 == cpend)
                break;
        /* at a word */
            while (*cp2 != ' ' && cp2 < cpend)  {
                if (x1 >= wwd - 1)  {
                    /* wrap the word */
                    svcp = cp1 + (wwd - x1);
                    while (*--cp1 != ' ')    {
                        *cp1 = ' ';
                        --cp2;
                    }
                    x1 = 0;
                    blkbeg++;
                    cp1 = svcp;
                }
                *cp1++ = *cp2++;
                x1++;
            }
            if (cp2 < cpend)     {
                *cp1++ = ' ';
                x1++;
            }
        }
    while (cp1 < cpend)
        *cp1++ = ' ';
    blkbeg++;
    if (blkbeg <= blkend)
        delete_block();
    blkbeg = blkend = 0;
    display_text();
    findlast();
}
```

continued...

...from previous page

```c
/* -------- test for a blank line ---------- */
static int blankline(int line)
{
    char *cp;
    int x;

    cp = topptr + (line-1) * wwd;
    for (x = 0; x < wwd; x++)
        if (*(cp + x) != ' ')
            break;
    return (x == wwd);
}

/* -------------- delete a word -------------- */
static void delete_word(int x, int y)
{
    int wct = 0;
    char *cp1, *cp2;

    cp1 = cp2 = curr(x, y);
    if (*cp2 == ' ')
        while (*cp2 == ' ' && x + wct < wwd)    {
            wct++;
            cp2++;
        }
    else    {
        while (*cp2 != ' ' && x + wct < wwd)    {
            wct++;
            cp2++;
        }
        while (*cp2 == ' ' && x + wct < wwd)    {
            wct++;
            cp2++;
        }
    }
    movmem(cp2, cp1, wwd - x - wct);
    setmem(cp1 + wwd - x - wct, wct, ' ');
    display_text();
    findlast();
}
```

continued...

9 The Window Text Editor

...from previous page

```c
/* ----------- delete a line --------------- */
static void delete_line(int y)
{
    char *cp1, *cp2;
    int len;

    cp1 = bfptr + y * wwd;
    cp2 = cp1 + wwd;
    if (cp1 < lstptr)    {
        len = endptr - cp2;
        movmem(cp2, cp1, len);
        lstptr -= wwd;
        setmem(endptr - wwd, wwd, ' ');
        display_text();
    }
}

/* ----------- delete a block ------------- */
static void delete_block()
{
    char *cp1, *cp2;
    int len;

    if (!blkbeg || !blkend) {
        putchar(BELL);
        return;
    }
    cp1 = topptr + blkend * wwd;
    cp2 = topptr + (blkbeg - 1) * wwd;
    len = endptr - cp1;
    movmem(cp1, cp2, len);
    setmem(cp2 + len, endptr - (cp2 + len), ' ');
    blkbeg = blkend = 0;
    lstptr -= (cp1 - cp2);
    display_text();
}
```

continued...

...from previous page

```
/* ------- move and copy text blocks -------- */
static void mvblock(int y, int moving)
{
    char *cp1, *cp2, *hd;
    int len;
    if (!blkbeg || !blkend) {
        putchar(BELL);
        return;
    }
    if (lineno(y) >= blkbeg-1 && lineno(y) <= blkend-1) {
        error_message("Can't move/copy a block into itself");
        return;
    }
    len = (blkend - blkbeg + 1) * wwd;
    if ((hd = malloc(len)) == 0)
        return;
    cp1 = topptr + (blkbeg-1) * wwd;
    movmem(cp1, hd, len);
    cp2 = topptr + lineno(y) * wwd;
    if (moving) {
        if (lineno(y) > blkbeg-1)
            cp2 -= len;
        do_display_text = 0;
        delete_block();
        do_display_text = 1;
    }
    if (cp2+len <= endptr)  {
        movmem(cp2, cp2 + len, endptr - cp2 - len);
        movmem(hd, cp2, len);
    }
    free(hd);
    blkbeg = blkend = 0;
    display_text();
}
/* -------------- copy a block ---------------- */
static void copy_block(int y)
{
    mvblock(y, FALSE);
    findlast();
}
```

continued...

9 The Window Text Editor

...from previous page

```c
/* --------- move a block ------------- */
static void move_block(int y)
{
    mvblock(y, TRUE);
}

/* ------- find the last character in the buffer -------- */
static void findlast()
{
    register char *lp = endptr - 1;
    register char *tp = topptr;

    while (lp > tp && (*lp == ' ' || *lp == '\0')) {
        if (*lp == '\0')
            *lp = ' ';
        --lp;
    }
    if (*lp != ' ')
        lp++;
    lstptr = lp;
}

/* ------- go to the end of the data in the buffer ------- */
static void find_end(int *x, int *y)
{
    int ct;

    bfptr = lstptr;
    ct = (lstptr - topptr) % wsz;
    bfptr -= ct;
    if (bfptr + wsz > endptr)
        bfptr = endptr - wsz;
    *y = (ct / wwd);
    *x = 0;
    downward(y);
}
```

continued...

...from previous page

```c
/* -------- carriage return -------- */
static void carrtn(int *x, int *y, int insert)
{
    int insct;
    char *cp, *nl;
    int ctl = 2;

    cp = curr(*x, *y);
    nl = cp + ((cp - topptr) % wwd);
    if (lineno(*y) + 2 < lines)
        if (insert && nl < endptr)   {
            insct = wwd - *x;
            while (ctl--)   {
                if (endptr > cp + insct)    {
                    movmem(cp, cp+insct, endptr-insct-cp);
                    setmem(cp, insct, ' ');
                }
                else if (ctl == 1)
                    setmem(cp, endptr - cp, ' ');
                cp += insct * 2;
                insct = *x;
            }
        }
    *x = 0;
    downward(y);
    if (insert) {
        test_para(*x, *y);
        display_text();
    }
    if (lineno(*y) + 2 < lines)
        if (insert)
            if ((lstptr + wwd) <= endptr)
                if (lstptr > curr(*x, *y))
                    lstptr += wwd;
}
```

continued...

9 The Window Text Editor

...from previous page

```c
/* ------- move the buffer offset back one position ------ */
static void backspace(int *x, int *y)
{
    if (*x == 0)     {
        *x = wwd - 1;
        upward(y);
    }
    else
        --(*x);
}

/* -------- move the buffer offset forward one word ------ */
static void fore_word(int *x, int *y, char *bf)
{
    while (*bf != ' ')  {
        if (spaceup(x, y, &bf) == 0)
            return;
        if (*x == 0)
            break;
    }
    while (*bf == ' ')
        if (spaceup(x, y, &bf) == 0)
            return;
}

static int spaceup(int *x, int *y, char **bf)
{
    if (*bf == lstptr)
        return 0;
    (*bf)++;
    forward(x, y);
    return 1;
}
```

continued...

...from previous page

```
/* -------- move the buffer offset backward one word ------ */
static void back_word(int *x, int *y, char *bf)
{
    spacedn(x, y, &bf);
    while (*bf == ' ')
        if (spacedn(x, y, &bf) == 0)
            return;
    while (*bf != ' ')  {
        if (*x == 0)
            return;
        if (spacedn(x, y, &bf) == 0)
            return;
    }
    spaceup(x, y, &bf);
}

static int spacedn(int *x, int *y, char **bf)
{
    if (*bf == topptr)
        return 0;
    --(*bf);
    backspace(x, y);
    return 1;
}


/* ----- move the buffer offset forward one position ------ */
static void forward(int *x, int *y)
{
    int ww = wwd;

    (*x)++;
    if (*x == ww)   {
        downward(y);
        *x = 0;
    }
}
```
continued...

9 The Window Text Editor

...from previous page

```c
/* ------- move the buffer offset down one position ------ */
static int downward(int *y)
{
    if (*y < wht - 1)    {
        (*y)++;
        return 1;
    }
    else if ((bfptr + wsz) < endptr)    {
        bfptr += wwd;
        scroll(wnd, UP);
        disp_line(wht-1);
        return 1;
    }
    return 0;
}

/* -------- move the buffer offset up one position ------ */
static void upward(int *y)
{
    if (*y)
        --(*y);
    else if ((topptr + wwd) <= bfptr)    {
        bfptr -= wwd;
        scroll(wnd, DN);
        disp_line(0);
    }
}

/* ---- display all the lines in a window ------ */
static void display_text()
{
    int y = 0;

    if (do_display_text)
        while (y < wht)
            disp_line(y++);
}
```

continued...

...from previous page

```c
/* ---------- Display a line -------- */
static void disp_line(int y)
{
    int x = 0, atr = WNORMAL;

    if (blkbeg || blkend)
        if (lineno(y) >= blkbeg-1)
            if (lineno(y) <= blkend-1)
                atr = WACCENT;
    while (x < wwd) {
        displ(wnd, x+1, y+1, *(bfptr+y * wwd+x), atr);
        x++;
    }
}

/* ---------- set insert/exchange cursor shape ----------- */
static void insert_line()
{
    set_cursor_type(inserting ? 0x0106 : 0x0607);
}
```

PROGRAM DESCRIPTION: editor.c

Editor.c contains several **#define** statements that control tab settings in the editor window. The TAB global is set to 4 to establish tab stops every four characters. The other globals—NEXTTAB, LASTTAB, and PREVTAB—are macro expressions coded to make the functions more legible. The **curr** macro returns a pointer to the character in the edit buffer that corresponds to the **x** and **y** coordinate arguments. The **lineno** macro returns the line number in the buffer that is represented by the window's line number as expressed by the **y** argument.

9 The Window Text Editor

Several external variables are declared and computed to reduce the number of computations in the code and to make the code more legible. The **wht** variable is the height of the window's text area; it does not include the window's border characters. The **wwd** variable is the width of the window's text area without the border characters. The **wsz** variable is the size of the window's text area. The **lines** variable is the number of lines the text buffer can hold. The **endptr** pointer points to the last character position in the text buffer, plus one. The **lstptr** pointer points to the last nonspace character in the buffer. The **topptr** pointer points to the first character in the buffer. The **bfptr** pointer varies as the user pages and scrolls through the buffer; it always points to the character in the buffer that is in the upper left corner of the window.

The **text__editor** function is called to allow the user to enter and modify text in the buffer. The external variables are computed, and the cursor is positioned at the initial coordinates of 0,0. As the user types characters, function keys and control characters are tested. If the user presses the Enter key, the **carrtn** function is called. The Down arrow key calls the **downward** function. The PgUp and PgDn keys call **upward** and **downward** for as many lines as are in the window. <Tab> and <Shift/Tab> reposition the **x** coordinate to the next or previous tab stop. <Ctrl/Right arrow> and <Ctrl/Left arrow> call the **fore__word** or **back__word** function. <Ctrl/B> positions the **y** coordinate at the bottom of the screen. <Ctrl/T> positions the **y** coordinate at the top of the screen. <Ctrl/Home> sets the coordinates to 0,0, resets **bfptr** to the top of the buffer, and calls **display__text** to redisplay the screen. The Home key sets the **x** coordinate to zero. <Ctrl/End> uses **find__end** to locate the last character in the buffer and displays the text. <End> uses **find__end** to position the **x** coordinate to the end of the current line. The <Up arrow> key calls the **upward** function. <F2> and <Esc> cause text entry to be completed. <Left arrow> and <backspace> move the cursor one position to the left by calling **backspace**. <Backspace> then drops into the code for the Del key, which deletes the character under the cursor with the **movmem** function. <Alt/D> calls **delete__line**. <Ctrl/D> calls **delete__word**. <Ins> toggles the **inserting** flag and calls **insert__line** to change the shape of the cursor. <F3> calls **erase__buffer**. <F4> calls **paraform**. <F5> and <F6> set the **blkbeg** and **blkend** variables to the value of the current line. Then, they call **display-text** so the block will be shown in reverse video colors. <F7>, <F8>, and <F9> call **move__block**, **copy__block**, and **delete__block** respectively. <F10> sets the **blkbeg** and **blkend** variables to 0 and calls **display__text**. <Right arrow> calls **forward**.

If the typed character is none of the above and is a displayable ASCII character, it is to be copied into the buffer. First, a test is made to ensure that the character will not go past the end of the buffer or that it will not push the last character past the end as a result of the Insert mode. Then, if the Insert mode is on, the current line is shifted one character to the right. The character is written into the buffer. If this addition appends the last character in the buffer, the **lstptr** pointer is adjusted, and the current line is displayed.

Next, the function tests for a word wrap condition. If the last character on the line is not blank, a word must be wrapped. The function scans forward until it reaches the end of the buffer or finds two blank spaces. Then, it shifts the text one position to the right, beginning with the next line, past the line with the word to wrap, and up to the scanned position. This procedure creates a space between the wrapped word and the text on the next line. The **lastword** function is called to see if the new character is in the last word or if the word wrap is the result of an insert into an earlier word on the line. This test will tell the program how to reposition the cursor after the word is wrapped. The results of this test are saved in **svlw**. The x coordinate is set to the end of the line. If the character before the last character is not blank, the **back__word** function is used to position the x coordinate at the beginning of the last word. The **carrtn** function is called to logically insert a newline at the current x position. (The newline is not actually inserted because of the rectangular buffer structure. The text is shifted and spaces are inserted.) The cursor is positioned at the character past the character just added to the buffer.

Regardless of the word wrap, the **forward** function is called to advance the x coordinate.

The **erase__buffer** function opens a window and asks the user to verify the Erase command. If the command is verified, the function clears the buffer and resets all pointers and variables.

The **lastword** function tests to see if the x coordinate passed to it is in the last word on the line represented by the y coordinate.

The **last__char** function repositions the x coordinate to one plus the last displayable character on a line.

9 The Window Text Editor

The **test__para** function tests to see if a paragraph should be reformatted. The Scroll Lock keyboard toggle must be off and there must be more trailing spaces on the current line than there are characters in the first word of the next line. If these conditions are true, **test__para** calls **paraform** and reformats the paragraph. The **trailing__spaces** function counts trailing spaces on a line, and the **first__wordlen** function counts characters in the first word in the next line.

The **paraform** function reformats a paragraph. As previously mentioned, paragraphs are defined as all text up to the next two empty lines. The **paraform** function is called as the result of the user pressing the <F4> key or as the result of the **test__para** function deciding that an automatic paragraph reformat should occur. In the latter situation, the **blkbeg** and **blkend** variables have not been set to define a block that will become the paragraph, so the function sets the variables. **Blkbeg** is set to the current line. The function scans forward, looking for two blank lines or the end of the buffer and sets **blkend**.

To reformat a paragraph, the function begins by scanning past leading spaces. When a nonspace word is found, the function begins copying that word to the beginning of the buffer. When a space is found, the function returns to the logic that eliminates leading spaces. If, while copying a word, the function encounters the end of a line, it backs up to the beginning of the word, inserting spaces into the buffer as it goes. Since this logic can compress the space occupied by a group of words, the function pads the paragraph with spaces. Then, since one or more lines might have been eliminated, the **delete__block** function is used to delete those lines.

The **blankline** function tests to see if a specified line is all blanks.

The **delete__word** function deletes a word from the buffer. If the current **x** coordinate is on a blank, it deletes the blanks up to the beginning of the next word; otherwise, it deletes the word from the **x** coordinate past the blanks following the word to the beginning of the next word.

The **delete__line** function deletes a line by shifting the text. First, the function computes the address of the first character in the current and next line. Then, the function computes the amount of text to be shifted as being the distance from the next line to the end of the buffer. The text is shifted, and the **lstptr** variable is adjusted. The end of the buffer is padded with spaces, and the text is displayed.

The **delete_block** function works in a manner similar to that of **delete_line** but operates on a block of text rather than a single line.

The **mvblock** function is used to move and copy a block of text. First, a hold buffer is allocated, and the block of text is moved into the hold buffer. If the operation is a move rather than a copy, the **delete_block** function is called to delete the block of text from the buffer. The buffer is shifted to the right, beginning at the current line, to make room for the block being moved or copied. The text in the hold buffer is moved into the space opened by this shift. The hold buffer is deallocated, and the window is displayed by a call to **display_text**.

The **copy_block** and **move_block** functions are called to copy and move blocks. They use **mvblock** to perform the operation.

The **findlast** function locates the last significant character in the buffer and resets the **lstptr** pointer to one past that character.

The **carrtn** function effects a carriage return line-feed on the user's cursor within the text buffer. It computes the address of the first character of the next line from the current character position. If the Insert mode is on, the function must allow the splitting of a line, which is achieved by shifting the buffer to the right from the cursor position to the end of the current line and padding the opened area with spaces. Then, the new line must be similarly shifted and padded to account for its shorter length after the split. The **downward** function is used to move the coordinates to the next (possibly new) line, and, if Insert mode is on, the **lstptr** pointer is adjusted.

A number of functions are called to position the edit coordinates in one direction or another. Among these functions are **find_end**, **backspace**, **fore_word**, **spaceup**, **back_word**, **spacedn**, **forward**, **downward**, and **upward**.

AN EXAMPLE: THE NOTEPAD

Listings 9.2, 9.3, and 9.4 provide an example of using the window text editor for an on-line notepad. Listing 9.2, **note.c**, is the **main** function that calls the example function in Listing 9.3, **notepad.c**. Notepad.c is maintained separately because it is integrated into the menu example in Chapter 10 and the memory-resident utility in Chapter 12.

9 The Window Text Editor

Listing 9.4, **note.prj**, is the project make file that Turbo C uses to build the program.

Notepad.c operates on a file named in an external array. For this example, the array is defined in **note.c** and is the file named **note.pad**. If the file exists, **notepad.c** reads it into the buffer.

Notepad.c establishes a window, assigns it a border, a title, and colors, and then displays it. **Notepad.c** then calls the **text__editor** function. When the **text__editor** function returns, **notepad.c** deletes the window and locates the line in the buffer where the last significant text is written. Then, **notepad.c** writes the text to the notepad file.

Listing 9.2: note.c

```c
/* ----- note.c ------ */

#include "twindow.h"

void notepad(void);
char notefile [] = "note.pad";

main()
{
    load_help("tcprogs.hlp");
    notepad();
}
```

Listing 9.3: notepad.c

```c
/* --------------- notepad.c ----------------- */

#include <stdio.h>
#include <mem.h>
#include "twindow.h"

#define LWID 60
#define WHT 10
#define PADHT 20

char bf [PADHT] [LWID];
extern char notefile[];

void notepad()
{
    WINDOW *wnd;
    FILE *fp, *fopen();
    int i, ctr = 0;

    set_help("notepad ", 0, 0);
    setmem(bf, sizeof bf, ' ');
    if ((fp = fopen(notefile, "rt")) != NULL)    {
        while (fread(bf [ctr], LWID, 1, fp))
            ctr++;
        fclose(fp);
    }
    wnd = establish_window
        ((80-(LWID+2))/2, (25-(WHT+2))/2, WHT+2, LWID+2);
    set_border(wnd, 3);
    set_title(wnd, " Note Pad  ");
    set_colors(wnd, ALL, BLUE, AQUA, BRIGHT);
    set_colors(wnd, ACCENT, WHITE, BLACK, DIM);
    display_window(wnd);
    text_editor(wnd, bf[0], (unsigned) LWID * PADHT);
    delete_window(wnd);
    ctr = PADHT;
```

continued...

9 The Window Text Editor

...from previous page

```
    while (--ctr)   {
        for (i = 0; i < LWID; i++)
            if (bf [ctr] [i] != ' ')
                break;
        if (i < LWID)
            break;
    }
    fp = fopen(notefile, "w");
    for (i = 0; i < ctr+1; i++)
        fwrite(bf[i], LWID, 1, fp);
    fclose(fp);
}
```

Listing 9.4: note.prj

```
note
notepad (twindow.h)
editor (twindow.h, keys.h)
thelp (twindow.h, keys.h)
twindow (twindow.h, keys.h)
ibmpc.obj
```

To run the example, enter the following command.

```
C>note
```

You will see the display shown in Figure 9.2. The first time you run the program, the notepad is blank. If you enter text into the notepad, it is saved in the disk file named **note.pad** when you exit the program by pressing <Esc> or <F2>. Subsequently, when you run the program, the notepad is displayed with the text entered earlier.

The Window Text Editor 9

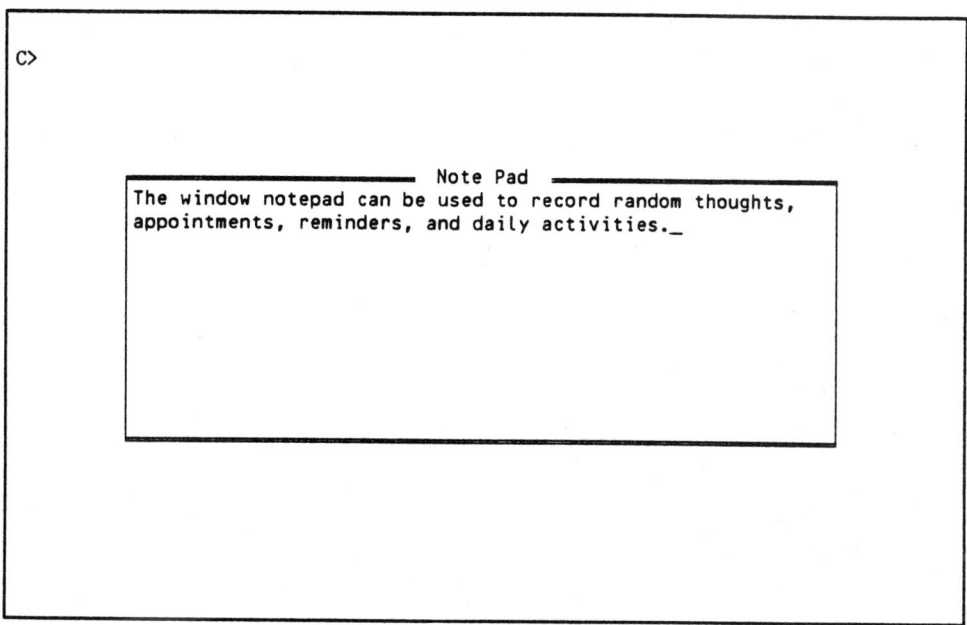

Figure 9.2   The Notepad

Use the editor commands shown in Figure 9.1 to enter text into the notepad. Press <F1> for a screen display of the command list.

SUMMARY

There is one additional feature to add to the list of the window library's capabilities. The software now has all the functionality necessary to support individual, window-based processes. The software can provide on-line help, data-entry templates, and a text editor. The next feature, presented in Chapter 10, will support a hierarchical menu structure that is implemented in windows and that uses a sliding menu bar and pop-down menus to execute functions in an application.

CHAPTER 10

WINDOW MENUS

10 Window Menus

Until now, you have been addressing areas of an interactive system's user interface that are related to specific operations. For the entry of data fields, there is a forms-oriented data entry capability; for the entry of text, there is a window text editor; to help the user with these operations, there is context-sensitive help; and to support each of these operations, there is a library of window functions. Everything that has been discussed so far addresses the support of a single operation at a time. But an on-line interactive program usually includes several operations the user can perform. These operations are chosen more often by the user than by the program because they exist among a group of multiple independent selections, and the user knows better than the software which operation should be performed next.

MENUS

Many techniques exist for listing such selections for the user. Most of these techniques are called **menus**. The executive processes of a system will display menus to the user and let the user select an operation. These executive processes are as much a part of the user interface as anything that has been discussed so far.

You saw an example of the use of one kind of menu in Chapter 6 in the example program named **poetry.exe**. That menu provided a list of options in a window. The user made a selection by pressing the key that corresponded to one of the options or by moving a cursor bar onto the desired selection and pressing the Enter key. Such a menu technique is common, effective, and easy to understand.

Another popular format for menus, one often seen in computers with a graphics user interface and a mouse, is the **sliding bar menu**. This format has a horizontal menu at the top of the screen with pop-down vertical menus under each of the selections in the horizontal menu. The user moves a sliding bar cursor from selection to selection in the horizontal menu. Vertical menus pop up below the horizontal selection, and the user moves another bar cursor up and down the selections in the vertical menu.

The advantage of this menu technique is that it occupies a minimum of screen space, leaving the displays of the application mostly in the user's view. The vertical menus are pop-up windows, so they temporarily cover but do not destroy the screen images under them. Figure 10.1 is an example of such a menu. Users of Borland's Superkey will recognize this menu.

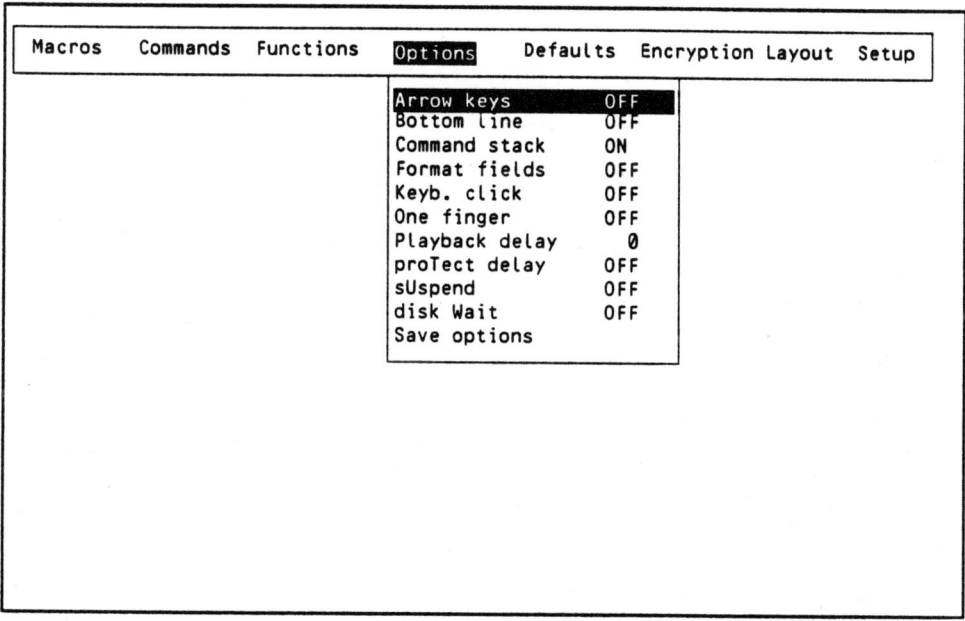

Figure 10.1   An Example of a Menu

10 Window Menus

THE WINDOW MENU EXECUTIVE PROCESS

This chapter introduces a menu driver function that uses the sliding bar menu technique just described. The menus are built as windows and are controlled by a series of tables provided by the calling program. These tables describe the selections in the sliding menu bar and those in each of the vertical pop-up menus. The menu driver function serves as a general-purpose executive process for your program. It manages the user interface by controlling the display of menus and the user's entry of selections. It then manages the execution of the applications functions in your program. The entire process is driven by the set of menu tables that you code into your program.

The primary menu table is an array of **MENU** structures. The **MENU** structure is defined in **twindow.h** (see Chapter 6). This array has an entry for each of the selections in the sliding bar menu. Each selection entry contains the selection's displayed name and some pointers to describe the contents of the vertical pop-up menu that is associated with the horizontal selection. These pointers include a pointer to an array of selection names for the pop-down menu and a pointer to an array of C function pointers. The names are displayed in the pop-up menu; the functions are provided by the application program and are executed when the user makes the corresponding menu selection.

The hierarchy of menus has two levels. The first is represented by selections on the horizontal menu and is limited to six selections, which is the number of selections you can fit on one line. Each selection at this level delivers a pop-up menu at the second level. The pop-up menu is limited to 21 selections, which is the maximum number of lines a pop-up menu can support. Each selection at this level executes a caller-provided applications function.

To have additional levels in your menu hierarchy, you describe additional menu table sets and make recursive calls to the executive menu function. Because the menu function is reentrant, a selection at the second-level pop-up menu can open a new horizontal menu.

The application program provides the menu arrays, and thus describes the menu hierarchy. The example given in Listing 10.3 (presented later in this chapter) illustrates the arrays. That discussion includes a screen image that results from those example arrays and describes their entries in detail.

THE MENU FUNCTION

To use the window menus in this chapter, you provide the **MENU** array, the arrays that the **MENU** array points to, and the applications functions that are executed when pop-up menu selections are made by the user. Then, you call the **menu_select** function, which is described next.

void menu_select(char *name, MENU *mn)

This function activates the menu process by displaying the horizontal sliding bar menu and waiting for the user to key in a selection. The **name** pointer is the name that appears as the title of the sliding menu bar. The **mn** pointer points to the array of **MENU** structures in the calling program. This array and those pointed to by the **MENU** array define the menu hierarchy to the menu process.

Once **menu_select** has displayed the horizontal menu, the user can move the sliding bar cursor by using the left and right arrow keys. If the user presses the Esc key, the process returns to the function that called **menu_select**. If the user presses Enter, the pop-up menu associated with the current menu bar selection is popped up.

While a vertical pop-up menu is visible, the user can press the right and left arrow keys to move among the other selections on the menu bar. In this mode, the pop-up menu is deleted, and the next one is popped up. If the user presses Esc, the current pop-up menu is deleted, and the process returns to the sliding menu bar routine described in the previous paragraph. The user can use the up and down arrow keys to move the pop-up menu selection bar up and down among the selections. To select an item, the user presses Enter. This keystroke will hide the pop-up menu and the sliding menu bar and will call the function pointed to by the entry in the pop-up's function pointer array that corresponds to the selection. The functions are provided by the calling software.

10 Window Menus

When the called function returns, the menus are restored, and the menu process continues with the pop-up menu routine just described.

SOURCE LISTING: tmenu.c

Listing 10.1 is **tmenu.c**, the library functions that support the previously described menu processes.

(Listing 10.1 on next page)

Window Menus 10

Listing 10.1: tmenu.c

```c
/* ------------ tmenu.c ------------ */

#include <stdio.h>
#include <conio.h>
#include <stdlib.h>
#include "keys.h"
#include "twindow.h"

extern int VSG;

WINDOW *open_menu(char *mnm, MENU *mn, int hsel);
int gethmenu(MENU *mn, WINDOW *hmenu, int hsel);
int getvmn(MENU *mn, WINDOW *hmenu, int *hsel, int vsel);
int haccent(MENU *mn, WINDOW *hmenu, int hsel, int vsel);
void dimension(char *sl[], int *ht, int *wd);
void light(MENU *mn, WINDOW *hmenu, int hsel, int d);

/* ------------- display & process a menu ----------- */
void menu_select(char *name, MENU *mn)
{
    WINDOW *open_menu();
    WINDOW *hmenu;
    int sx, sy;
    int hsel = 1, vsel;

    curr_cursor(&sx, &sy);
    cursor(0, 26);
    hmenu = open_menu(name, mn, hsel);
    while (hsel = gethmenu(mn, hmenu, hsel))    {
        vsel = 1;
        while (vsel = getvmn(mn, hmenu, &hsel, vsel))   {
            delete_window(hmenu);
            set_help("", 0, 0);
            (*(mn+hsel-1)->func [vsel-1])(hsel, vsel);
            hmenu = open_menu(name, mn, hsel);
        }
    }
    delete_window(hmenu);
    cursor(sx, sy);
}
```

continued...

10 Window Menus

...from previous page

```c
/* ------- open a horizontal menu ------- */
static WINDOW *open_menu(char *mnm, MENU *mn, int hsel)
{
    int i = 0;
    WINDOW *hmenu;

    set_help("menu    ", 30, 10);
    hmenu = establish_window(0, 0, 3, 80);
    set_title(hmenu, mnm);
    set_colors(hmenu, ALL, BLUE, AQUA, BRIGHT);
    set_colors(hmenu, ACCENT, WHITE, BLACK, DIM);
    display_window(hmenu);
    while ((mn+i)->mname)
        wprintf(hmenu, " %-10.10s ", (mn+i++)->mname);
    light(mn, hmenu, hsel, 1);
    cursor(0, 26);
    return hmenu;
}

/* ------- get a horizontal selection ---------- */
static int gethmenu(MENU *mn, WINDOW *hmenu, int hsel)
{
    int sel;

    light(mn, hmenu, hsel, 1);
    while (TRUE)    {
        switch (sel = get_char())   {
            case FWD:
            case BS:    hsel = haccent(mn, hmenu, hsel, sel);
                        break;
            case ESC:   return 0;
            case '\r':  return hsel;
            default:    putchar(BELL);
                        break;
        }
    }
}
```

continued...

...from previous page

```
/* --------pop down a vertical menu --------- */
static int getvmn(MENU *mn,WINDOW *hmenu,int *hsel,int vsel)
{
    WINDOW *vmenu;
    int ht = 10, wd = 20;
    char **mp;

    while (1)   {
        dimension((mn+*hsel-1)->mselcs, &ht, &wd);
        vmenu = establish_window(2+(*hsel-1)*12, 2, ht, wd);
        set_colors(vmenu, ALL, BLUE, AQUA, BRIGHT);
        set_colors(vmenu, ACCENT, WHITE, BLACK, DIM);
        set_border(vmenu, 4);
        display_window(vmenu);
        mp = (mn+*hsel-1)->mselcs;
        while(*mp)
            wprintf(vmenu, "\n%s", *mp++);
        vsel = get_selection(vmenu, vsel, "");
        delete_window(vmenu);
        if (vsel == FWD || vsel == BS)  {
            *hsel = haccent(mn, hmenu, *hsel, vsel);
            vsel = 1;
        }
        else
            return vsel;
    }
}

/* ----- manage the horizontal menu selection accent ----- */
static int haccent(MENU *mn,WINDOW *hmenu,int hsel,int sel)
{
    switch (sel)    {
        case FWD:
            light(mn, hmenu, hsel, 0);
            if ((mn+hsel)->mname)
                hsel++;
            else
                hsel = 1;
            light(mn, hmenu, hsel, 1);
            break;
```

continued...

10 Window Menus

...from previous page

```
            case BS:
                light(mn, hmenu, hsel, 0);
                if (hsel == 1)
                    while ((mn+hsel)->mname)
                        hsel++;
                else
                    --hsel;
                light(mn, hmenu, hsel, 1);
                break;
            default:
                break;
        }
        return hsel;
}

/* ---------- compute a menu's height & width --------- */
static void dimension(char *sl[], int *ht, int *wd)
{
    unsigned strlen(char *);

    *ht = *wd = 0;
    while (sl [*ht])    {
        *wd = max(*wd, strlen(sl [*ht]));
        (*ht)++;
    }
    *ht += 2;
    *wd += 2;
}

/* ---------- accent a horizontal menu selection ---------- */
static void light(MENU *mn, WINDOW *hmenu, int hsel, int d)
{
    if (d)
        reverse_video(hmenu);
    wcursor(hmenu, (hsel-1)*12+2, 0);
    wprintf(hmenu, (mn+hsel-1)->mname);
    normal_video(hmenu);
    cursor(0, 26);
}
```

Window Menus   10

PROGRAM DESCRIPTION: tmenu.c

The **menu_select** function is called to process a menu that is described in an array of MENU structures. This function saves the current cursor location, and positions the cursor to an off-screen location. Then **open_menu** is called to open and display the horizontal menu at the top of the screen. A **while** loop processes horizontal menu selections until the user presses the Esc key. In each loop iteration, **getmenu** is called. When **gethmenu** returns a zero value, the user has pressed the Esc key. When **gethmenu** returns a non-zero value, the user has made one of the selections on the horizontal menu. The returned value specifies the user's selection. Another **while** loop processes the pop-down menu associated with the selection. Each iteration of this loop calls **getvmn**, which processes the pop-down menu. If the user presses Esc, **getvmn** returns zero; otherwise, **getvmn** returns a selection value. The horizontal menu window is deleted, and the function associated with the pop-down selection is called. When the function returns, **open_menu** is called to re-establish the horizontal menu.

The **open_menu** function opens a long window across the top of the screen. This window will be the horizontal menu. The menu selections are displayed in the window from the MENU table. The first of the selections is accented by the **light** function.

The **gethmenu** function reads the keyboard for menu selections or menu cursor bar movements. If the user presses the right or left arrow keys, the **haccent** function is called to move the cursor bar. If the user presses the Esc key, zero is returned. If the user presses the Enter key, the value associated with the current selection is returned.

The **getvmn** function processes the pop-down menus under the horizontal menu selection. The pop-down menu is established as a window, and its selections are displayed from the MENU tables. The function **get_selection** (see Chapter 6) is called to get a selection from the user. When the selection is returned, the pop-down window is deleted. If the user pressed the right or left arrow key, the **haccent** function is called to advance or retreat the horizontal menu bar cursor, and processing of the new pop-down menu proceeds here in **getvmn**; otherwise, the value returned from **get_selection** is returned to the caller of **getvmn**.

10 Window Menus

WINDOW MENU EXAMPLE

Listings 10.2, 10.3, and 10.4 provide the example program that illustrates menu processing. This example builds and executes a menu that integrates all the example window functions from Chapters 6 through 9.

Listing 10.2, **menu.c**, is a small driver program that calls the example program, **exec.c**, shown in Listing 10.3. **Exec.c** is separate because it is included in the memory resident example in Chapter 12. Listing 10.4, **menu.prj**, is the project make file that Turbo C uses to build the example program.

Listing 10.2: menu.c

```
/* ---------- menu.c ---------- */
#include "twindow.h"
void exec(void);

char notefile [] = "note.pad";

main()
{
    load_help("tcprogs.hlp");
    exec();
}
```

Listing 10.3: menu.prj

```
menu.c
exec.c (twindow.h, keys.h)
testmove (twindow.h, keys.h)
promote (twindow.h, keys.h)
ccolor (twindow.h, keys.h)
fasttest (twindow.h)
notepad (twindow.h)
ordent (twindow.h)
maxims (twindow.h, keys.h)
poems (twindow.h, keys.h)
editor (twindow.h, keys.h)
entry (twindow.h, keys.h)
thelp (twindow.h, keys.h)
tmenu (twindow.h)
twindow (twindow.h, keys.h)
ibmpc.obj
```

(Listing 10.4 on next page)

10   Window Menus

Listing 10.4: exec.c

```c
/* ----------- exec.c --------- */
#include <stdio.h>
#include "twindow.h"
/*    ------ local prototypes -------- */
void testmove(void);
void promote(void);
void ccolor(void);
void fasttest(void);
void notepad(void);
void ordent(void);
void poems(void);
void maxims(void);
/* ---------- menu tables --------- */
char *dselcs[] = {
    " move ",
    " promote ",
    " colors ",
    " fast ",
    NULL
};
char *pselcs[] = {
    " notepad ",
    " orders ",
    " poetry ",
    " sayings ",
    NULL
};
static void (*dfuncs[])()={testmove,promote,ccolor,fasttest};
static void (*pfuncs[])()={notepad,ordent,poems,maxims};
static MENU tmn [] = {
    {" demos ",     dselcs, dfuncs},
    {" programs ",  pselcs, pfuncs},
    {NULL,NULL,NULL}
};

void exec()
{
    menu_select(" TC Executive ", tmn);
}
```

Window Menus 10

To run the example program, enter the following command:

C>menu

The screen shown in Figure 10.2 will be displayed, which is the horizontal sliding bar menu. In the example, only two selections are given, but a sliding bar menu has room for a total of six selections.

Refer now to the array of **MENU** structures named **tmn** in Listing 10.4, **exec.c**. There are two entries in this array, one for each selection on the horizontal menu. The **MENU** structure is defined in **twindow.h** (see Chapter 6) and has three members: a pointer to the selection name, a pointer to an array of names for the pop-up menu selections, and a pointer to an array of function pointers.

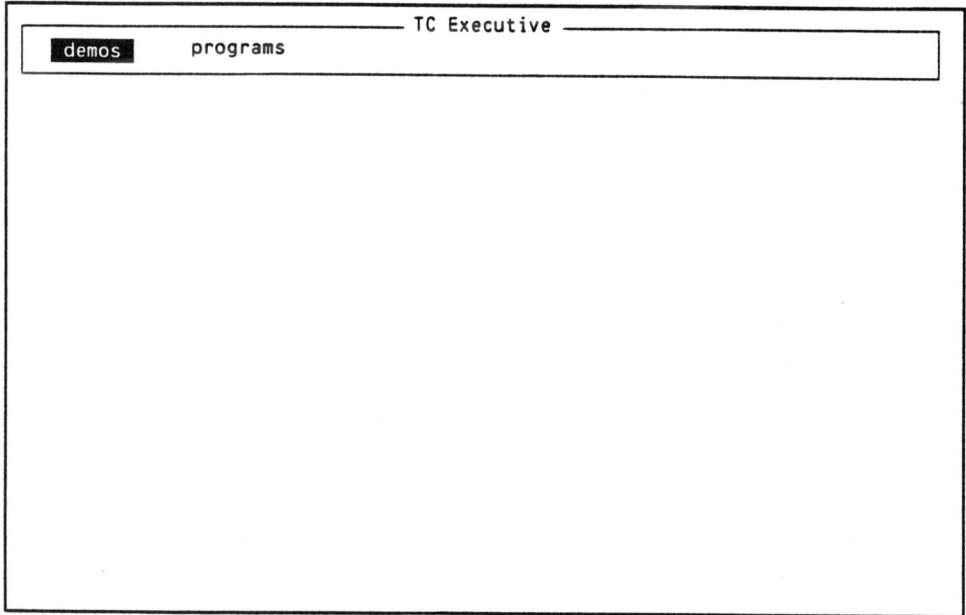

Figure 10.2 The Horizontal Sliding Bar Menu

10 Window Menus

Use the right and left arrow keys to move the sliding menu bar from selection to selection on the horizontal menu. With the menu bar on the **demos** selection, press the Enter key. You will see the display shown in Figure 10.3, which is the pop-up menu associated with the **demos** selection. Refer back to Listing 10.3 to the first entry in the **tmn** array, the one for the **demos** selection. The **dselcs** address points to an array of character pointers initialized with the selection names you see in the **demos** pop-up menu, and the **dfuncs** address points to an array of function pointers. Each of these pointers is the address of one of the example functions from earlier chapters. Move the pop-up menu's cursor bar up and down. When you reach your selection, press Enter. You have just executed one of the example functions. When you return from that function (as explained in the chapter that describes whichever function you chose — usually with the Esc key), the horizontal and pop-up menus are back in place, and you may continue the selections. Press the Esc key to delete the pop-up menu, and press the Esc key again to delete the horizontal menu and exit the program.

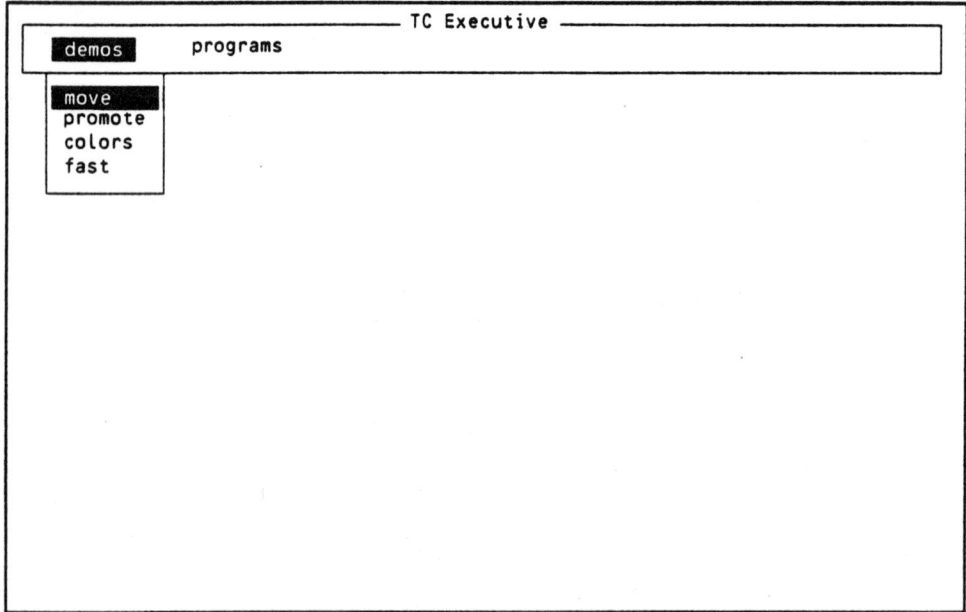

Figure 10.3   A Pop-Up Menu

SUMMARY

The library of window functions is now complete. It supports the level of software development that traditionally has been available from vendors of window libraries at costs many times the price of this book. Versions of this software have been used for developing large, complex software systems, and those systems are installed and running in dozens of installations.

In the chapters that follow, the subject of memory-resident utilities is addressed. The window functions in this book can be included in normal, single-task DOS programs, or they can be installed into a program category that resides in memory and executes at the touch of a key. Techniques and examples for developing such a program are presented in the following chapters.

CHAPTER 11

MEMORY-RESIDENT PROGRAMS

11 Memory-resident Programs

Throughout this book, "PC" refers to the IBM PC, its family, and compatible computers; however, the personal computer was not always what has come to be known as the PC. When personal computers were first developed, they existed principally in the concern and domain of hobbyists who designed and built them. As microcomputer technology matured, personal computers evolved from home-built kits to store-bought appliances. Software and operating system evolution followed suit. The earliest operating systems were little more than BASIC or Pascal shells that provided language environments and simple file managers. These systems were usually oriented to specific computers, with no compatibility between different systems. As the hardware evolved in the appliance direction, operating systems began to stabilize. Among them were Apple-DOS, NorthStar DOS, TRSDOS, and CP/M. The systems all shared the following characteristics:

- execution of a single program for a single user at a time
- support of a directory-driven file system
- support of language interpreters, assemblers, and compilers
- program and data file incompatibility between systems

One operating system had an attribute not shared by the others. With great insight, Gary Kildall designed CP/M to be a generic operating system. Although originally developed as a software development environment for the Intel MDS, CP/M is not soft-wired to any single model or brand of computers. CP/M consists of the basic disk operating system (BDOS), console command processor (CCP), and basic I/O system (BIOS). The BIOS is the hardware-specific code—the code that manages the console, the printer, and the disk system. By writing a custom BIOS, a computer manufacturer can adopt a mature, accepted operating system with thousands of available programs. Because it is adaptable, CP/M became the industry standard operating system for personal computers using 8080 or Z80 microprocessors.

The 8080 and Z80 microprocessors can address only 64K of memory, so CP/M was built as a single-user, single-task operating system. A multi-user version named MP/M was developed, but it never became the industry favorite that CP/M was, mainly because it was slow—the 8080 is not a fast processor—and because personal computers are not particularly suitable for multi-user tasks.

Memory-resident Programs 11

The DOS that operates the PC is an adaptation of an operating system developed to run on the 8086, with a distinct resemblance to CP/M. Microsoft bought it from its original creator, Seattle Computer Products, and IBM licensed it from Microsoft. DOS still resembles CP/M in many ways. DOS consists of three modules similar in function to the BDOS, CCP, and BIOS of CP/M, and its command line user interface is almost identical to that of CP/M. DOS has additional features not found in CP/M, such as pipes, filters, input/output redirection, file date/time stamps, and a hierarchical file directory structure. DOS is still a single-user, single-task operating system that resembles CP/M in many ways.

Early IBM PCs closely resembled their 8080 and Z80 ancestors; they had 64K of memory, floppy disks, and a processor not much faster than the Z80. The single-task DOS was adequate and appropriate for that computer, but the PC has three architectural characteristics (other than the IBM logo) that made it destined to grow. The 8088 microprocessor can address 1 megabyte of memory; it has a vectored interrupt structure; and the PC's keyboard and video display are an integral part of the computer rather than a video terminal connected to the computer through a serial data port. These characteristics lend themselves to the limited style of multi-tasking that has evolved on the PC and that is now known as the **Terminate-and-Stay-Resident (TSR)** program.

TSR programs—with sufficient memory, an interrupt structure, and memory-mapped video display—are natural enhancements to the otherwise bland user environment of the single-user, single-task DOS. To extend DOS in such a way, you must be able to install permanent memory-resident programs into the DOS architecture.

DOS includes two functions that allow a program to declare itself resident. The two DOS functions are similar with minor differences. The 0x31 function of DOS interrupt 0x21 terminates the program currently running, but allows it to remain resident. DOS will not attempt to use memory declared by the resident program as its own. DOS interrupt 0x27 performs the same function but restricts the length of the resident program to 64K.

11 Memory-resident Programs

The two TSR functions are provided by DOS not to support memory-resident utility programs but so that system developers can write interrupt service routines (**ISR**s) to manage custom input/output hardware devices such as a mouse, digitizing tablet, or joystick. These devices are not standard parts of PC architecture and, as such, have no standard software interface in DOS.

The ISR environment can support another kind of program not necessarily associated with a custom device but that extends the user interface of the computer. Such programs are TSR programs; two of the most popular types of TSR programs are the keyboard enhancer program and the desktop accessory. **Keyboard enhancers** such as Prokey and Superkey allow the user to assign sequences of characters to a function key, an <Alt> key combination, or any other key. **Desktop accessories** such as Sidekick and Homebase provide notepads, calculators, calendars, telephone dialers, and other desktop aids that pop up at the press of a key.

Other TSR programs include spelling checkers, outline processors, print spoolers, extensions to the DOS command processor, debugging aids, and alarm clocks. These programs and numerous other resident processes are readily available from commercial vendors, from public domain software sources, or from source code published in magazines.

This chapter introduces and explains such a class of PC programs, which is known by a number of names, among them **pop-up**, **TSR**, **memory-resident utility**, and **desktop accessory**. Such programs are unique because when one is executed, it remains resident in memory and often does not go away until you reboot the computer. While resident, it executes (or pops up) when called.

A typical TSR program is activated by an external event—usually what is called a **hot key**. A hot key is a keystroke formed when the user presses a combination of keys that are reserved for the execution of the utility program. Naturally, this keystroke would be one that is not commonly used for other tasks.

Activation of a TSR program causes any other currently running program to be suspended while the TSR executes. When the TSR terminates, the interrupted program resumes. This interrupted process can be a transient program, another TSR program, or DOS itself.

Memory-resident Programs 11

Loading a number of TSR utilities into memory coerces DOS — essentially a single-task operating system — into becoming a limited, somewhat crippled multitasking operating system.

INTERRUPTS

To understand the nature of memory-resident programs, you must understand system interrupts because such programs use the interrupt structure of DOS and the PC. This discussion is by no means an exhaustive treatment of interrupts, and you are encouraged to explore the matter with texts dedicated to the architecture of the 8086/80286 and the PC. This explanation addresses what interrupts are and how they are used, but it does not go into detailed specifics. It is restricted to the knowledge that you need about interrupts to understand memory-resident programs.

An **interrupt** is a momentary suspension of the sequential procedure of a program that allows another procedure to execute. When the interrupt is complete, the interrupted procedure resumes as if no interruption had occurred. The two procedures can be unrelated; the interrupted procedure might never be affected by the consequence of the interrupt. The two procedures can be interdependent; the interrupted procedure might be modified by the interrupting procedure. An interrupt can be generated by an event external to the current program, or it can be generated as the result of an action by the interrupted program. It can be caused by a hardware event or a programmed software instruction.

Interrupt Vectors

There are 256 different interrupts in the PC's architecture, numbered 0 to 0xff. Some of these interrupts are defined for use by the processor. For example, interrupt 0 is the divide-by-zero interrupt. Others are defined in the PC's architecture for invoking functions in the ROM-BIOS. Others are defined by DOS for its use. Remember that the 8088/8086/80286 family is a microprocessor; the PC is a computer based on the microprocessor; and DOS is the operating system. Each of these three architectural layers has its own reserved set of interrupts. The remaining interrupts are available for use by applications programs and device interrupt service routines.

11 Memory-resident Programs

Each interrupt is represented by a four-byte address vector stored in the computer's memory. These vectors are located in absolute memory locations 0 to 0x3ff. When an interrupt occurs, the contents of the processor's flags register and the four-byte address presently being processed are pushed onto the stack. Further interrupts are disabled, and processing is transferred to the address stored in the interrupt vector associated with the interrupt that occurred. The program code located at that address must save any machine registers it plans to use, do its job, restore the machine registers, and execute a return instruction that pops the interrupted program's address and flags register so the interrupted program's processing will resume where it left off.

Hardware Interrupts

Hardware interrupts are caused by events physically attached by hardware design to particular interrupt vectors. For example, the PC keyboard is attached to interrupt 9. Pressing a key causes the processor to interrupt the running program in the manner just described and to transfer to the address stored in the interrupt vector associated with interrupt 9. That vector is at memory location 0x24 (9 * 4 bytes).

Software Interrupts

Software interrupts are caused when the current program executes the INT machine instruction with an interrupt number as an operand. No distinction is made between this interrupt and a hardware interrupt. The ISR cannot tell the difference, and, in fact, nothing prevents a program from executing a designated hardware interrupt as a software interrupt.

DOS, THE SINGLE-TASK OPERATING SYSTEM

You can gain an understanding of the operating environment of TSR programs by looking at the environment in which transient programs operate. DOS was designed to support the execution of a single task at a time. The operating system manages the loading and execution of a task and responds to requests for input and output services. It manages the placement of disk directories and files, deals with the system clock, writes to the system printer, writes to the video console, and returns characters typed at the keyboard. DOS is, in essence, a hierarchical file and unit-record device server that supports a single user running a single task. It serves that purpose well.

When DOS is first booted, and before any programs are executed, the memory space from 0 to the 640K upper limit supported by the PC (or whatever your machine contains) is allocated as shown in Figure 11.1. The lower 0x400 memory locations are reserved for interrupt vectors. Above the vectors is the DOS program. Next are device driver programs that are loaded when DOS is booted. For example, if you use a RAM disk or the **ANSI.SYS** console driver, those device drivers are located above DOS. Above the device drivers is the resident portion of the DOS command processor program. This program processes the DOS command line and executes programs, and it is split into a resident portion and a transient portion. The **Transient Program Area (TPA)** is above the resident command processor. When the user runs a program from the command line, the program is loaded into the TPA. At the top of the TPA is the transient portion of the command processor. A user program is allowed to use the memory that the transient command processor occupies. If that memory is used, the resident command processor will reload the transient command processor when the user program terminates.

11 Memory-resident Programs

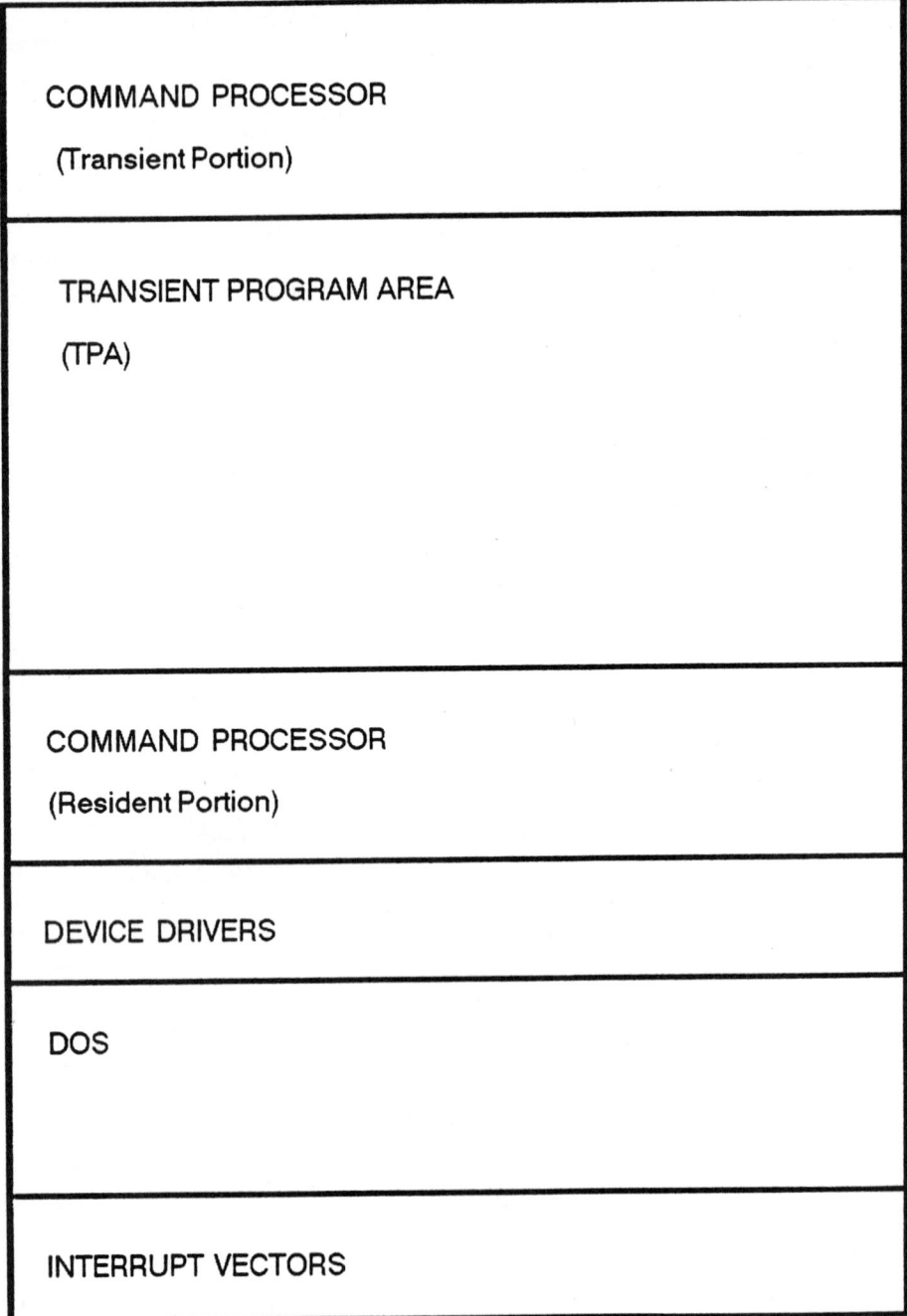

Figure 11.1 The DOS Memory Map

Memory-resident Programs 11

When the command processor loads a program, the program begins execution. When the program needs DOS support, such as for a file operation, it calls DOS by invoking a software interrupt and passes function parameters in registers. DOS takes over and executes the function. The calling program remains suspended until the DOS function is completed. The results of DOS functions are returned in registers and in the setting of the carry flag.

This sequence of events describes the typical single-task operating system environment. Nothing in DOS provides for the co-residency of user programs, co-execution of user programs, or cognizance by DOS of more than one task in memory at a time. The only way that more than one task can be active in memory is for all but one of them to be memory-resident in the manner designed for interrupt service routines. According to DOS, such programs are not tasks but ISRs to support the single task that might be running. DOS allows a task to spawn a subordinate task, but only one of them can be active at a time. The spawning task remains dormant until the spawned task terminates.

One rule for an orderly ISR is that it must avoid DOS function calls if it could be executed as the result of an interrupt of DOS itself. ISRs executed exclusively from transient programs that issue software interrupts have no such restriction, but an ISR asynchronous to the execution of the running program (a timer or keyboard ISR, for example) may not call DOS. The software industry has known for some time that TSR programs should, when popped up, avoid DOS function calls. As long as a resident program reads the keyboard by using ROM-BIOS functions and writes the screen with either ROM-BIOS calls or direct video memory accesses, the program runs without problems, but when such a program attempts to use DOS functions for anything, the system crashes. DOS functions are not reentrant; when a resident program interrupts a DOS function and then calls a DOS function, the system goes off into the weeds. This non-reentrant characteristic of DOS seems to restrict TSR programs to operations that can be performed within the limits of memory and ROM-BIOS resources. That restriction is no big sacrifice. As you learned from the way the window functions are built, you can get along nicely without DOS if all you need are the keyboard and the screen, but no file operations are permitted for a resident program, and programs need files.

11 Memory-resident Programs

To this anomaly the DOS developers added a wrinkle; they included a print spool program named **PRINT.COM**. **Spool** is an acronym from earlier times meaning "simultaneous peripheral operation on-line." A **print spooler** allows the computer to print a file while the user does something else that does not require the printer. The **PRINT.COM** program is a TSR program that remains resident, maintains a print queue, and prints named files while the computer and DOS environment are available to the user. The presence of a program that reads disk files, reads and writes a print queue file, and churns out pages on the printer while the user does anything else suggests that DOS is performing some multitasking without letting on to the rest of the world how it is done.

That suggestion and the inquisitive nature of a generation of hackers led, of course, to the discovery of DOS's limited multitasking capability. For some time, the keys to the coffer were held close; those who understood techniques for writing fully functioning TSR utilities kept the secret because they were selling TSR programs and supposedly wanted to stifle competition. As will happen, though, others broke the code and spilled the beans. Today, a careful researcher can piece together the steps necessary to write such a program by reading stacks of technical magazines and hundreds of conversations on electronic bulletin board services. By the time you read this book, more books like this one might be published to help explain the concept.

TERMINATE-AND-STAY-RESIDENT PROGRAMS

When DOS is running and at the command processor prompt, TSR programs are executed as if they were normal transient programs. In fact, neither DOS nor the command processor has any way of knowing that these programs will become resident until they terminate by using one of the two TSR functions. When the program terminates, it instructs DOS how much memory to reserve. As far as DOS is concerned, this action simply increases the lower address of the TPA to just above the memory-resident program, decreasing the amount of memory available to a user program by the size of the resident program. Figure 11.2 shows the system memory map with two TSR programs in place.

Memory-resident Programs 11

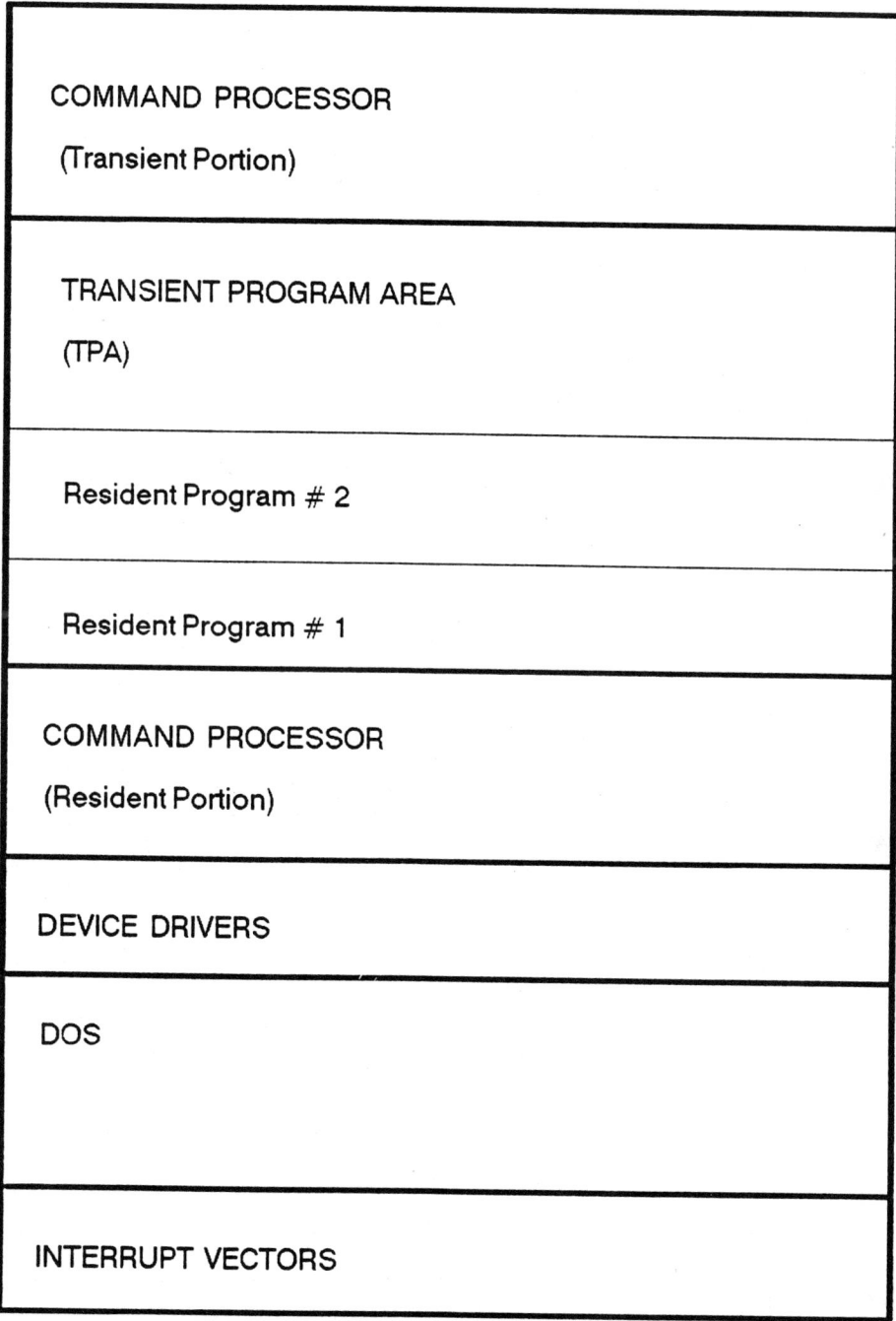

Figure 11.2 The DOS Memory Map with Two TSRs

11 Memory-resident Programs

TSR programs come in two varieties: interrupt service routines and memory-resident utilities. The difference between the two varieties is minor, but a clear difference exists.

Interrupt Service Routines

An ISR responds to an interrupt generated by a hardware device or a program and usually exists to support a hardware device. An ISR that responds to the system timer interrupt is one example. An example program in Chapter 12 shows how you can use the system timer interrupt to display the date and time on the screen. The ISR that comes with the Microsoft Mouse is named **MOUSE.COM** and operates on hardware interrupts that are based on the movement of the mouse. MOUSE.COM also processes software interrupts when applications programs query the ISR to determine the mouse's location and the condition of its buttons. Memory-resident utilities can include several such ISRs.

Memory-Resident Utilities

Memory-resident utilities are ISRs that usually involve no special hardware but respond to a defined hot key and run their processes at user request. The utilities preserve the condition of the computer when they interrupt it and restore the previous condition when done. A typical memory-resident utility program uses window techniques to communicate with the user because the pop-up nature of a window lends itself to a process that must restore everything to an undisturbed state when finished.

What Should Be Resident?

As you proceed with this chapter and the next, you will learn how to write TSR utilities in Turbo C. You might develop a tendency to build everything as a resident program and have everything available at the touch of a hot key, but restrain yourself. Not everything can or should be resident.

Memory-resident Programs 11

Remember, as you add resident programs, the size of the TPA is decreased. You can shrink it to a point where not enough memory remains to run normal programs. You might find yourself rich in pop-up utilities but without enough memory to build a small spreadsheet or compose a memo in your word processor.

Remember also that you are straining the design limits of DOS when you insert the first resident program into memory. It is not surprising that TSR programs from different sources do not coexist peacefully. Further, some TSRs do not perform well when certain transient programs are run.

Some TSR programs insist on being loaded after all other resident programs are loaded; they want to be the first in the chain of programs that attach themselves to interrupts. Since only one program can be loaded last, the various ones that must be last cannot be run together. Sidekick is so intent on being last that it will steal the timer interrupt from any resident program loaded after it.

Such shenanigans are the result of an industry trying to shoehorn multi-tasking into DOS. To their credit, TSR developers have tried to agree on some TSR program standards. They attempted a collaboration and a definition of a well-behaved TSR program, but no such standard has yet been published. There have also been attempts to define behavior for transient programs so they will coexist harmoniously with well-behaved resident programs. Developers of PC software have traditionally dealt with single-task DOS and PC hardware limitations in predictable fashion. To overcome the performance penalties of DOS, many developers have bypassed it, scanning the keyboard and poking into video memory to achieve the desired program performance. This method assumes that DOS is a single-task operating system, and no other program is competing for those resources. These assumptions get in the way of the TSR program that is trying to be the second task without stepping on the first.

11 Memory-resident Programs

Borland is promoting a TSR environment manager called **Sidekick Plus**. This package provides the TSR engine and arbitrator for a family of TSRs, all of which are developed within the Sidekick Plus guidelines and run under the Sidekick Plus environment. The advantage of this approach is that the problems of TSR incompatibility are solved. Apparent disadvantages are that the user must have a Sidekick Plus package to run the TSRs developed by cooperating vendors, and not all vendors of TSRs will cooperate; non-cooperating TSRs might not run with cooperating TSRs.

A programmer needs guidelines for deciding whether a utility program should be a TSR or a normal, transient program. Following are tests to apply to programs you are writing:

- **Size of the utility.** If the program cannot be compiled and linked with the tiny memory model—64K code, data, and stack—then it probably should not be a TSR. This self-imposed restraint might prevent you from loading memory with utilities at the expense of other programs the user needs. The TSR driver software in Chapter 12 works with tiny-model programs as well as small-model programs.

- **How often the utility is needed.** Don't write a resident income tax preparation utility. A program run as infrequently as once a day should not be resident. A program run once an hour could be memory-resident. Do not overload the system with seldom-used TSR programs.

- **Resources needed by the utility.** If a program must allocate much memory or degrades its performance when memory is limited, it should not be resident. A resident program can be popped up while any other program is running; the other program might have all or most of the memory itself. If the current transient program is a .COM file, DOS thinks the current program has all the memory. You might not be able to get any memory at all without a lot of dark byte-twiddling.

- **Pop-up nature of the utility's task.** If the program is used in conjunction with other programs that the user runs, it is a good candidate for a TSR. For example, an outline processor is a handy pop-up while you are running a word processor. The same is true for an on-line thesaurus. A calculator and notepad are relevant any time. A C language syntax checker would be a useful pop-up utility to have while you are using your program editor to write C code. Not all utility programs, however, should be on-line at the touch of a key.

- **Execution time for the utility program.** The advantage of a pop-up utility is that it is available instantly, and you can run it without closing down whatever else you are doing. The time savings are irrelevant if the utility program takes all day to run.

(People devour efficiency. A few years back, users were content if a data base query response came from the data center overnight. Now, they grumble if they must save their spreadsheet and return to DOS to use their modem program.)

BUILDING TSR UTILITIES

A number of problems must be solved when you write a TSR program. Some of the problems are minor, some are helped by the Turbo C extensions to the standard library, and some are downright thorny. Assembly language solutions are often easier to build than C solutions, but, to the extent possible, this book addresses those problems by using as much C code as possible.

11 Memory-resident Programs

Getting Resident

To be a TSR, a program must declare itself resident. This area is one of the few places in which the documented features of DOS help the programmer. The two DOS TSR functions have already been mentioned. To use them, you must know the size of the program. To know the size of the program, you must know how Turbo C programs are built, which will be explained shortly. Once a program has executed, attached itself to its interrupt vectors, and done everything that is required for a resident program, it must call one of the two TSR functions. The functions are similar in what they do, and the DOS 0x21, function 0x31 function is the preferred technique for declaring a resident program. Following is a code fragment showing how a Turbo C program becomes resident:

```
#include <dos.h>
static struct REGS rg;
unsigned int sizeprogram;

rg.x.ax = 0x3100;
rg.x.dx = sizeprogram;
intdos(&rg, &rg);
```

The **sizeprogram** integer must be initialized to the length of the program in paragraphs. A paragraph is 16 bytes.

Is the TSR Program Already Resident?

Remember, DOS does not know that your program is resident or what its name is after it terminates (the information is available, but DOS doesn't know it). If you execute a TSR program several times, several copies of it will be resident unless it has a way to test to see if a copy of itself is already in memory.

The simplest way for a TSR program to see if it is already resident is to use one of the unused interrupt vectors as a vehicle for communicating with the TSR. When first executed, the TSR can execute the interrupt, looking for a returned value. First, the vector must be examined to see if it has a pointer in it. If the value is not returned as expected, the utility is not already resident, so it attaches itself to that vector and declares itself resident. By attaching itself to the vector, it becomes an interrupt service routine that returns the expected value from the interrupt. A subsequent attempt by the user to load the same utility will result in the expected value being returned to the new copy of the utility, and the program will not declare itself resident.

The interrupt vectors from 0x60 through 0x67 are usually available, and you can choose one of them, but there are problems with this approach. If you arbitrarily select one of these vectors, you have no assurance that another program from another source will not also select the same vector. Remember, the design of DOS assumes one task at a time and that a task can have any of the available vectors it wants.

A preferred method is to have the attached interrupt vector point to a signature in the memory of the utility. The **signature** is a string of characters that should be unique to the program. Rather than executing the interrupt when it is first loaded, the program will scan the interrupts from 0x60 through 0x67. If any of them points to the signature, the program is resident; if not, the program appropriates an unused interrupt vector and sets the pointer. Unfortunately, there is no way to prevent other programs from grabbing your vector. Nothing is for sure.

Finding an unused interrupt vector is a matter of testing each one for a **null value**. A vector with a null value is one that is available. The interrupts numbered 0x60 to 0x67 are documented as those that are available for applications programs to use.

Once you have found and appropriated an interrupt vector, besides determining residency, you might want to use it for other kinds of communication with the program. Some TSRs allow themselves to be used to change run-time parameters. A subsequent execution of an already resident TSR can pass new parameters to the resident copy of itself by way of the communication interrupt vector. The vector can point to an ISR in the resident program; the signature can be an offset in the same segment as the ISR. Having found the signature, the second invocation of the program can communicate with the first through the vector. The TSR driver program in Chapter 12 illustrates this technique.

11 Memory-resident Programs

Capturing an Interrupt

You will want to capture more than just a communications interrupt vector; you will need to capture the vectors that will allow your TSR to be executed once it is resident. Remember, interrupting events execute a resident program when those interrupting events execute the ISR code pointed to by interrupt vectors.

Capturing an interrupt vector is easy in Turbo C. The **setvect** function provides a one-line way to perform the task. You must have declared an interrupt function, and you must know which vector you are going to attach to the vector. Then, issue the following function call:

```
setvect(vno, isr);
```

The **vno** parameter is an integer value between 0 and 255, and the **isr** parameter is the address of a function that is declared to be an **interrupt** function. The declaration would look like the following:

```
void interrupt isr();
```

Chaining Interrupts

If you attach to interrupts that are used by other programs, you must chain those interrupts so that all programs that need them will see them. For example, if you attach your program to the timer interrupt and make no provision for the rest of the system to use the interrupt, the other processes that are timer-event-driven will be disabled for as long as your program is installed and keeps the attachment. In this case, the system clock would shut down.

Other interrupts you will attach are the keyboard interrupt, the DOS function interrupt, the BIOS disk function interrupt, and other interrupts that exist to support the TSR. In each of these cases, you must chain the interrupt to the other processes that need it.

Memory-resident Programs 11

Interrupts are chained in the initialization code of the program. To chain an interrupt, read the address stored in the interrupt vector. That address is where the interrupt has been going prior to the execution of your TSR. The Turbo C function library includes the **getvect** function for reading the contents of an interrupt vector. You declare an **interrupt** function pointer and direct **getvect** to write the vector's address into the pointer, as follows:

```
void interrupt (*oldisr)();

oldisr = getvect(vno);
```

Next, write the address of your ISR into the interrupt vector by using the **setvect** function previously described.

In your ISR, which is usually executed after the program has declared itself resident and terminated, you must provide for the execution of the old ISR. Sometimes, you will do this as soon as your ISR is executed and before you do anything with the interrupt. Other times, you will process the interrupt yourself and then give the old ISR a shot at it. These concepts are discussed and illustrated in Chapter 12.

How Big is the TSR Program?

When your program declares itself resident, it must specify its size so that DOS knows how much memory to set aside for it. You can be safe and declare every program to be 64K bytes, but this strategy would unnecessarily consume memory. It is easy to figure the size of an assembly language program, but the configuration of a C program is somewhat hidden from the programmer. To compute the program's size, you must look at how the Turbo C compiler builds your program.

Figure 11.3 shows the memory map of a typical Turbo C tiny-model program. The **Program Segment Prefix (PSP)** is a DOS construct at the beginning of every program that will be discussed later. The code, which is the machine language that executes the functions, follows the PSP. Data variables declared as static or external and initialized when they are declared follow the code. Uninitialized static and external variables follow the initialized variables. The **heap** is next. The heap is the block of memory from which dynamic memory allocations are made.

11 Memory-resident Programs

The size of the heap depends on how much memory your program is going to allocate. The **stack** is above the heap and grows downward. When the program is first executed, the top of the stack is at the top of the 64K memory space that the tiny-model program occupies. As the program uses stack space, the stack pointer grows downward. The amount of stack required by the program depends on the depth to which function calls are nested and the amount of local data used by those functions. Each call to a function pushes the parameters for that function on the stack and causes some registers to be saved on the stack. If the function has local, automatic variables, the stack pointer is moved further down because these variables are also stored on the stack. A function that is called recursively and that has a lot of parameters and automatic variables will use a lot of stack.

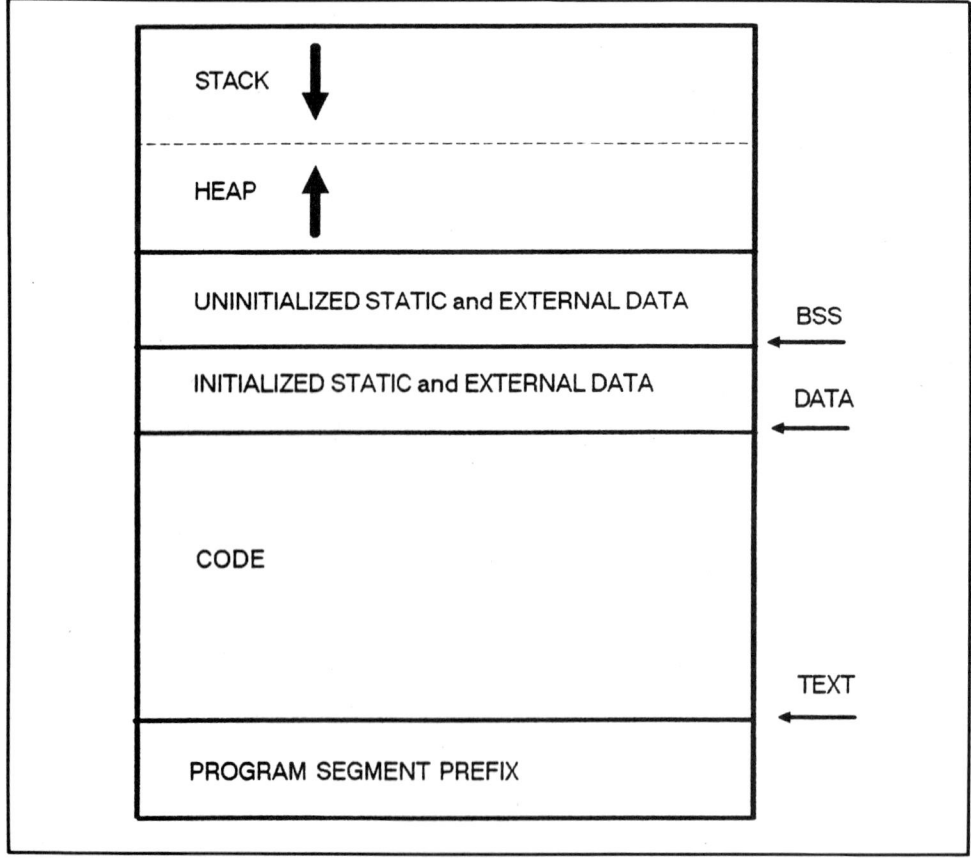

Figure 11.3 A Turbo C Tiny-Model Program Memory Map

Memory-resident Programs 11

Because of the dynamic nature of the heap and stack, you must use some guesswork to determine the program's length.

You can guess at the length of a program by looking at the MAP file generated by the **TLINK** program. At the beginning of the map is a block such as the following:

```
Start   Stop    Length  Name      Class

00000H  010BAH  010BBH  _TEXT     CODE
010C0H  013D8H  00319H  _DATA     DATA
013DAH  013DDH  00004H  _EMUSEG   DATA
013DEH  013DFH  00002H  _CVTSEG   DATA
013E0H  013E5H  00006H  _SCNSEG   DATA
013E6H  014EDH  00108H  _BSS      BSS
014EEH  014EEH  00000H  _BSSEND   BSSEND
```

The rightmost column labeled **class** tells which of the segments is represented by the values to the left. CODE contains code, DATA contains initialized variables, and BSS contains uninitialized variables. The **Stop** column for the BSSEND entry gives the address (in hexadecimal) of the top of the uninitialized variable space and, therefore, the start of the heap. A program that used no stack and no heap would be this size, plus 256 for the PSP.

To estimate your heap size, examine your use of the Turbo C memory allocation functions. If you are using the window functions from prior chapters, you can estimate their heap requirements by estimating the size and number of windows that will be concurrently established. Each window allocates a Save buffer equal to its height multiplied by its width multiplied by two. The heap buffer for a window is returned to the heap when the window is deleted, so the important consideration is the maximum number of windows that are established at one time. You must estimate the other heap demands of your program by reviewing your own use of the Turbo C memory allocation functions. If your program allocates memory as a function of external influences, such as data dependencies or user inputs, be sure that your error-checking is thorough and your error-handling is appropriate. Never call the **exit** function from a memory-resident program, regardless of the error.

11 Memory-resident Programs

Once you have determined your heap size, you can estimate its top and, therefore, the bottom of the stack. Next, you must estimate the top of the stack. When the program is first executed, the top of the stack is at the 64K mark, which is where the Turbo C startup code places it. When the program terminates to stay resident, it will tell DOS its size, and DOS will use memory above the TSR program for other programs. When the TSR is popped up, it must establish its stack pointer at a location inside the TSR and not inside another program. If you tell DOS that the program is less than 64K, the stack pointer must be established at a location somewhere below the 64K mark.

The best way to find the optimum top of the stack is by trial and error. First, get your program working as a 64K program, and then begin to move the top of your stack down. With each experimental move of the stack, stress the program with tests that use the most heap and stack. Continue these experiments until the program begins to crash the system or behave in peculiar ways. Then, move the top of the stack back up to a safe location. With this stack setting, use the program extensively before you believe that the stack is safe from the heap.

It would be better if there were a more scientific and precise way to find the program size, but this approach works and seems to be the only reliable method.

Context Switching

When the TSR is first executed, it enjoys all the resources that DOS provides to a normal task. After it has declared itself resident and terminated, those resources are given to other programs or, when no program is running, to the DOS command processor. When the TSR is executed as the result of the hot key, the program is a parasite to the interrupted program. DOS does not realize that a different task is running; those resources still belong to the interrupted task. Somehow, the system pointers to those resources must be changed so that the TSR is the acknowledged running task. Changing such resources among tasks is called **context switching** in a multitasking environment, and a multitasking DOS switches the context. In the single-task DOS of the PC, however, DOS does no context switching, so the interrupting task must switch its own context in and out.

Memory-resident Programs **11**

The Stack

All programs need a stack. The TSR has a stack when it terminates, but when it interrupts another program, the PC's stack segment and stack pointer point to the interrupted program's stack. Since stacks push down and pop up, and since such a device promotes reentrant programs, you might reason that the best approach is to use the interrupted program's stack. In fact, many assembly language TSRs do just that, but to do so, they must severely restrict their use of stack space. First, you have no idea how much stack the interrupted program will provide. Second, DOS guarantees that it will have a stack with enough space for the registers only. C is a stack-intensive language, and you need more stack space than DOS guarantees, which means that a TSR must switch to its own stack when it interrupts another process.

Switching to your own stack means you must save the stack segment register before you make the switch. This saved value is returned to the register before the TSR returns to the interrupted program. The stack segment and pointer registers can be addressed directly in Turbo C through the use of pseudo-variables with the names __SS and __SP. When the TSR declares itself resident, it saves its own stack segment and knows the size of the program. When the TSR is popped up and has saved the stack context of the interrupted program, the TSR must reestablish its own stack. It performs this task by setting the stack segment register to the value saved when it was becoming resident and setting the stack pointer register to a value computed from the TSR program's size.

If the TSR is reentrant, i.e., if it can interrupt itself, this stack switching can fail. The second time you switch the stack, you overwrite the save area for the stack register. To avoid this, you must write resident programs that are not reentrant. This restriction is no great loss; memory-resident utilities needn't be reentrant. You don't need to interrupt your calculator to run another calculation.

To prevent a TSR from being reentrant, set a flag when it is popped up. The flag remains set until the TSR returns to the interrupted process. If the TSR is requested a second time (by a chance bump of the hot key, perhaps), it senses the setting of the flag and declines to run.

11 Memory-resident Programs

The Program Segment Prefix (PSP)

The PSP is a 256-byte control area at the front of every program in memory. The prefix contains many fields that DOS uses to manage the processing environment of the program. Figure 11.4 is an illustration of the PSP. The following discussion addresses each of the fields in the PSP. Note that many of these fields are not officially acknowledged by Microsoft or IBM. They are used in the manner described here, but their use or modification by applications programs is neither endorsed nor sanctioned by the vendors. Knowledge of these fields is the gift of those inquisitive hackers who dissect DOS and publish their findings. Except where otherwise specified, these characteristics are true for the versions of DOS that are in popular use — versions 2.0, 2.1, 3.0, 3.1, 3.2, and 3.3. DOS 4.0 is not published in the U.S., and, it is alleged, future versions of DOS will support multitasking and the 80286/80386 microcomputers only. It is safe to use the PSP fields documented here in the manner discussed. Many popular commercial PC programs do just that.

INT Call to Process Terminator (PSP:0)

This field contains an INT 0x20 machine instruction; its purpose is to support programs that are converted from CP/M to DOS. Under CP/M, programs terminated themselves with a call or jump to memory location 0.

Top of Memory Segment Address (PSP:2)

When a program is executed, DOS allocates a block of memory into which the program is loaded. This field contains the segment address of the top of that block of memory.

Terminate Handler Address (PSP:0xa)

When a program is executed, DOS saves the previous contents of the interrupt 0x22 vector in this field. When the program terminates, DOS restores the vector by using this saved field. The 0x22 interrupt vector points to the DOS program termination handler.

Memory-resident Programs 11

INT Call to DOS Process Terminator	0000
Top of Memory Segment Address	0002
0	0004
Call Instruction to DOS Function Handler	0005
Terminate Handler Address (INT 0x22)	000A
Ctrl – Break Handler Address (INT 0x23)	000E
Critical Error Handler Address (INT 0x24)	0012
Segment Address of Parent Process's PSP	0016
File Handle Array	0018
Segment Address of Environment Block	002C
Stack Address at Time of DOS Function Call	002E
Size of File Handle Array	0032
Segment:Offset Address of File Handle Array	0034
Reserved	0038
File Control Block # 1	005C
File Control Block # 2	006C
Command Tail / Disk Transfer Area	0080

Figure 11.4 The Program Segment Prefix

11 Memory-resident Programs

Ctrl-Break Handler Address (PSP:0xe)

When a program is executed, DOS saves the previous contents of the interrupt 0x23 vector in this field. When the program terminates, DOS restores the vector by using this saved field. The 0x23 interrupt vector points to the DOS Ctrl-Break handler.

Critical Error Handler Address (PSP:0x12)

When a program is executed, DOS saves the previous contents of the interrupt 0x24 vector in this field. When the program terminates, DOS restores the vector by using this saved field. The 0x24 interrupt vector points to the DOS critical error handler.

Note that DOS restores the previous three vectors when a TSR program terminates and declares itself resident. If the TSR needs to intercept these interrupts, it must attach itself to them each time it is popped up.

Segment of Parent's PSP (PSP:0x16)

The program that owns this PSP was executed as the result of another program's call to DOS. The executing program is called the **parent** program. Usually, the parent program is the DOS command processor, COMMAND.COM, although any program can be the parent of another. This field in the PSP contains the PSP segment address of the parent program.

The command processor has no parent other than DOS; therefore, this field in the command processor's PSP contains the segment address of the command processor's own PSP, which is effectively a pointer to itself.

File Handle Table (PSP:0x18)

This field is an array of twenty bytes, each of which represents a file handle. When a program opens a file, DOS returns a handle for the program to use when it calls DOS to read and write records in the file. (C programs that use the stream I/O functions do not directly address this handle—they use the **FILE** pointer defined in **stdio**; however, the standard C library functions that support stream I/O use these handles in a manner that hides them from the calling program.) These file handles are subscripts into this array. The elements of this array are subscripts into a DOS array of file control tables.

Environment Block Segment Address (PSP:0x2c)

This field is the segment address of the environment block that DOS establishes for a program when the program is executed. The environment block is an allocated block of memory that can be deallocated by a task if it has no need for the environment settings.

Stack Address during DOS Function Calls (PSP:0x2e)

When a program calls a DOS function, DOS saves the program's current stack segment and pointer registers in this field. Then, DOS switches to its own stack for the execution of the function. Prior to returning to the program, DOS uses the saved values in this field to restore the program's stack segment and pointer registers.

Size of File Handle Table (PSP:0x32)

This field is an integer count of the number of entries in the file handle table. Normally, this count contains the value 20. Note that this field has no value or use in versions of DOS prior to version 3.0.

Address of File Handle Table (PSP:0x34)

This field is a long pointer to the file handle table; its segment value is usually the same as the PSP's segment address, and its offset is usually 0x18. Note that this field has no value or use in versions of DOS prior to version 3.0.

11 Memory-resident Programs

The previous two fields are probably intended to allow a program to extend the maximum to 20 files that it can have concurrently open. By allocating a longer table, putting its entry count and address in these fields, and copying the 20 values from the PSP into the new program, a program can increase its maximum file open count to that specified in the FILES= statement of the CONFIG.SYS file in the boot disk's root directory.

File Control Block #1 (PSP:0x5c)

This field is a file control block built by DOS if the command line that executes a program has a file name as its first parameter.

File Control Block #2 (PSP:0x6c)

This field is a file control block built by DOS if the command line that executes a program has a file name as its second parameter.

The previous two fields are provided to support programs converted from the CP/M environment.

Command Tail/Disk Transfer Area (PSP:80)

This last field is also a carry-over from the CP/M influence. When the program is executed, everything on the command line, beginning with the second character after the program's name, is parsed into a string of words in the command tail. Leading and extra white space is eliminated. The first byte of the command tail is a count of characters the tail contains.

Once the program is underway, this field is the **Disk Transfer Area**, the read and write buffer for files opened under the older File Control Block DOS functions. This field is also used by the DOS functions that manipulate file directories.

Memory-resident Programs 11

Context-Switching the PSP

Each program has a PSP. To DOS, the only real PSP is the one at the front of the last program executed. DOS allows programs to spawn the execution of other programs, and the new program inherits PSP values from its parent, but, since DOS only recognizes one active task at a time, it knows about only one PSP.

The PSP contains several interesting fields, but the one of most interest for this discussion is the array of 20 file handles. A program is allowed to open up to 20 files at a time. Each file is assigned a handle, and that handle is an element of the array in the PSP. The array has room for 20 handles, and the first five entries are assigned to the **stdin**, **stdout**, **stderr**, **stdaux**, and **stdprn** logical devices when the program is first executed. As a program opens files, the new handles are stored in the PSP array. Array entries that have not been used contain a -1 value. The program addresses the files as subscripts into the array. The array values are subscripts into a DOS table of files.

If a TSR begins, opens a file, then declares itself resident and terminates, the handle for that file is stored in the TSR's PSP. When the TSR is popped up, DOS thinks the interrupted program is still running. If the TSR makes a DOS call in reference to the file it opened when it was first executed, DOS looks into the PSP of the interrupted program for the handle. This action will confuse matters; if the corresponding array entry in the interrupted program's PSP contains an entry, the file reference will be to the interrupted program's file and not to the TSR's file. If the interrupted program has not used that entry in its PSP, DOS will think that it is being asked to refer to an unopened file.

The solution would seem to be one of the following:

- Don't open files at initialization of the TSR; open them when it interrupts the other program. This method uses entries from the interrupted program's PSP for the TSR's files.

- Don't use the handle files of DOS 2.0 and above. Use the older File Control Block (FCB) logic from DOS 1.1. Those functions do not use PSP array entries. The FCB tables are maintained in the data space of the programs that use them.

11 Memory-resident Programs

- Switch PSP pointers in DOS when the TSR interrupts, and switch them back when it returns.

Each of these approaches has its disadvantages:

- There are two disadvantages to using the interrupted program's PSP array for TSR file handles. First, the nature of the TSR might be such that opening and closing files presents an unacceptable performance penalty each time the program is popped up. Second, there is no way to be sure that the interrupted program's PSP will have enough array space for the TSR's handles.

- Using FCB functions has two disadvantages. First, a file opened with FCB functions must be in the currently logged-on subdirectory of the system when the file is opened. No DOS path subdirectories may be used in the file specification when it is opened. Second, all Turbo C standard library file operations assume the use of the more flexible handle files. To use FCB functions, you must develop equivalent functions to replace the standard **open**, **close**, **read**, **write**, **fopen**, **fclose**, **fget**, **fput**, **fprintf**, etc. functions.

- There are no documented DOS functions for modifying the address of the PSP as DOS recognizes it. There is a documented DOS function for reading the current PSP (INT 0x21, Function 0x62), but it is available only with DOS Versions 3.0 and higher. Two undocumented DOS INT 0x21 functions (0x50 and 0x51) set and get the address of the PSP, but they are not reliable in DOS versions 2.0 and 2.1 for use in TSR programs. They share a stack with certain DOS functions that might be interrupted by a TSR, and if the TSR uses functions 0x50 and 0x51 while interrupting these other DOS functions, the system will crash. You may use these functions only if your TSR is to run with DOS versions 3.0 and greater. The address of the PSP has come to be called the **Process ID (PID)**. The two undocumented DOS functions are called **GetPID** and **SetPID**.

Memory-resident Programs **11**

The solution is none of the above. A TSR must be able to use files, but all the obvious solutions have disadvantages. Working substitutes for the **GetPID** and **SetPID** functions are needed. One approach is to determine through experimentation the address where DOS stores the PID. This address, of course, depends on the version of DOS and might be unique to a particular OEM's issue of a DOS version. Tabling and using these values are shaky measures at best.

A better approach is to determine the PID addresses at run-time when the TSR is executed. You can find the addresses where DOS stores the PID by using the following procedure. First, the present PID is retrieved by using the **GetPID** function. Next, the memory occupied by DOS is searched for a copy of the PID value. Once such a value is found, its address is saved, and the PID is changed to an artificial value by using the **SetPID** function. The value at the found address is examined to see if it has changed to the artificial PID. If so, an address of where a PID is stored in DOS has been identified and is now saved. The original PID is restored, and the search proceeds. Versions of DOS below 3.0 keep the PID in two locations. DOS Versions 3.0 and greater maintain one PID. The PID addresses and the original PID of the TSR are saved before the TSR declares itself resident and terminates. When the TSR is popped up, one of the saved PID addresses is used to read the interrupted program's PID. This value is saved, and the TSR's PID is restored to DOS. When the resident program is about to return, it restores the interrupted program's PID to the DOS locations.

This approach is used in the TSR driver functions in Chapter 12.

The Disk Transfer Area (DTA)

The second half of the PSP is the DTA, a 128-byte buffer where DOS reads and writes any disk files that are opened for use with the FCB functions. DOS also uses this area for functions that deal with directory searches.

The Turbo C library has functions that read and set the address of the DTA. **Getdta** returns the current DTA address, and **setdta** changes the DTA address to a different location. The functions have the following format:

11 Memory-resident Programs

```
#include <dos.h>
char far *dta;

dta = getdta();

setdta(dta);
```

A TSR must save the DTA address of the program it interrupts and establish its own DTA address if the TSR will use any DOS functions that write to the DTA. Upon return to the interrupted program, the TSR must restore the DTA address to the address of the interrupted program. The interrupt might have occurred after the interrupted program set the DTA address and before the program was done with it.

Since the TSR will be in C, you cannot be certain that it will not change or use the DTA. Actions of functions in the C library are not necessarily known, and the best course is the safe one. The TSR driver program in Chapter 12 preserves the DTA for the interrupted program.

The Keyboard Interrupt (9)

When the user presses the hot key, the TSR must interrupt whatever the system is doing and start itself. To do this, the program must watch the keyboard for the hot key. An understanding of this process requires an understanding of how keyboard interrupt and data scan codes work.

A key press generates interrupt 9, and processing takes over at the ISR pointed to by the interrupt 9 vector. The ISR must read the keyboard data port and process the keystroke. The PC keyboard does not generate the ASCII value your program sees when it issues the **get_char** function; the keyboard generates a scan code that can be read from the keyboard's input data port. Each key on the keyboard has its own value. The ISR must determine from this value which key or keys are pressed and what to make of them.

The ROM-BIOS has a keyboard ISR that reads the scan codes, translates them into ASCII values, and inserts them into a keyboard buffer. Programs (including DOS) that read the keyboard read from this buffer. The ROM-BIOS maintains a status byte that indicates whether the Alt, Right Shift, Left Shift, or Ctrl keys are being pressed. A program can read the current value of these keys by retrieving that status byte from the ROM-BIOS. Chapter 12 includes illustrations of the scan code and keyboard status byte values.

A TSR can attach itself to the interrupt 9 vector. The interrupt 9 ISR in the TSR must chain to the previous contents of the interrupt 9 vector so that the ROM-BIOS keyboard services continue. Before chaining, however, the TSR's ISR can read the scan code and status byte to see if the hot key has been pressed.

If the TSR avoids all DOS function calls, the interrupt 9 ISR can execute the pop-up function immediately. If the TSR wants to use DOS functions, the ISR must not execute the pop-up but must flag the presence of the hot key and return. Other ISRs will observe the hot key flag and execute the pop-up when it is safe to do so. One ISR that watches for an acceptable time to execute the pop-up is the timer interrupt ISR.

The Timer Interrupt

The PC is interrupted 18.2 times a second by the system timer, which uses interrupt vector 0x1c to execute the timer ISR. Chapter 12 includes a resident clock program run by the timer interrupt. Hot key TSRs also must use the timer interrupt, so they will attach a timer ISR to interrupt vector 0x1c. Since the program cannot execute until it is safe to use DOS functions, the keyboard ISR sets a flag when the hot key is pressed as just described. The TSR uses a timer interrupt to see if the flag is set and, if it is set, to see if it is safe to use DOS functions. If these two conditions are met, the timer ISR can call the TSR's pop-up functions.

As with the keyboard interrupt, the timer ISR of a TSR must chain the timer interrupt to other programs that have it attached ahead of the TSR.

11 Memory-resident Programs

The DOS Reentrancy Problem

You have been reading about the problems of using DOS from inside a TSR pop-up program. If the program interrupts DOS and wants to use DOS, DOS is not reentrant. It is not enough to say that you will avoid interrupts while DOS is running. Sometimes, DOS is running a keyboard input function when you press the hot key. The TSR cannot wait for the system to arrive at a non-DOS keyboard function—the user wants the pop-up now, and DOS has the system.

The Two DOS Stacks

DOS maintains two stacks. When DOS is executing one of the lower functions numbered 0 to 12, it uses one stack; when it is executing any other function, it uses the other stack. In either case, DOS saves the caller's stack segment and pointer registers in a single location for each group; therefore, neither of the groups is reentrant. The first caller's saved stack registers would be overwritten by those of the second caller.

DOS is better described as semi-reentrant. When functions 0 to 12 are interrupted, it is safe to call any of the other functions. When any of the other functions is interrupted, it is safe to use functions 0 to 12.

There is no problem avoiding DOS functions 0 to 12. These functions manage the DOS console input and output. They are easy to forsake because there are other ways to manage the screen and keyboard, and those other ways offer better performance than the DOS functions. The upper functions are not so easy to avoid. They do everything else, including file management, which is necessary in a resident program.

Since you can avoid functions 0 to 12 but need the others, the two-stack situation works for you. If you can be sure that your interrupts will always occur outside of the upper DOS functions, no reentrancy problem will exist. You manage the problem by flagging a hot key interrupt and delaying its process until DOS is outside of an unsafe function. The unsafe functions are fast functions; they do their operation and return quickly, so there is no undue wait.

Because the TSR is triggered by a hot key interrupt, and because keyboard interrupts occur regardless of what DOS is doing, you need a way to determine if DOS is unsafe. The DOS Busy Flag provides that information.

Memory-resident Programs **11**

The DOS Busy Flag (0x34)

DOS Function 0x34 returns the DOS segment address and an offset to a special flag that DOS maintains. That flag is called the **DOS Busy Flag**. When DOS is about to go into one of the unsafe functions, it sets this flag. When the unsafe function completes, DOS clears the flag.

When the resident program first executes, it uses DOS function 0x34 to find the address of the DOS Busy Flag. The address is saved to be used by the timer ISR. When the hot key is pressed, the keyboard ISR sets a flag. At every tick of the system clock, the timer ISR examines the hot key flag. If the hot key flag is set, the timer ISR looks at the DOS Busy Flag. If that flag is set, the timer ISR returns, doing nothing for the resident program. At each successive tick of the clock, the timer ISR watches the DOS Busy Flag. When the flag finally indicates that DOS is no longer busy, the timer ISR clears the hot key flag and pops up the TSR.

This procedure works some of the time. At other times, DOS stays busy until the user does something other than press the hot key, for example, when the command processor is waiting at the system prompt for the user to type a command. If the user presses the hot key, the keyboard ISR sets the hot key flag, but, because DOS is busy, the timer ISR never pops up the TSR. To cope with this condition, DOS uses the **DOSOK** interrupt vector.

The DOSOK Interrupt (0x28)

There are frequent periods during which DOS is busy when DOS knows that you can use the upper DOS functions. One of these times is when DOS is waiting for a keystroke. When DOS knows that it is busy but that it is safe to use its upper functions, DOS calls the **DOSOK** interrupt number 0x28. The whole purpose of the **DOSOK** interrupt is to tell TSRs (specifically, the DOS **PRINT.COM** spool program) that the programs can use the upper DOS functions. If no TSRs are attached to the 0x28 interrupt vector, the vector simply points to an interrupt return (IRET) machine instruction. The 0x28 interrupt vector is a software interrupt; an ISR that is attached to it executes when another program performs the INT 0x28 machine instruction.

11 Memory-resident Programs

TSRs can attach themselves to the **DOSOK** interrupt vector and use its invocation to tell if DOS can be used. The TSR's **DOSOK** ISR tests for the hot key flag. If the hot key flag is set, the ISR clears the hot key flag and pops up the TSR. If not, the ISR returns to the program that called the **DOSOK** interrupt. In either case, the ISR chains the interrupt vector to any other TSR that might be attached to it.

The **DOSOK** interrupt is called when DOS is busy; however, a TSR executed from this function cannot be interrupted by another TSR unless the running TSR also makes occasional calls to INT 0x28. The reason for this limitation is that when DOS calls the **DOSOK** interrupt, the DOS Busy Flag is set. While the TSR is running, the DOS Busy Flag will remain set, and if the user presses the hot key for another TSR, that program's timer ISR will wait for the DOS Busy Flag to be reset, which will not happen while the TSR is running. This situation will always happen when the first TSR is popped up while the DOS command processor is waiting for a user command.

To allow a second TSR to interrupt a first, each TSR must call the **DOSOK** interrupt at appropriate times. The most appropriate time is while the TSR is waiting for a keystroke. If you refer to the **get_char** function in Chapter 4, you will see that it calls the 0x28 interrupt while it is waiting for a keystroke. The purpose for that call is to support the TSR concepts discussed here and used in Chapter 12.

The Disk ROM-BIOS Interrupt (0x13)

You never want to interrupt a disk operation. If your TSR is allowed to interrupt the system while a disk seek, read, or write operation is underway, the latent time used by the TSR can generate disk errors for the interrupted program. If the TSR is allowed to interrupt a seek-read operation or a seek-write operation, particularly after the seek and before the read/write, the TSR's use of the disk system could throw the interrupted program's disk processing out of whack. To avoid these circumstances, a TSR will attach itself to the ROM-BIOS disk processing interrupt vector for interrupt 0x13. If any process calls this interrupt, the TSR sets a flag and then chains to the prior interrupt vector for 0x13. When the 0x13 interrupt is completed, the TSR's ISR clears the flag. This flag is tested by the timer ISR and DOSOK ISR. If disk operations are in effect, the TSR is not allowed to interrupt.

The DOS Critical Error Interrupt (0x24)

When DOS encounters a critical error, it calls the Critical Error Interrupt, number 0x24. For example, if you try to access a diskette with the drive door open, DOS senses a not ready condition and calls the critical error interrupt. If a program does not attach itself to the 0x24 interrupt vector, all critical errors are handled by an ISR in the DOS command processor. The command processor writes the dreaded "Abort, Retry, or Ignore" message on the screen. The ISR returns a value to DOS that specifies what DOS should do about the error.

Assume that no program has attached itself to the 0x24 vector. Your TSR interrupts a transient program. Your TSR tries to read a diskette, and the drive door is open. The DOS command processor takes over and asks the user whether it should abort, retry, or ignore. The user types "A," and DOS attempts to abort. If your TSR swapped PSP addresses, DOS tries to abort the TSR. DOS does not know that there is a transient program in an interrupted condition and does not return to it, even though its memory is still allocated by DOS. The system is amuck. If your TSR did not swap PSP addresses, DOS aborts the transient program and does not return to the TSR.

Suppose the transient program attached itself to the 0x24 interrupt vector. Your disk error will execute the interrupted transient program's critical error ISR.

A TSR must attach itself to the 0x24 interrupt vector whether or not it intends to do anything about the errors. The vector is attached when the TSR program is popped up and restored when the TSR program is about to return to the interrupted program. Under no circumstance should the TSR tell DOS to abort the process. Most TSR programs simply ignore the errors and tell DOS to also ignore the errors, figuring that the user can tell when something is wrong. The critical error interrupt is not chained. This approach has peril. If another TSR program (a spooler, for example) has attached itself to the 0x24 vector and is popped up after your TSR program, it will get your errors. If the program was popped up ahead of your TSR program, your program will get its errors and tell DOS to ignore them, which is a problem you cannot solve without writing a system-wide, smart critical error handler ISR. Remember, DOS is a single-task operating system.

11 Memory-resident Programs

The DOS Ctrl-Break Interrupt (0x23)

When the user presses the Ctrl-Break key, DOS displays the ^C token at the current cursor location on the screen and calls interrupt 0x23. The 0x23 ISR provided by DOS causes immediate termination of the current program. You do not want the TSR program terminated in this fashion; it has too many interrupt vectors attached to it, and a transient program might be above it in memory. If you merely intercept the interrupt, you run the risk that another program loaded behind yours attached itself to the interrupt and will do something inappropriate with the Ctrl-Break while your TSR program is running.

DOS includes a function (0x33) that allows a program to read the current status (enabled/disabled) of the Ctrl-Break process and to set the status. When a TSR program is popped up, it should read the current status of the Ctrl-Break process. Then, the TSR should disable the Ctrl-Break process. When the TSR program is ready to return to the interrupted process, the TSR program should restore the Ctrl-Break status to its former setting. It is not necessary to attach a TSR program to the Ctrl-Break interrupt vector.

If you disable the Ctrl-Break process in the manner just described and the user presses Ctrl-Break when the TSR program is running, the interrupted program will be terminated when the TSR program returns. If all TSRs use the same logic, only transient programs will be terminated by the Ctrl-Break interrupt.

Running the TSR Utility Program

A TSR program has two stages of execution. The first stage is when it is run by the user from the command line. The program executes its initialization code, saves its own context, attaches itself to the interrupts it requires, and terminates by using a DOS TSR function, thereby declaring itself resident.

The second stage is when the TSR program is executed as the result of one of the interrupts to which it has attached itself. In most cases, the program chains the interrupt as described above. Then, the program determines if it can execute, based on several critical system indicators. If it can execute, it saves the context of the interrupted program, restores its own context, executes its functions, restores the interrupted program's context, and returns to the interrupted program.

Memory-resident Programs 11

Terminating a TSR Utility Program

There will be occasions when you will want to terminate a TSR program, which is not a simple procedure. Remember, DOS does not know about the program because to DOS, the program terminated when it became resident; therefore, to terminate a TSR program, you must do what DOS would have done if the program had been transient.

Termination of a TSR program involves the following steps:

1. **Instruct the program to terminate itself.** You might use a second hot key, or you might use the communications interrupt vector that points to the program's signature and tells the program that it is already resident. This approach is used in the TSR driver program in Chapter 12. In this approach, the user, knowing that the program is resident, runs it a second time, giving it a command line parameter instructing it to terminate. The program searches for its signature by scanning the interrupt vectors, as previously described. When the program has found its signature, it has also found its interrupt vector. Through the interrupt vector, it sends a termination command to the resident copy of itself, which tells the resident version of the program to take the next several steps to terminate itself.

2. **Restore the interrupt vectors to their prior contents.** You may or may not be able to perform this task. If another TSR program was loaded after yours and it chained interrupts, you will effectively disable it if you replace the old vectors. Also, the other TSR, if it is terminated later, will replace the vectors with pointers into your program. These vectors could point into never-never land because your program is about to give its space back to DOS. Before you can restore interrupt vectors, you must determine if your program still owns them. To determine if you still own the interrupts, you must compare the vectors to the addresses of your ISRs. If any vector has changed, you do not own it; therefore, you cannot terminate the program—you must merely suspend it.

11 Memory-resident Programs

To further complicate matters, the termination of your program with another TSR above it will result in fragmented memory in the TPA. DOS will reallocate such fragments if programs request memory allocation, but DOS will not use this space to load another program. Remember, DOS—the single-task operating system—does not understand the concept of fragmented programs because it does not understand multiple programs.

3. **Close all files opened by the TSR program.** When a transient program terminates, DOS automatically closes all files by scanning the program's file handle array in the PSP and closing any entries still in use. Remember, these entries are offsets to an array DOS maintains. When a TSR program terminates to stay resident, DOS does not close the TSR's open files; therefore, your TSR termination routine must do it. If you do not close the files, the DOS file table entry is not released, and is not available for subsequent use by other programs. Successive loading and termination of a TSR program that does not close its files will exhaust the DOS file table and crash the system.

   Entries in the PSP file handle array represent files at the handle level. These entries are equivalent to the low-level unbuffered input/output functions in C. The C language functions that perform buffered stream input/output maintain their own internal buffers and pointers and might require flushing prior to closing. Flushing is a C library operation rather than a DOS operation. You will want to close all such files by calling the standard **fclose** function. Files that the TSR opened with the **open** and **creat** functions can be closed with the **close** function.

4. **Return the program's memory to the DOS memory allocation pool.** You can use the DOS 0x49 function for this process. There are at least two blocks allocated. One is the program's environment block; its address is in the PSP at offset 0x2c. The other block is the PSP itself. If the program has other blocks allocated, they too must be returned to DOS. Chapter 12 demonstrates a technique for scanning the DOS Memory Control Block chain to find and deallocate all blocks assigned to a program.

Memory-resident Programs 11

Suspending and Resuming a TSR Utility Program

When you suspend a TSR program, you do not remove it from memory; you simply tell it to stop interrupting. A flag is set that tells the keyboard ISR to ignore the hot key. A resume command will clear the flag. You can use the communications interrupt vector to tell the program to suspend or resume itself.

The TSR driver program in Chapter 12 uses these techniques to terminate, suspend, and resume a TSR program.

SUMMARY

This chapter describes the operating environment of the Terminate-and-Stay-Resident utility program. Chapter 12 will step you through the TSR program process with two example programs. The first program is an on-line clock program that maintains a constant screen display of the current time and date. The second program is more interesting; it is a general-purpose TSR driver program. You link your Turbo C program with the driver, follow a few conventions for initializing the environment, and your Turbo C program becomes a TSR utility program. The assumptions are that the utility program will interrupt the system when the user presses a hot key; that it will open, close, read, and write disk files; that it uses ROM-BIOS functions for keyboard input and direct video memory accesses to manage its screen displays; and that it never exits to DOS.

CHAPTER 12

BUILDING TURBO C MEMORY-RESIDENT PROGRAMS

12 Building Turbo C Memory-resident Programs

This chapter demonstrates how the TSR concepts from Chapter 11 are put into practice in a Turbo C program. The functions in this chapter provide a driver program that you link with your Turbo C program to turn it into a TSR utility. Few limitations exist on the nature of the applications utility program. The primary one is that it must not use any C functions that call the DOS interrupt 0x21 with functions numbered from 0 to 12, which means that all keyboard and screen input/output must be managed by BIOS calls or direct video memory reads and writes. The examples use the window functions from earlier chapters, and these functions obey the conventions just stated. Additionally, the TSR program must be compiled with either the tiny or small memory model of Turbo C.

Chapter 10 demonstrated the window menu functions by integrating all the prior examples into one executable program controlled by a window menu. This chapter uses the same integrated example program but turns it into a TSR utility program.

The integrated example program uses the DOS file functions and, therefore, all the DOS protection measures described in Chapter 11. Because of the complexity of that problem and to ease your introduction to TSR programming, the first example developed here does not require these extreme measures.

A TSR EXAMPLE: THE ON-LINE CLOCK

Listing 12.1 is **clock.c**, a simple TSR utility that provides a constant date and time display in the upper right corner of the screen. **Clock.c** makes no DOS calls after it is resident, so it does not need to protect against DOS reentrancy.

12 Building Turbo C Memory-resident Programs

Making the Program Resident

The main function of **clock.c** prepares for and declares residency. First, it saves its stack pointer, which will allow it to reestablish its own stack when it runs as a TSR program. Next, **clock.c** uses **getvect** to read the current value of the timer (0x1c) interrupt vector, after which **clock.c** uses **setvect** to establish the function named **newtimer** as the timer ISR. The TSR stack pointer is established as a function of the TSR's declared size, and the address of video RAM is determined on the basis of the value returned by the **vmode** function. DOS functions are used to retrieve the date and time.

The Divide-by-Zero Interrupt Vector

Another consideration for Turbo C TSRs involves the **divide-by-zero interrupt vector**. When a Turbo C program is started, it begins execution within its startup code. The startup code establishes initial stack and heap values and calls your program's main function. Startup code resides in the files named **c0t.obj** for tiny model programs and **c0s.obj** for small model programs. These files are distributed with Turbo C. The startup code contains a divide-by-zero ISR, which is attached to the divide-by-zero interrupt vector before the **main** function is called. When the **main** function returns, the divide-by-zero vector is restored to its previous address. A return from a **main** function in a normal, transient program signifies that the program has completed and is ready to terminate. But TSR programs do not terminate by returning from the **main** function. They use one of the DOS TSR functions, and the divide-by-zero vector is never restored. The implication is that a divide-by-zero error in another program will be processed by the ISR in the TSR's startup code. The TSR does not want this to happen, and neither does the other program; therefore, the TSR must take steps to restore the vector before terminating and becoming resident.

12 Building Turbo C Memory-resident Programs

Borland distributes the source code for the Turbo C startup code. It is in two source files named **c0.asm** and **rules.asi**. You will need to modify the **c0.asm** file and assemble it twice—once for the tiny and once for the small memory models. The location where **c0.asm** saves the vector is named **ZeroDivVector**. As distributed, this variable is local to the **c0.asm** program module. So that your TSR C program can restore the divide-by-zero interrupt vector to the value saved in this variable, you must change **ZeroDivVector** to a public symbol. Turbo C adds an underscore character to the beginning of external variable names, so you must change each occurrence of the name to **_ZeroDivVector**. Then you must replace the statement in **c0.asm** where **ZeroDivVector** is declared with this statement:

```
PubSym@ ZeroDivVector <dd 0>, __CDECL__
```

Assemble the file twice with the following commands:

```
C>masm c0,c0t /ML /D__TINY__;
C>masm c0,c0s /ML /D__SMALL__;
```

These commands will create two files named **c0t.obj** and **c0s.obj**. Replace the distributed Turbo C files with these new files.

Note in **clock.c** the declaration of the **ZeroDivVector** interrupt function pointer. This external pointer is the one you just made public in the startup code. In the **main** function, before declaring itself resident, **clock.c** uses the **setvect** function to restore the divide-by-zero interrupt vector to its original value. **Clock.c** then terminates and declares itself resident.

Building Turbo C Memory-resident Programs 12

If you do not have an assembler program and cannot reassemble the startup code, you can allow your TSR to handle the divide-by-zero error the first time it occurs. When the error occurs in another program, the Turbo C startup code ISR will display an error message and terminate the program, which is exactly what the DOS divide-by-zero interrupt handler does. Since DOS is now terminating a program, it restores the divide-by-zero interrupt vector to its own ISR address, and your TSR no longer gets into the act. This approach is unclean, but it will work. Of course, you must remove the references to **ZeroDivVector** in **clock.c** and **resident.c** described later.

Executing the Timer ISR

At every tick of the clock, which occurs 18.2 times each second, the **newtimer** ISR function is called. **Newtimer** is declared as a Turbo C interrupt function. This declaration means that when the function is called, the registers are saved on the stack and the data segment register is pointed to the data segment of the program in which the ISR is linked. The interrupt declaration also guarantees that when the function returns, the registers are popped off the stack, and the IRET interrupt return machine instruction is executed. IRET is the usual way to exit from an ISR. It pops the program counter, the code segment register, and the flags register, accounting for the pushes that occur with an interrupt.

Chaining to the Old Timer

When **newtimer** is executed, it first calls the ISR that is pointed to by the **oldtimer** function pointer. This action chains the interrupt to its earlier vector and assures that other programs using the timer (for example, DOS) will be advised of the tick. **Newtimer** tests the **running** flag, which is a flag that **newtimer** will set to tell itself it is running so it will not be reentered.

12 Building Turbo C Memory-resident Programs

Saving and Switching the Stack Context

Newtimer now saves the stack segment and pointer registers. These values are those belonging to the interrupted process. The stack register values that **clock.c** saved when it was executed are written into the registers so that **clock.c** can use its own stack and be free from violating the stack depth of the program it interrupted.

Computing the Time

Newtimer now counts the ticks. If 18 ticks (19 every fifth time to account for the 18.2 ticks/second) have occurred, a new clock value is computed for the screen display.

The date and time are written into the upper left corner of the screen; the interrupted program's stack registers are restored; and **newtimer** returns.

Note that **newtimer** will not roll the date over at midnight, nor will it adjust its display if you use the DOS date or time commands to change the clock value. This program merely serves to illustrate the workings of the simplest TSR program. If you don't work past midnight, you can use it to keep a date and time reminder on the screen. It refreshes the screen with every tick, so screen scrolling by other programs will not prevent its operation. As an experiment, you might try adding an alarm clock function to **clock.c**. Include the time for the alarm to sound as a command line parameter when **clock.exe** is first executed. Then, each time the clock value changes, compare it to your programmed alarm time. When the times are equal, sound the audible alarm (avoiding DOS calls, of course). Later, when you know how to use the TSR's communications interrupt vector, you can modify **clock.c** to set and change the alarm from the command line after the clock TSR is resident. You can add comments to the alarm with the window functions and the window editor. Such meanderings of the imagination are how world-famous desktop accessory programs are born.

Building Turbo C Memory-resident Programs 12

Clock.c uses the timer interrupt. If you load it after Sidekick, the clock will stop running while Sidekick is popped up. Because the newtimer ISR simply counts the seconds rather than reading the DOS time, this suspension by Sidekick will cause the clock readout to be incorrect. Sidekick steals the timer interrupt vector back from any TSR program that is loaded behind Sidekick and causes this condition. Beware of Sidekick when you are loading your TSRs.

To run the clock TSR, enter the following command:

```
C>clock
```

(Listing 12.1 on next page)

12 Building Turbo C Memory-resident Programs

Listing 12.1: clock.c

```c
/* ---------- clock.c ------------ */
#include <dos.h>

void interrupt (*oldtimer)();
void interrupt newtimer();
extern void interrupt (*ZeroDivVector)();
#define sizeprogram 375
unsigned intsp, intss;
unsigned myss, stack;
static union REGS rg;
struct date dat;
struct time tim;
unsigned vseg;
int running = 0;
char bf[20];
unsigned v;
char tmsk [] = " %2d-%02d-%02d %02d:%02d:%02d ";
int ticker = 0;
static struct SREGS seg;

main()
{
    segread(&seg);
    /* ------ save stack of resident program -------- */
    myss = _SS;
    /* --------- prepare timer interrupt vectors -------- */
    oldtimer = getvect(0x1c);
    setvect(0x1c, newtimer);
    stack = (sizeprogram - (seg.ds - seg.cs)) * 16 - 300;
    vseg = vmode() == 7 ? 0xb000 : 0xb800;
    /* ---- get the current date and time ------ */
    gettime(&tim);
    getdate(&dat);
    /* ---- restore zero divide interrupt vector --- */
    setvect(0, ZeroDivVector);
    /* ----- terminate and stay resident ------- */
    rg.x.ax = 0x3100;
    rg.x.dx = sizeprogram;
    intdos(&rg, &rg);
}
```

continued...

...from previous page

```c
/* ----- timer isr ------- */
void interrupt newtimer()
{
    (*oldtimer)();
    if (running == 0)    {
        running = 1;
        disable();         /* set resident stack */
        intsp = _SP;
        intss = _SS;
        _SP = stack;
        _SS = myss;
        enable();
        if (ticker == 0)    {   /*count ticks (18.2/second)*/
            ticker = (((tim.ti_sec % 5) == 0) ? 19 : 18);
            tim.ti_sec++;
            if (tim.ti_sec == 60)    {
                tim.ti_sec = 0;
                tim.ti_min++;
                if (tim.ti_min == 60)    {
                    tim.ti_min = 0;
                    tim.ti_hour++;
                    if (tim.ti_hour == 24)
                        tim.ti_hour = 0;
                }
            }
            /* ----- build the date/time display ------- */
            sprintf(bf,tmsk,dat.da_day,dat.da_mon,dat.da_year
                % 100,tim.ti_hour, tim.ti_min, tim.ti_sec);
        }
        --ticker;
        /* ----- display the date and time -------- */
        for (v = 0; v < 19; v++)
            vpoke(vseg, (60 + v) * 2, 0x7000 + bf[v]);
        disable();        /* reset the interrupted stack */
        _SP = intsp;
        _SS = intss;
        enable();
        running = 0;
    }
}
```

12 Building Turbo C Memory-resident Programs

Listing 12.2 is **clock.prj**, the project make file that the Turbo C environment uses to build **clock.exe**.

Listing 12.2: clock.prj

```
clock
ibmpc.obj
```

THE TSR DRIVER PROGRAMS

To expand the ability of a TSR program to use DOS functions while it is popped up, this chapter includes two supporting C source files that, once adapted to and linked with your program, make a TSR out of an otherwise standard Turbo C program. One of the C source files contains the **main** function for the program and is the place where your program-specific parameters and code will be placed. The other file is a general-purpose TSR driver program that manages the attachment to interrupt vectors, the interrupts themselves, the arbitration of DOS and BIOS contentions, the TSR calls, the determination if the program is already resident, the suspension and resumption of the TSR program, and the removal of the TSR from memory.

The third program module in the configuration is your utility program, which must abide by a few TSR rules in order to operate in this environment. These rules are as follows:

- The program must be built with the tiny or small memory model.

- The program must not use the DOS functions 0 to 12.

- If the program changes the current working disk directory, it must restore the original directory before returning to the interrupted program.

- The program should avoid the use of floating point operations.

- The program must never terminate or exit to DOS.

Building Turbo C Memory-resident Programs 12

You might wonder why you should avoid floating point math. The Turbo C floating point package uses a number of interrupt vectors, which are attached during a call to the package from Turbo C's startup code. The vectors are not restored until after a C program exits and returns to the startup code. Unlike the divide-by-zero vector, the save area for these vectors—which include the nonmaskable interrupt vector 2—are not maintained in the startup code; therefore, they are not accessible to the TSR program in the same manner that the divide-by-zero save area was made accessible. If a TSR program terminates and removes itself, these vectors are never restored.

This chapter uses **exec.c** from Chapter 10 and all the window example programs as the example utility program that will become a TSR.

Operation of the Three Program Modules

The three program modules for a TSR are **popup.c**, **resident.c**, and your utility Turbo C program. **Popup.c** (Listing 12.3) and **resident.c** (Listing 12.4) constitute the TSR driver program. **Popup.c** is the module that you modify to the requirements of your TSR, and **resident.c** is the module that remains fixed for all TSRs. The discussion that follows will jump between the functions in **popup.c** and **resident.c,** since they are closely related in supporting your TSR utility program.

Popup.c is the part of the driver program that you modify to suit your program's requirements. Besides any custom code that you will need, **popup.c** has several variables that you must initialize with values that describe your program.

Size of the TSR

The unsigned variable named **sizeprogram** is where you specify the size of your program in paragraphs. (A paragraph is 16 bytes.) You read in Chapter 11 how you determine what this value should be. Until your program is operational, you should assign a large number to **sizeprogram.** Tiny model programs can be no bigger than 64K (4096 paragraphs); small model programs can be no bigger than 128K (8192 paragraphs).

12 Building Turbo C Memory-resident Programs

Hot Key Assignment

Your hot key value is assigned by the combination of the unsigned variables, **scancode** and **keymask**. When a key is pressed, the 09 ISR reads the keyboard input port, which returns a scan code. Each key on the keyboard has a scan code. Figure 12.1 shows these scan codes. You want to assign a key combination that is unlikely to interfere with other programs' keys. It is good policy to avoid function keys, Alt key combinations, or Ctrl key combinations because many programs use them. The best choice is an unlikely combination such as Alt-period.

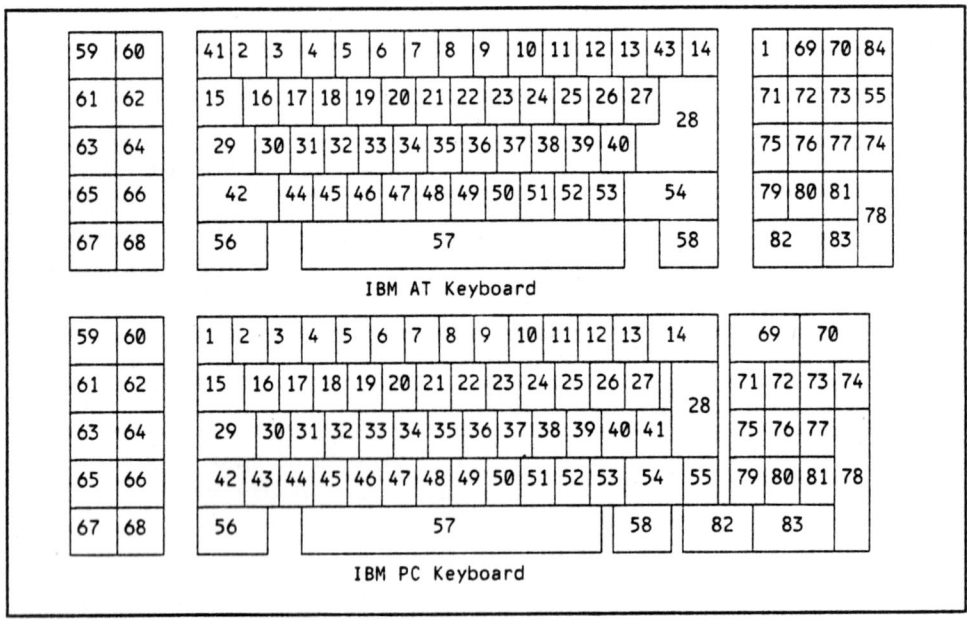

Figure 12.1 The Keyboard Scan Codes

Building Turbo C Memory-resident Programs 12

Reading a combination of keys is made easy by a status mask at address 0:417 that contains bits for the Ctrl, Alt, Shift, Ins, Caps Lock, and Scroll Lock keys. The mask tells which of these toggle/shift keys are presently being pressed. Figure 12.2 shows the position of these key values in the mask. If the bit corresponding to the key is set to one, the key is being pressed. By sensing the specified scan code and determining that the specified toggle/shift key is depressed, the TSR keyboard ISR can determine that the hot key combination has been pressed. To specify these values, you initialize the **scancode** and **keymask** variables in **popup.c**. As shown in the listing, **scancode** is 52, the code for the period key, and **keymask** is 8, the code for the Alt key. The hot key is, therefore, Alt-Period.

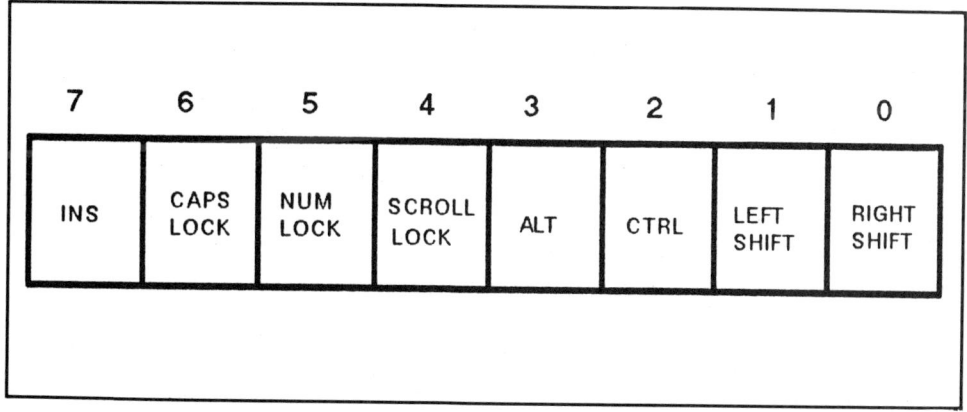

Figure 12.2 The Keyboard Status Mask

The TSR Signature

The **popup.c** program also provides the TSR's signature, which is used to check if the TSR is already resident when the user runs it from the DOS command line. The character array named **signature** is a null-terminated string that serves this purpose.

12 Building Turbo C Memory-resident Programs

When first run, **popup.c** calls the function named **resident**. **Resident** is a function in **resident.c**, and its purposes are to determine if the program is already resident and, if not, to appropriate and assign a communications interrupt vector. **Resident** assigns this vector by scanning the user interrupt vectors from 0x60 to 0x67. If any of these vectors contains a value, the segment half of that value is combined with the program signature's offset. This offset is the signature's character pointer, which is an offset from the data segment register of the program. The segment half of the vector is summed with the difference between the program's code and segment registers.

Remember that the segment register taken from the interrupt vector is suspected to be the code segment of the original TSR program when it was first executed. The signature would be in the TSR's data space as well as in the data space of the copy of the TSR that is now testing to see if it can become resident. But the segment address needed is the data segment address of the TSR, which is not stored in the interrupt vector. The data segment of the TSR must be computed.

The program looking at the interrupt vector is a second copy of the TSR (assuming the TSR is already resident), so the difference between its code and data segments will be the same as that of the resident copy of the TSR. With this convoluted algorithm, you have the segments and offsets of the signature in the suspected TSR and the would-be TSR. These two signatures are compared, and if they are equal, the TSR is already resident, and the **resident** function returns the found interrupt vector to the **main** function of **popup.c**. If the signatures are not equal, the scan continues until all user vectors have been examined. If it is determined that the TSR is not yet resident, then the first available vector is appropriated and attached to the communications ISR of the TSR. A zero value is returned to the **main** function of the TSR to tell it that it can become resident.

Building Turbo C Memory-resident Programs 12

The Communications Interrupt Vector

If the **main** function finds that a TSR version of itself is resident, it next tests for command line parameters. The technique used allows subsequent executions of the same TSR to pass parameters to the resident copy of the TSR. Remember that there are two copies of the TSR in memory: a resident copy and a transient copy just executed. The transient copy can communicate with the resident copy by way of the communications interrupt vector returned when the TSR reported that it was already resident. Three parameters are used in the typical TSR, but you might add others. The standard three allow the user to terminate, suspend, and resume the resident TSR. If one of these commands is in the command tail, as indicated by the **argc**, **argv** convention, then a software interrupt is generated with the **ax** register set to a value indicating the desired action. This interrupt is generated in the **main** function of the TSR's transient copy.

Look further down the listing of **popup.c**. The interrupt function named **ifunc** is the TSR's communications ISR. When the **main** function of the transient copy issues the interrupt, the communications ISR in the resident copy is called. The ISR tests the value of **ax** upon entry and performs the appropriate routines. At the very least, it should call the **terminate**, **restart**, or **wait** functions in **resident.c**. You will insert other logic here to manage other modifications to the TSR's runtime environment.

The **wait** and **restart** functions in **resident.c** simply set and clear a flag that tells the keyboard ISR to ignore the hot key while the TSR is suspended.

The **terminate** function in **resident.c** must determine if the TSR can terminate and, if so, must presume to undertake what DOS does when a program terminates. This process will be discussed after you understand how the TSR becomes resident.

12 Building Turbo C Memory-resident Programs

Preparing for Residency

If the function named **resident** tells the **main** function in **popup.c** that the TSR is not yet in memory, then **popup.c** must prepare itself to become resident. Your TSR will want to open files and do any other housekeeping for when it is popped up. The **popup.c** program used for the examples in this chapter calls **load_help** to set up the help functions from Chapter 7, sets up the DOS path specification for the **notepad** function from Chapter 9, and prints a sign-on message. Then it calls **resinit**, the function in **resident.c** that does everything else needed to get the TSR resident.

First, **resinit** saves the stack segment register for stack context switching when the TSR is popped up. Next, the address of the DOS Busy flag is read by using DOS function 0x34. The **getdta** function delivers the address of the Disk Transfer Area for the TSR. This address is also used in later context switching. The address of the PID is retrieved and saved. This technique is explained in Chapter 11. The interrupt vectors for the timer, keyboard, disk, and **DOSOK** are read and saved for interrupt chaining, and the TSR's ISRs are attached to those interrupts. The TSR's stack pointer is computed to be 300 bytes less than the TSR's size, and the divide-by-zero vector is restored to what it was before Turbo C's startup code appropriated it. Then, the DOS TSR function is used to terminate the program, leaving it resident.

The Disk ISR

As the computer runs programs and the programs use DOS, DOS uses the ROM-BIOS disk interrupt vector (0x13) to read and write sectors of disk data. Remember in Chapter 11 that you were cautioned never to interrupt a disk operation. The Disk ISR in **resident.c** is given the name **newdisk**, and it protects the disk operations from interruption by your TSR. A flag is set for vector 0x13 upon entry to the chained ISR and cleared when the ISR returns. If that flag is set when the TSR is otherwise ready to pop up, the TSR will delay its execution until the flag is cleared.

Building Turbo C Memory-resident Programs 12

Note the tricky code in **newdisk**. A Turbo C interrupt function pushes all registers on the stack, sets the **ds** register to the data segment of the program containing the interrupt function, and then the code of the interrupt function is begun. When the function returns, the registers are popped, and the IRET machine instruction is executed. This instruction pops the program counter, code segment, and flags registers, effecting a return to the interrupted program with all registers as they were when the interrupt occurred.

Everything works until you have an ISR that wants to return a condition in the carry flag. The IRET machine instruction restores the flags, including the carry flag, to their condition when the interrupt was called. Several DOS and BIOS software interrupts use the carry flag to indicate a condition to the caller of the interrupt. The ROM-BIOS 0x13 interrupt service uses the carry flag this way; therefore, the code in the Disk ISR does some gyrations to preserve the carry flag and see that it gets returned to the caller of the interrupt. When the **olddisk** interrupt chain returns, there are values in the **ax** register and the carry flag that must be returned to the caller. The **ax** register value is taken from the Turbo C **_AX** pseudo variable and placed in the **ax** integer variable that is one of the parameters to the interrupt function. Turbo C uses this vehicle to allow you to modify the contents of the registers that will be popped when the function returns. There is no pseudo-variable for the flags register, and the program wants to avoid in-line assembly code, so the following hacker's trick is used. The **newcrit** function just below the **newdisk** function can be called, and it will write the flags register that was pushed on the stack when it was called into the external variable named **cflag**. When **newcrit** returns, **cflag** is written into the stack where the old flags value was saved. When the function returns, the flags resulting from the **olddisk** chained call will be popped into the flags register.

These measures are extreme, to say the least. They are based on understandings of how Turbo C uses registers and the workings of the interrupt function's entries and returns. The measures are certainly not portable to any other compiler much less to another computer. They might not even be portable to a future version of Turbo C if Borland decides to change how things are done. Assembly language programmers might chide you for using these techniques when a clean assembly language program could manage the job nicely. Such criticism is valid, but this programming trick is an exercise in pushing Turbo C to the limits of its performance. This author is pleased with the level of support to the TSR problem that the Turbo C solution provides.

12 Building Turbo C Memory-resident Programs

The Critical Error ISR

The interrupt function named **newcrit** is the attached Critical Error ISR. It is not attached when the TSR declares itself resident, but only temporarily when the TSR is popped up. Its purpose is to avoid the confusion of an abort by a critical error while the TSR has contexts switched from where DOS had them. The Critical Error ISR returns a zero value in the **ax** register to DOS. This value tells DOS to ignore the error.

The Keyboard ISR

The interrupt function named **newkb** is the keyboard ISR for the TSR. It reads the keyboard data port and tests for the specified scan code that matches the TSR's hot key. If the scan code matches, the keyboard status byte is retrieved and matched against the **keymask** variable. If that code matches and the TSR is not in a suspended condition, the hot key has been activated. The function resets the keyboard hardware so that it will not interrupt again and then tests to see if the TSR is currently popped up. If not, a flag is set that says the hot key was pressed, and the function returns.

If the scan code or status mask does not match the hot key, the function chains to the old keyboard vector and returns.

The Timer ISR

Each tick of the timer causes an execution of the timer ISR **newtimer** in resident.c. Before it does anything else, it chains to the earlier address of the timer interrupt vector. Then, it tests to see if the hot key was pressed. If so, it tests the DOS Busy flag. If DOS is not busy, **newtimer** tests to see if a disk operation is in process. If not, it resets the timer interrupt, turns off the flag that says the hot key was pressed, and calls the **dores** function to get the TSR utility running.

Building Turbo C Memory-resident Programs 12

The DOSOK ISR

The **DOSOK** interrupt is serviced by the ISR named **new28** in **resident.c**. It chains to any earlier **DOSOK** ISR and tests the hot key flag. If the hot key has been set, it tests to make sure that DOS is busy. If so, it resets the hot key flag and calls **dores**.

Executing the TSR Utility

The **dores** function is called when the TSR has determined that it is safe to execute the TSR. **Dores** first sets a flag that says it is running. This flag prevents the keyboard ISR from allowing another press of the hot key to start the TSR in a reentrant call. Then, the interrupted program's stack registers are saved, and the stack is pointed to the TSR's local stack.

The critical error interrupt vector is saved and the TSR's critical error ISR is attached to the vector. The current Ctrl-Break setting is saved, and Ctrl-Break interrupts are disabled.

The interrupted program's DTA address is saved, and the DTA is set to that of the TSR. The same process is done for the PID. Then, the TSR utility function named **popup** in **popup.c** is called. The **popup** function saves the current cursor, calls the utility program, restores the cursor and returns. In the listing of **popup.c**, the function named **exec** is called. You would substitute the name of your program's entry function.

When the **popup** function returns, the PID, DTA, critical error interrupt vector, Ctrl-Break setting, and interrupted program's stack are restored to the values they contained before the TSR took over, and the TSR returns to the interrupted program.

Terminating the TSR

When the user terminates the TSR by executing it a second time with the "quit" command line parameter, the second copy of the TSR calls the resident copy through the communications interrupt vector. The **terminate** function in **resident.c** first tests to see if the TSR can be terminated by testing to see if any of the interrupt vectors have changed. If so, the TSR is suspended. If not, the TSR can be terminated.

12 Building Turbo C Memory-resident Programs

Termination of the program involves three procedures. First, all files must be closed. When DOS terminates a program, it closes all open files by checking all 20 entries in the PSP's file handle array. This procedure closes files at the handle level and does not account for stream files that are open and might need to be flushed. So that these files might be closed, the **terminate** function calls a function named **closefiles** in **popup.c** to have it close all open files.

The second procedure is to restore all interrupt vectors to their original values before the TSR attached itself to them.

The final step is to de-allocate all memory blocks that have been allocated to the TSR. Memory is allocated to a program from two places — from DOS and from the program through a DOS function. Those two kinds of memory blocks are allocated in the same way and also can be de-allocated in the same way.

Memory Blocks and Memory Control Blocks

A DOS-allocated block of memory consists of a 16-byte **Memory Control Block (MCB)** followed by the memory block that is allocated. The MCB contains the following fields:

- A one-byte token that identifies the MCB. All but the last MCB in the chain will have the value 0x4d in this token. The last MCB will have the token value 0x5a.

- The two-byte PID of the process that owns the memory. If a memory block is free, this field has a zero value.

- The two-byte size of the block in paragraphs. This size does not include the MCB. The MCB is followed immediately by the memory block that it represents. MCB-memory blocks sets are contiguous in memory. The segment address of the next MCB can be computed from the address and contents of the current MCB. The MCB's address plus the size of the memory block plus one will equal the address of the next MCB in the chain. If you have the address of the first memory block allocated by DOS, you can trace the chain.

Building Turbo C Memory-resident Programs 12

DOS has a function (undocumented, of course) that can be used to derive the address of the first MCB in its chain. This function, number 0x52, returns a segment address in the **es** register and an offset in the **bx** register. The effective address of this segment:offset pair minus two is the address of a word that is the segment address of the first MCB in the DOS memory allocation chain.

To delete the memory owned by the TSR program, the DOS memory allocation chain is traced. Every block that contains the TSR's PID in the MCB is deleted by a call to DOS function 0x49. When this procedure is completed, the TSR has been terminated and removed from memory.

SOURCE LISTINGS: popup.c, resident.c

Following are Listings 12.3 and 12.4, the two source files that constitute the TSR driver program. These files, when compiled and linked with the utility program, will build a TSR program.

(Listing 12.3 on next page)

12 Building Turbo C Memory-resident Programs

Listing 12.3: popup.c

```c
/* ---------- popup.c ---------- */

#include <dos.h>
#include <stdio.h>
#include <string.h>
#include <dir.h>
#include "twindow.h"

static union REGS rg;

unsigned sizeprogram = 48000/16;
unsigned scancode = 52;
unsigned keymask = 8;
char signature [] = "POPUP";

char notefile[64];

/* -------- local prototypes ---------- */
int resident(char *, void interrupt (*)());
void resinit(void);
void terminate(void);
void restart(void);
void wait(void);
void resident_psp(void);
void interrupted_psp(void);
void exec(void);

main(argc, argv)
char *argv[];
{
    void interrupt ifunc();
    int ivec;

    if ((ivec = resident(signature, ifunc)) != 0)    {
        /* ----- TSR is resident ------- */
        if (argc > 1)    {
            /* ---- there is a command line parameter --- */
            rg.x.ax = 0;
            if (strcmp(argv[1], "quit") == 0)
                rg.x.ax = 1;
```
continued...

...from previous page

```
            else if (strcmp(argv[1], "restart") == 0)
                rg.x.ax = 2;
            else if (strcmp(argv[1], "wait") == 0)
                rg.x.ax = 3;
            if (rg.x.ax)      {
                /* -- call the communications interrupt -- */
                int86(ivec, &rg, &rg);
                return;
            }
        }
        printf("\nPopup is already resident");
    }
    else    {
        /* ------ initial load of TSR program ------ */
        load_help("tcprogs.hlp");
        getcwd(notefile, 64);
        if (*(notefile+strlen(notefile)-1) != '\\')
            strcat(notefile, "\\");
        strcat(notefile, "note.pad");
        printf("\nResident popup is loaded");
        /* ---- T&SR --------- */
        resinit();
    }
}

/* -------- TSR communications ISR ---------- */
void interrupt ifunc(bp,di,si,ds,es,dx,cx,bx,ax)
{
    if (ax == 1)                /* "quit" */
        terminate();
    else if (ax == 2)           /* "restart" */
        restart();
    else if (ax == 3)           /* "wait" */
        wait();
}
```

continued...

12 Building Turbo C Memory-resident Programs

...from previous page

```
/* -------- close files when terminating ---------- */
closefiles()
{
    extern FILE *helpfp;

    resident_psp();     /* switch to TSR PID */
    if (helpfp)
        fclose(helpfp); /* close the help file */
    interrupted_psp();  /* switch to int'd PID */
}

/* -------- the popup TSR utility function --------- */
popup()
{
    int x, y;

    curr_cursor(&x, &y);
    exec();                    /* call the TSR C program here */
    cursor(x, y);
}
```

Listing 12.4: resident.c

```c
/* -------- resident.c --------- */

#include <dos.h>
#include <stdio.h>

static union REGS rg;
static struct SREGS seg;
static unsigned mcbseg;
static unsigned dosseg;
static unsigned dosbusy;
static unsigned enddos;
char far *intdta;
static unsigned intsp;
static unsigned intss;
static char far *mydta;
static unsigned myss;
static unsigned stack;
static unsigned ctrl_break;
static unsigned mypsp;
static unsigned intpsp;
static unsigned pids[2];
static int pidctr = 0;
static int pp;
static void interrupt (*oldtimer)();
static void interrupt (*old28)();
static void interrupt (*oldkb)();
static void interrupt (*olddisk)();
static void interrupt (*oldcrit)();
extern void interrupt (*ZeroDivVector)();
void interrupt newtimer();
void interrupt new28();
void interrupt newkb();
void interrupt newdisk();
void interrupt newcrit();
extern unsigned sizeprogram;
extern unsigned scancode;
extern unsigned keymask;
static int resoff = 0;
static int running = 0;
static int popflg = 0;
```

continued...

12 Building Turbo C Memory-resident Programs

...from previous page

```
static int diskflag = 0;
static int kbval;
static int cflag;

void dores(), pidaddr();

/* -------- establish & declare residency --------- */
void resinit()
{
    segread(&seg);
    myss = seg.ss;
    /* ------ get address of DOS busy flag ---- */
    rg.h.ah = 0x34;
    intdos(&rg, &rg);
    dosseg = _ES;
    dosbusy = rg.x.bx;
    /* ----- get address of resident program's dta ----- */
    mydta = getdta();
    /* -------- get addresses of PID in DOS ------- */
    pidaddr();
    /* ----- get original interrupt vectors ----- */
    oldtimer = getvect(0x1c);
    old28 = getvect(0x28);
    oldkb = getvect(9);
    olddisk = getvect(0x13);
    /* ----- attach vectors to resident program ----- */
    setvect(0x1c, newtimer);
    setvect(9, newkb);
    setvect(0x28, new28);
    setvect(0x13, newdisk);
    /* ------ compute stack pointer ------- */
    stack = (sizeprogram - (seg.ds - seg.cs)) * 16 - 300;
    /* ---- restore zero divide interrupt vector --- */
    setvect(0, ZeroDivVector);
    /* ----- terminate and stay resident ------- */
    rg.x.ax = 0x3100;
    rg.x.dx = sizeprogram;
    intdos(&rg, &rg);
}
```

continued...

...from previous page

```c
/* ------ BIOS disk functions ISR ------- */
void interrupt newdisk(bp,di,si,ds,es,dx,cx,bx,ax,ip,cs,flgs)
{
    diskflag++;
    (*olddisk)();
    ax = _AX;        /* for the register returns */
    cx = _CX;
    dx = _DX;
    newcrit();       /* to get current flags register */
    flgs = cflag;
    --diskflag;
}

/* -------- critical error ISR ---------- */
void interrupt newcrit(bp,di,si,ds,es,dx,cx,bx,ax,ip,cs,flgs)
{
    ax = 0;
    cflag = flgs;    /* for newdisk */
}

/* ----- keyboard ISR ------ */
void interrupt newkb()
{
    if (inportb(0x60) == scancode)  {
        kbval = peekb(0, 0x417);
        if (!resoff && ((kbval & keymask) ^ keymask) == 0)  {
            /* --- reset the keyboard ---- */
            kbval = inportb(0x61);
            outportb(0x61, kbval | 0x80);
            outportb(0x61, kbval);
            outportb(0x20, 0x20);
            /* ---- set hotkey indicator ---- */
            if (!running)
                popflg = 1;
            return;
        }
    }
    (*oldkb)();
}
```

continued...

12 Building Turbo C Memory-resident Programs

...from previous page

```
/* ----- timer ISR ------- */
void interrupt newtimer()
{
    (*oldtimer)();
    if (popflg && peekb(dosseg, dosbusy) == 0)
        if (diskflag == 0) {
            outportb(0x20, 0x20);
            popflg = 0;
            dores();
        }
}

/* ----- DOSOK ISR -------- */
void interrupt new28()
{
    (*old28)();
    if (popflg && peekb(dosseg, dosbusy) != 0) {
        popflg = 0;
        dores();
    }
}

/* ------ switch psp context from interrupted to TSR ----- */
resident_psp()
{
    /* ------ save interrupted program's psp ----- */
    intpsp = peek(dosseg, *pids);
    /* ----- set resident program's psp ----- */
    for (pp = 0; pp < pidctr; pp++)
        poke(dosseg, pids [pp], mypsp);
}

/* ---- switch psp context from TSR to interrupted ---- */
interrupted_psp()
{
    /* ----- reset interrupted program's psp ----- */
    for (pp = 0; pp < pidctr; pp++)
        poke(dosseg, pids [pp], intpsp);
}
```

continued...

...from previous page

```c
/* ------ execute the resident program ------- */
void dores()
{
    running = 1;
    disable();
    intsp = _SP;
    intss = _SS;
    _SP = stack;
    _SS = myss;
    enable();
    oldcrit = getvect(0x24);/* redirect critical error    */
    setvect(0x24, newcrit);
    rg.x.ax = 0x3300;       /* get ctrl break setting     */
    intdos(&rg, &rg);
    ctrl_break = rg.h.dl;
    rg.x.ax = 0x3301;       /* turn off ctrl break logic  */
    rg.h.dl = 0;
    intdos(&rg, &rg);
    intdta = getdta();      /* get interrupted dta        */
    setdta(mydta);          /* set resident dta           */
    resident_psp();         /* swap psps                  */
    popup();                /* execute resident program   */
    interrupted_psp();      /* reset interrupted psp      */
    setdta(intdta);         /* reset interrupted dta      */
    setvect(0x24, oldcrit); /* reset critical error       */
    rg.x.ax = 0x3301;       /* reset ctrl break           */
    rg.h.dl = ctrl_break;
    intdos(&rg, &rg);
    disable();              /* reset interrupted stack    */
    _SP = intsp;
    _SS = intss;
    enable();
    running = 0;
}
```

continued...

12 Building Turbo C Memory-resident Programs

...from previous page

```
static int avec = 0;

/* ------- test to see if the program is already resident
      if not, attach to an available interrupt ---------- */
unsigned resident(signature, ifunc)
char *signature;
void interrupt (*ifunc)();
{
    char *sg;
    unsigned df;
    int vec;

    segread(&seg);
    df = seg.ds-seg.cs;
    for (vec = 0x60; vec < 0x68; vec++) {
        if (getvect(vec) == NULL)    {
            if (!avec)
                avec = vec;
            continue;
        }
        for (sg = signature; *sg; sg++)
            if (*sg!=peekb(peek(0,2+vec*4)+df,(unsigned)sg))
                break;
        if (!*sg)
            return vec;
    }
    if (avec)
        setvect(avec, ifunc);
    return 0;
}
```

continued...

...from previous page

```c
/* -------- find address of PID ---------- */
static void pidaddr()
{
    unsigned adr = 0;

    /* ------- get the current pid --------- */
    rg.h.ah = 0x51;
    intdos(&rg, &rg);
    mypsp = rg.x.bx;
    /* ----- find the end of the DOS segment ------- */
    rg.h.ah = 0x52;
    intdos(&rg, &rg);
    enddos = _ES;
    enddos = peek(enddos, rg.x.bx-2);
    /* ---- search for matches on the pid in dos ---- */
    while (pidctr < 2 &&
           (unsigned)((dosseg<<4) + adr) < (enddos<<4))     {
        if (peek(dosseg, adr) == mypsp) {
            rg.h.ah = 0x50;
            rg.x.bx = mypsp + 1;
            intdos(&rg, &rg);
            if (peek(dosseg, adr) == mypsp+1)
                pids[pidctr++] = adr;
            /* ---- reset the original pid ------ */
            rg.h.ah = 0x50;
            rg.x.bx = mypsp;
            intdos(&rg, &rg);
        }
        adr++;
    }
}
```

continued...

12 Building Turbo C Memory-resident Programs

...from previous page

```
/* -------- terminate function ----------- */
static resterm()
{
    closefiles();   /* close TSR files */
    /* ----- restore the interrupt vectors ----- */
    setvect(0x1c, oldtimer);
    setvect(9, oldkb);
    setvect(0x28, old28);
    setvect(0x13, olddisk);
    setvect(avec, (void interrupt (*)()) 0);
    /* ---- get the seg addr of 1st DOS MCB ---- */
    rg.h.ah = 0x52;
    intdos(&rg, &rg);
    mcbseg = _ES;
    mcbseg = peek(mcbseg, rg.x.bx-2);
    /* ---- walk thru mcb chain & release memory ----- */
    segread(&seg);
    while (peekb(mcbseg, 0) == 0x4d)     {
        if (peek(mcbseg, 1) == mypsp)    {
            rg.h.ah = 0x49;
            seg.es = mcbseg+1;
            intdosx(&rg, &rg, &seg);
        }
        mcbseg += peek(mcbseg, 3) + 1;
    }
}
/* --------- terminate the resident program --------- */
terminate()
{
    if (getvect(0x13) == (void interrupt (*)()) newdisk)
        if (getvect(9) == newkb)
            if (getvect(0x28) == new28)
                if (getvect(0x1c) == newtimer)   {
                    resterm();
                    return;
                }
    resoff = 1;  /* another TSR is above us, merely suspend */
}
```

continued...

...from previous page

```
/* ------------- restart the resident program --------- */
restart()
{
    resoff = 0;
}

/* ------- put the program on hold -------- */
wait()
{
    resoff = 1;
}
```

THE TSR APPLICATION PROGRAM

In **popup.c**, the function named **popup** is called when the resident program driver determines that the hot key has been pressed and it is safe to use DOS. The **popup** function saves the cursor location, calls a function named **exec**, restores the prior cursor position, and returns. The function named **exec** is the entry function of the TSR utility program — in this case, the example program from Chapter 10. There is little else for you to know about **exec**, since you learned all about it in earlier chapters. It works just like its **menu.exe** transient program version, but now its name is **popup.exe**, and it is a memory-resident utility TSR program. Listing 12.5 is the project make file for building **popup.exe** from within the Turbo C environment.

12 Building Turbo C Memory-resident Programs

Listing 12.5: popup.prj

```
popup (twindow.h)
exec (twindow.h, keys.h)
testmove (twindow.h, keys.h)
promote (twindow.h, keys.h)
ccolor (twindow.h, keys.h)
fasttest (twindow.h)
notepad (twindow.h)
ordent (twindow.h)
maxims (twindow.h, keys.h)
poems (twindow.h, keys.h)
editor (twindow.h, keys.h)
entry (twindow.h, keys.h)
thelp (twindow.h, keys.h)
tmenu (twindow.h, keys.h)
twindow (twindow.h, keys.h)
resident
ibmpc.obj
```

To run the resident utility program built by Turbo C with the project make file in **popup.prj**, enter the following command:

```
C>popup
```

This command will load the TSR and cause it to terminate and stay resident. Before terminating, the program displays the following message:

```
Resident popup is loaded
```

If you were to run it a second time, it would sense that it was already resident and would display the following message:

```
Popup is already resident
```

Once the TSR is resident, you can execute it with command line parameters that cause it to suspend, resume, or terminate itself. These three commands are as follows:

```
C>popup wait
C>popup restart
C>popup quit
```

TESTING A TSR PROGRAM

If you write a TSR program and try to test it as a TSR program, you will experience some inconvenience. First, you will not be able to use the Turbo C environment for interactive testing. A TSR program is installed from the command line and run with a hot key. Next, until the terminate function is working or if other programs are installed above the TSR, you must remove it by rebooting the computer. Further, because it has attached itself to interrupt vectors, its loops and aborts can hang up your system. The TSR program is not easy to test as a TSR program.

A better approach is to test the TSR program as a transient program. All the DOS interfaces to establish and operate the TSR in the memory-resident environment are managed by **popup.c** and **resident.c**. Why not bypass these operations until your program is reasonably well-tested? As you saw in the example TSR in this chapter, the utility part of the program was developed and tested apart from the TSR operations. In fact, that part was used as an example of some capabilities that are unrelated to the TSR discussion. You can test your TSR programs in the same way.

The simplest way to test the TSR program is to link it without **popup.c** or **resident.c** but with a stub program that provides a main function and any of the utility initialization code that you will put into **popup.c**. The **menu.c** program in Chapter 10 is an example of such a stub program.

Another technique is to link the utility program with **popup.c** and **resident.c** just as if you were building a TSR, but with one change. In place of the call to the **resinit** function from the main function in **popup.c**, insert calls to the **popup** and **closefile** functions in **popup.c**. The program will have the appearance, structure, and size of its TSR version, but will function as a transient program.

12 Building Turbo C Memory-resident Programs

Using either technique, you test the program by running it. Instead of becoming resident, the program behaves as if the hot key had been pressed. It executes once and terminates.

Once the program is tested, you can relink it as a TSR and test it in the memory-resident environment. Begin with the **sizeprogram** variable at a high value and reduce it gradually in the manner described in Chapter 11.

The final test is to see how your program fares in the company of other TSR programs. This test is sometimes a crap shoot. Many of the popular TSR programs will not play together, so you should select those with which you want to be compatible and run tests that involve loading them all in various sequences until you arrive at a working arrangement. Write this arrangement into the installation procedures in your user's guide.

SUMMARY

With the software in this chapter, you have completed the tool collection that allows you to write memory-resident utility programs in Turbo C for the IBM PC. Those programs can be developed and tested in the Turbo C Integrated Development Environment as normal, transient DOS programs. They can employ the window, data entry, text entry, and menu functions from the earlier chapters in this book. When they are operational, they can be integrated with the tools of this chapter to turn them into fully functioning memory-resident utility programs.

EPILOGUE

Hackers at heart will feel empathy for the work that went into this software. A hacker is a person who dissects computer systems to see how they work. The term has lately acquired a sinister connotation because of its treatment in the movies and press, but I prefer its earlier meaning and do not wish to give it up just yet. A programmer who nourishes an interest in the techniques and principles that underlie these C language functions will find a kindred body of hackers who explore and share their findings. You might be content to use these tools without question. But if you are of an inquisitive nature, they will compel you to dig further into the internals of the PC and DOS, and you will need help. Unless you work for Microsoft and have the source code for each version of DOS (and the time to read it), you must either ferret out the secrets of DOS yourself or partake of others' contributions.

I encourage you to join the Byte Information Exchange (BIX). Any recent issue of *Byte* magazine has information about how to join. There is more useful technical data in that service than in all the books, magazine articles, and reference manuals you might find. Learn and benefit from the shared work of those to whom this book is dedicated.

INDEX

A

accent, 93, 94
acline, 94
addfield, 161
add_list, 94
Algol, 10
ANSI, 11, 20
asm, 24
assembly language, 22, 49, 92, 285
attrib, 28

B

B, 10
backspace, 200, 203
back_word, 200, 203
BCPL, 10
BDS C, 11
beg_list, 94
BIX, 21, 306
blankline, 202
Borland International, 18, 41

C

c0.asm, 272
c0s.obj, 271
c0t.obj, 271
carrtn, 200, 201, 203
ccolor.c, 103, 105
chaining interrupts, 244
clear_message, 66, 94
clear_screen, 28
clear_template, 145, 146, 162, 165
clear_window, 63, 92
clock.c, 270, 272, 276
clock.prj, 278
close, 266
closefiles, 288
close_all, 64, 91
Color Graphics Adaptor, 45
color.c, 104
color.prj, 106

Combined Programming Language project, 10
command processor, 235
COMMAND.COM, 252
communications interrupt vector, 283
Compuserve, 21
CONFIG.SYS, 254
context switching, 248
context-sensitive help windows, 119
copy_block, 200, 203
CP/M, 11, 228, 250, 254
creat, 266
critical error interrupt, 263, 287
Ctrl-Break Interrupt, 264
curr, 199
curr_cursor, 29
cursor, 29

D

data entry field, 140
data entry template, 140
data entry windows, 139
data_entry, 146, 148, 163, 165, 166
data_value, 161, 163, 164
deaccent, 93, 94
delete_block, 200, 202, 203
delete_line, 200, 202
delete_window, 63, 91
delete_word, 200, 202
dget, 93, 94
Disk ROM-BIOS Interrupt, 262
Disk Transfer Area, 254, 257, 284, 287
displ, 93, 94
display-text, 200
display_text, 200, 203
display_window, 63, 91
disp_field, 161
divide-by-zero interrupt, 271
dores, 287
DOS Busy Flag, 261
DOS Busy flag, 286
DOSOK interrupt, 30, 261, 287

309

downward, 200, 203
dtitle, 92
Duncan, Ray, 5

E

editor, 21
editor.c, 180
endstroke, 163, 164
Enhanced Graphics Adaptor, 45
entry.c, 150
erase_buffer, 200, 201
errors, 23
error_message, 66, 94, 146, 166
establish_field, 144, 148, 161, 165
establish_window, 60, 91
exec, 287, 301
exec.c, 222, 279
exit, 247
extensibility, 14

F

fast.c, 106, 107
fast.prj, 108
fasttest.c, 108
FASTWINDOWS, 54, 59, 72
fclose, 266
FIELD structure, 72, 143, 144, 161
FIELDCHAR, 161
field_help, 144, 148, 165
field_protect, 144, 146
field_tally, 145, 146, 161
field_validate, 144, 146, 165
field_window, 144, 145, 162, 165
findlast, 203
find_end, 200, 203
first_wordlen, 202
forefront, 65, 99
fore_word, 200, 203
forward, 200, 201, 203
functions:
    accent, 93, 94
    acline, 94

addfield, 161
add_list, 94
backspace, 200, 203
back_word, 200, 203
beg_list, 94
blankline, 202
carrtn, 200, 201, 203
clear_message, 66, 94
clear_screen, 28
clear_template, 145, 146, 162, 165
clear_window, 63, 92
closefiles, 288
close_all, 64, 91
copy_block, 200, 203
curr, 199
curr_cursor, 29
cursor, 29
data_entry, 146, 148, 163, 165, 166
data_value, 161, 163, 164
deaccent, 93, 94
delete_block, 200, 202, 203
delete_line, 200, 202
delete_window, 63, 91
delete_word, 200, 202
dget, 93, 94
displ, 93, 94
display-text, 200
display_text, 200, 203
display_window, 63, 91
disp_field, 161
dores, 287
downward, 200, 203
dtitle, 92
endstroke, 163, 164
erase_buffer, 200, 201
error_message, 66, 94, 146, 166
establish_field, 144, 148, 161, 165
establish_window, 60, 91
exec, 287, 301
field_help, 144, 148, 165
field_protect, 144, 146
field_tally, 145, 146, 161
field_validate, 144, 146, 165
field_window, 144, 145, 162, 165
findlast, 203
find_end, 200, 203

first_wordlen, 202
forefront, 65, 99
fore_word, 200, 203
forward, 200, 201, 203
gethmenu, 219
getvmn, 219
get_char, 30, 121, 134, 258
get_selection, 65, 93, 109, 148, 219
haccent, 219
help, 128, 133
hide_window, 63, 92
ifunc, 283
init_template, 143, 144, 161, 165
insert_line, 200
insert_list, 94
insert_status, 162
lastword, 201
last_char, 201
light, 219
lineno, 199
load_help, 127, 133, 134, 145
menu_select, 213, 219
move_block, 200, 203
move_window, 64, 95
mvblock, 203
new28, 287
newcrit, 285, 286
newdisk, 284
newkb, 286
newtimer, 271, 273, 286
normal_video, 64, 164
notepad, 284
olddisk, 285
oldtimer, 273
open_menu, 219
paraform, 202
paraform., 200
popup, 287, 301
read_field, 162, 163
rear_window, 65, 99
redraw, 91
remove_list, 94
repos_window, 92
resident, 282, 284
resinit, 284
restart, 283

reverse_video, 64, 163
right_justify, 163
right_justify_zero_fill, 163
rmove_window, 65, 95, 96
scroll, 93
set_border, 61, 91
set_colors, 61, 91
set_cursor_type, 29, 162
set_help, 127, 129, 133, 134, 145, 163
set_intensity, 62, 91, 109
set_title, 62, 91
spacedn, 203
spaces, 163
spaceup, 203
terminate, 283, 287
test_para, 202
text_editor, 179, 200, 204
trailing_spaces, 202
upward, 200, 203
validate_date, 163
verify_wnd, 94
vmode, 28, 271
vpeek, 31, 50
vpoke, 31, 50
vrstr, 94
vsave, 94
vswap, 94
waddr, 93
wait, 283
wcursor, 63, 93
wframe, 92
wprintf, 63, 64, 92
wprompt, 144
wputchar, 63, 64, 92
hide_window, 54

G

getch, 122
getchar, 122
getdate, 166
getdta, 257, 284
gethmenu, 219
GetPID, 256
getvect, 245, 271

getvmn, 219
get_char, 30, 121, 134, 258, 262
get_selection, 65, 93, 109, 148, 219
Gibson, Jim, 11
Guthery, Scott, 11

H

haccent, 219
HBG, 133
help, 128, 133
helpfunc, 30, 128
helpkey, 30, 128, 163
HFG, 133
hide_window, 63, 92
HINT, 133
Homebase, 230
hot key, 230

I

ibmpc.c, 28, 32, 50, 72, 128, 162
ifunc, 283
In-line assembly code, 24
in-line assembly code, 31
init_template, 143, 144, 161, 165
insert_line, 200
insert_list, 94
insert_mode, 162
insert_status, 162
installation, 24
Integrated Development
    Environment, 19
interrupt 0, 271
interrupt 0x09, 258, 280
interrupt 0x13, 262, 284
interrupt 0x1c, 259
interrupt 0x21, 271
interrupt 0x21:
    functions 0-0x0c, 260
    function 0x31, 229
    function 0x33, 264
    function 0x34, 261, 284
    function 0x49, 266

function 0x50, 256
function 0x51, 256
function 0x52, 289
function 0x62, 256
interrupt 0x23, 264
interrupt 0x24, 263
interrupt 0x27, 229
interrupt 0x28, 261
interrupt 0x60-0x67, 282
interrupt 2, 279
interrupt function type, 23, 244
interrupt service routines, 238
interrupt vectors, 231
interrupts, 231

K

K&R, 10, 20
Kahn, Philippe, 19
Kernighan, Brian, 10
keyboard interrupt, 258, 280, 286
keyboard scan code, 259, 280
keyboard status byte, 259, 281
keymask, 280, 281, 286
keys.h, 30, 37, 128
Kildall, Gary, 228

L

LASTTAB, 199
lastword, 201
last_char, 201
layered window, 56
light, 219
lineno, 199
link, 22
Listings:
    ccolor.c, 105
    clock.c, 276
    clock.prj, 278
    color.c, 104
    color.prj, 106
    editor.c, 180
    entry.c, 150

exec.c, 222
fast.c, 107
fast.prj, 108
fasttest.c, 108
ibmpc.c, 32
keys.h, 37
maxims.c, 137
menu.c, 220
menu.prj, 221
move.c, 97
move.prj, 99
note.c, 204
note.prj, 206
notepad.c, 205
ordent.c, 168
order.c, 167
order.prj, 170
poems.c, 112
poetry.c, 111
poetry.prj, 117
popup.c, 290
popup.prj, 302
prom.c, 101
prom.prj, 103
promote.c, 102
resident.c, 293
sayings.c, 136
sayings.prj, 138
tcprogs.hlp, 126
testmove.c, 98
thelp.c, 130
tmenu.c, 215
twindow.c, 73
twindow.h, 66, 67
vidpoke.c, 47
load_help, 127, 133, 134, 145

M

make, 19, 22
MASM, 31, 50
MAXHELPS, 133
maxims.c, 134, 137
Memory Control Block, 266, 288
memory models, 25

memory-mapped video, 40
memory-resident utilities, 238
MENU structure, 72, 212
menu.c, 220
menu.prj, 221
menu_select, 213, 219
Monochrome Adaptor, 45
move.c, 97
move.prj, 99
move_block, 200, 203
move_window, 64, 95
movmem, 162, 200
MP/M, 228
mvblock, 203

N

new28, 287
newcrit, 285, 286
newdisk, 284
newkb, 286
newtimer, 271, 273, 286
NEXTTAB, 199
non-maskable interrupt, 279
normal_video, 64, 164
Norton, Peter, 44
note.c, 203, 204
note.prj, 204, 206
notepad, 284
notepad.c, 203, 205

O

olddisk, 285
oldtimer, 273
open, 266
open_menu, 219
ordent.c, 164, 168
order.c, 164, 167
order.prj, 164, 170

P

paraform, 202
paraform., 200
Pascal, 10
PID, 256, 284, 287
PL/I, 10
poems.c, 109, 112
poetry.c, 111
poetry.prj, 117
popup, 287, 301
popup.c, 279, 290
popup.prj, 302
Portability, 13
PREVTAB, 199
PRINT.COM, 236, 261
printf, 3, 64, 92
Process ID, 256
Program Segment Prefix, 250
project file, 22
Prokey, 230
prom.c, 101
prom.prj, 103
promote.c, 99, 102
prototypes, 72
pseudo-variables, 24, 249
putchar, 64

R

read_field, 162, 163
rear_window, 65, 99
redraw, 91
remove_list, 94
repos_window, 92
resident, 282, 284
resident.c, 279, 282, 283, 293
resinit, 284
restart, 283
reverse_video, 64, 163
Richards, Martin, 10
right_justify, 163
right_justify_zero_fill, 163
Ritchie, Dennis, 10
rmove_window, 65, 95, 96

rules.asi, 272

S

sayings.c, 134, 136
sayings.prj, 138
scancode, 280, 281
scanf, 3, 122
SCROLL, 92, 93
scroll, 93
SELECT, 93
setdta, 257
SetPID, 256
setvect, 244, 271
set_border, 61, 91
set_colors, 61, 91
set_cursor_type, 29, 162
set_help, 127, 129, 133, 134, 145, 163
set_intensity, 62, 91, 109
set_title, 62, 91
Sidekick, 21, 41, 174, 230, 275
Sidekick Plus, 240
signature, 281
sizeprogram, 279, 304
Small-C, 11
_SP, 249
spacedn, 203
spaces, 163
spaceup, 203
sprintf, 64, 92
_SS, 249
stacked window, 54
stdin, 122
stdio.h, 253
Superkey, 211, 230

T

TAB, 199
tcc, 19
TCCONFIG.TC, 24
TCINST, 20
tcprogs.hlp, 126, 134
terminate, 283, 287

terminating a TSR, 265
testmove.c, 95, 98
test_para, 202
text editor commands, 175
text_editor, 179, 200, 204
thelp.c, 130
Thompson, Ken, 10
timer interrupt, 259, 271, 275, 286
Tiny-C, 11
TLINK, 22, 247
tmenu.c, 215
trailing_spaces, 202
Transient Program Area, 233
TSR programs, 229, 236
Turbo C, 18
Turbo Pascal, 20
TURBOC.CFG, 24
twindow.c, 64, 72, 73
twindow.h, 31, 60, 66, 67, 143, 144, 146, 212, 223

U

UNIX, 10
upward, 200, 203

V

validate_date, 163
va_list, 92
va_start, 92
verify_wnd, 94
video attribute byte, 47
video refresh memory, 44
video snow, 48
video windows, 4, 40
vidpoke.c, 47
vmode, 28, 271
vpeek, 31, 50
vpoke, 31, 50
vrstr, 94
vsave, 94
vsprintf, 92
vswap, 94

W

waddr, 93
wait, 283
warnings, 23
WCURS, 92, 93
wcursor, 63, 93
wframe, 92
WINDOW structure, 60, 72, 92, 93, 161
window text editor, 173
Wizard C, 18, 23
WordStar, 21
wprintf, 63, 64, 92
wprompt, 144
wputchar, 63, 64, 92

X

X3J11 Technical Committee, 11

Z

ZeroDivVector, 272
Zolman, Leor, 11

ORDER FORM FOR
PROGRAM LISTINGS ON DISKETTE

*T*his diskette contains the complete program listings for all programs and applications contained in this book. By using this diskette, you will eliminate time spent typing in pages of program code.

*I*f you did not buy this book with diskette, use this form to order now:

*O*nly:
$20⁰⁰

MANAGEMENT INFORMATION SOURCE, INC.
P.O. Box 5277 • Portland, OR 97208-5277
(503) 222-2399

NAME (Please print or type)

ADDRESS

CITY   STATE   ZIP

*C*all free
1-800-MANUALS

☐ *Turbo C* diskette only $20.00
Please add $2.00 for shipping and handling.
Please check
☐ VISA   ☐ MasterCharge   ☐ American Express
☐ Check enclosed $ _____

ACCT.

EXP. DATE

SIGNATURE

MIS: PRESS

M A N A G E M E N T   I N F O R M A T I O N   S O U R C E ,   I N C .

RELATED TITLES FROM MIS:PRESS

TURBO C: MEMORY-RESIDENT UTILITIES, SCREEN I/O AND PROGRAMMING TECHNIQUES

Covers topics and techniques including memory management, ROM BIOS functions, programming screen input/output, and writing memory-resident utility programs in Turbo C.

Al Stevens 0-943518-35-0 $24.95 Book/Disk: $44.95

C DATA BASE DEVELOPMENT

All the tools programmers need for writing C data base programs — with complete, detailed instructions on how to use them.

Al Stevens 0-943518-33-4 $23.95 Book/Disk: $43.95

QUICK C

Quick C is the latest C compiler from Microsoft. This book provides a C language development environment for use by both beginning and advanced users. Includes an integrated editor and debugger. The code you develop is upward-compatible with the Microsoft C compiler.

Al Stevens, 0-943518-80-6 $24.95 Book/Disk: $49.95

ADVANCED DOS: MEMORY-RESIDENT UTILITIES, INTERRUPTS, AND DISK MANAGEMENT WITH MS AND PC DOS — SECOND EDITION

An indispensable resource for serious DOS programmers. Includes chapters on disk data storage, BIOS and DOS interrupts, utility programming, and memory-resident utilities. Addresses topics of DOS and Multitasking, subprograms and overlays, writing pop-ups, and reentrancy, and provides step-by-step exploration of the partition table, boot record, traverse paths, and more. Includes DOS 3.3.

Michael Hyman 0-943518-83-0 $22.95 Book/Disk: $44.95

MICROSOFT WINDOWS 2.0 PROGRAM DEVELOPMENT

A valuable source to help programmers increase their speed, productivity, and capabilities. Outlines specific procedures and techniques for programming in the unique, multiple-application environment of Microsoft Windows. Using C as the development language, this book includes detailed discussions of memory management, device independence communications interface, standard graphics interface, software and hardware compatibility, and more.

Michael Hyman 0-943518-34-2 $23.95 Book/Disk: $43.95

CONCISE GUIDE TO HYPERTALK

This book, based on Apple's HyperTalk language syntax, serves as a quick reference guide for users who want to create custom HyperCard applications. Information in each chapter is organized alphabetically for easy referencing. Brief examples of HyperTalk are used throughout the book to demonstrate key points.

Barry Shell 0-943518-84-9 $9.95

dBASE III PLUS POWER TOOLS

Outlines integrating data into spreadsheets and documents, accessing mainframe data, installing memory-resident utilities, debugging and compiling the program, and expanding dBASE III Plus into a comprehensive computing system.

Rob Krumm 0-943518-66-0 $21.95 Book/Disk: $40.95

LINEAR AND DYNAMIC PROGRAMMING WITH LOTUS 1-2-3 RELEASE 2

Explains and illustrates the basic concepts of Linear and Dynamic Programming within the Lotus 1-2-3 spreadsheet environment, with numerous examples from business and industry.

James Ho 0-943518-72-5 $19.95 Book/Disk: $39.95

Available where fine books are sold.

MANAGEMENT INFORMATION SOURCE, INC.
P.O. Box 5277 • Portland, OR 97208-5277
(503) 222-2399

Call free
1-800-MANUALS

M A N A G E M E N T   I N F O R M A T I O N   S O U R C E ,   I N C .